DANNY WILLIAMS

THE WAR
WITH OTTAWA

DANNY WILLIAMS

THE WAR
WITH OTTAWA

The inside story by a hired gun

Bill Rowe

FLANKER PRESS LIMITED
ST. JOHN'S
2010

Library and Archives Canada Cataloguing in Publication

Rowe, Bill, 1942-
Danny Williams : the war with Ottawa : the inside story
by a hired gun / Bill Rowe.

Includes index.
ISBN 978-1-897317-83-9

1. Williams, Danny, 1949-. 2. Newfoundland and
Labrador--Politics and government--21st century.
3. Canada--Politics and government--1993-2006.
4. Federal-provincial relations--Newfoundland and Labrador.
5. Federal-provincial relations--Canada. 6. Rowe, Bill, 1942-.
I. Title.

FC2177.2.R68 2010   C813'.6   C2010-905114-9

© 2010 by Bill Rowe

PRINTED IN CANADA

Mixed Sources
Cert no. SW-COC-001271
© 1996 FSC
FSC

This text of this book is printed on Ancient Forest Friendly paper, FSC certified, that is chlorine-free and 100% post-consumer waste.

Cover Design: Adam Freake

FLANKER PRESS
PO BOX 2522, STATION C
ST. JOHN'S, NL, CANADA
TOLL FREE: 1-866-739-4420
WWW.FLANKERPRESS.COM

15 14 13 12 11 10   1 2 3 4 5 6 7 8 9

  Canada Council
for the Arts   Conseil des Arts
du Canada   Newfoundland
Labrador

We acknowledge the financial support of the Government of Canada through the Book Publishing Industry Development Program (BPIDP) for our publishing activities; the Canada Council for the Arts which last year invested $20.1 million in writing and publishing throughout Canada; the Government of Newfoundland and Labrador, Department of Tourism, Culture and Recreation.

To my wife, Penelope Ayre Rowe, whose contribution to our province's cause was greater than anyone knew.

CONTENTS

Author's Note

During the months I spent as Premier Danny Williams's provincial representative in Ottawa, I kept a detailed personal journal. In it I reflected on important and amusing events as they occurred and I recorded my impressions of the intriguing characters involved, for better or for worse, on both sides of the battle lines.

That journal, augmented by memories, emails, conversations, and media clips, forms the core of this story.

Several short pieces from an early draft of the manuscript as a work-in-progress appeared as columns in the St. John's newspapers the *Independent* and the *Telegram*.

BILL ROWE, ST. JOHN'S

NEWFOUNDLAND AND LABRADOR

AUGUST 2010

— CHAPTER ONE —

Alpha Males at Work

WE KNEW THIS LATEST meeting between Premier Danny Williams and the prime minister of Canada was going to be frank, blunt, and edgy. The public war of words that had raged between them for weeks had made even veteran advisers on both sides uneasy. But nobody among us imagined that a fist fight might break out between the two aging statesmen.

The omens for this "summit" in Ottawa, at which Premier Williams, Premier John Hamm and Prime Minister Paul Martin would meet to resolve the dispute over how much money Newfoundland and Labrador and Nova Scotia could keep from their offshore oil and gas, were better than expected. Past exchanges of harsh language and personal insults in the media between Williams and Martin were being superseded now by friendly greetings and amicable handshakes all around. It was a fresh and affable beginning.

The three leaders were meeting on a November afternoon of 2004 in a private room off the prime minister's office in the Centre Block on Parliament Hill. Only the first ministers themselves and some note-taking aides were to be present in that room. The absence of bureaucrats was designed to encourage the premiers and the prime minister to come to grips directly with the issues without official interference. The idea worked—perhaps a little too well.

I was in a room next door with a dozen other federal and provincial minions from the prime minister's and the premiers' offices. We sat around a big circular table waiting for our masters, the legendary negotiators of hundreds of millions of dollars during their previous business careers, to emerge with the impressive fruit of their intellectual labours.

Despite the friendly entrance of their leader into the meeting room, staff members from the prime minister's office seemed to be in a state of agitation. If grace under pressure was an objective, this gang missed the target by a mile. Perhaps the aura of misery and defeat they exuded came from their secret knowledge that, contrary to his affable appearance, the PM intended to maintain his hard-nosed stance.

The top federal man in our room shook hands with the rest of us, displaying the demeanour of a man receiving mourners at a funeral home. A provincial adviser declared that we'd certainly like to achieve a win-win-win situation here, that is, a win for the feds, a win for Nova Scotia and a win for Newfoundland and Labrador. The PM's man batted that hope down with the grim reply that what we were trying to avoid here was a lose-lose-lose situation.

I said to myself that it was no wonder this Martin gang had turned Jean Chrétien's majority government into a bare minority. These guys were masters at spreading expectations of rout and grief. They lent credibility to the jibe that Paul Martin had eked out a win in the last election only because he had run against Stephen Harper; if he had run unopposed, he would have lost.

As we advisers settled in for the long wait, some of our time was filled with smartass remarks back and forth between the federal and provincial sides. One of the *federales* tried, as usual, to divide our two provinces over Danny Williams's stubbornness, which he characterized as self-defeating. "And when the good ship Terra Nova goes under," he prophesied, "remember that the Nova Scotia barnacles sticking to her hull will go down too."

A saucy Newfoundlander wondered how Paul Martin and his advisers had managed to achieve the impossible: "Explain to me again," he said, "the brilliant strategy you guys employed in the last election to snatch near-defeat from the jaws of victory."

But all this jabber was only a pallid aping of our leaders' words and actions in the other room. Most of the time, in fact, just about everyone around our table was glued to a BlackBerry, sending and receiving text messages. Often, someone would regale the rest of us by reading a message they'd just received, usually an ancient, recycled one-liner. "Here's one from Scott. 'Question: What's the difference between Stephen Harper's caucus and a cactus? Answer: With a cactus all the pricks are on the outside.'"

The BlackBerry wireless device had really come into its own over the past year or so, and everywhere you went in official Ottawa in those days, indoors and out, public servants were gawking at them and thumbing them, even when engaged in conversation. I didn't own a BlackBerry myself, and perhaps it was my lack of familiarity with them that would nearly startle me out of my skin this afternoon.

I had left our room for a few minutes and was just coming back when I noticed that instead of any sound of human voices inside, there was an eerie silence. I walked in, wondering. The ten or twelve officials were still sitting around the big table, but no one was saying a word. Their heads were bent forward and their hands were all out of sight under the table. Each of them was staring mutely down at his or her crotch in intense concentration. They were all bobbing up and down slightly and swaying a little in their chairs, with blissful expressions on their faces. Not one looked up at me or spoke. I stopped dead in my tracks. What the hell were they doing? My God, no—it couldn't be—they all looked like they were masturbating under the table.

I didn't know whether to tiptoe silently back out the door and run down the corridor, or to yell, "You people stop that this minute!" Then one of the men looked up and saw me. "Hi there," he said, with what seemed to me to be an alarmingly erotic smile. Everyone suddenly sat back and raised their hands above the table. They had not been engaged in self-abuse at all, at least not the regular kind. They were all clutching

BlackBerrys, into which they had just been lustily thumbing text. I had experienced my first encounter with a gaggle of government advisers participating in a group BlackBerry orgy. The shock has kept me BlackBerry-free to this day.

Premier Williams and Premier Hamm entered the room: the meeting was over. I could see from the ashen face of one note-taker with them, that something scary had happened there, too. "What's going on?" I whispered to him. He bent over and muttered in my ear, "It got very tense in there."

"Very tense" was an understatement of what had taken place, according to a source close to the prime minister who would soon give me his version of events. According to him, the two premiers had been firing their usual billion dollar demands at the prime minister, all three leaders progressing from candid to utterly no-guff on the question of what, exactly, Paul Martin had committed himself to. Whereupon, Danny and Paul abruptly levitated from their chairs and stood toe to toe, eyeball to eyeball, fists raised to punching position, shouting abuse and spittle into each other's faces.

Judging by the accusations they exchanged, their disagreement had moved away from oil money and to more personal issues. Which of them was the biggest fucking liar in the country and which of them had the tiniest balls. Only the intervention of a valiant note-taker, I was told, who wedged himself between them like an NHL referee, prevented a punch-up between the two senior statesmen. French writer Françoise Sagan would have been delighted. "I like men to behave like men," she wrote. "Strong and childish."

The intent of this latest gathering of the three first ministers was to correct the gross inequities of the Atlantic Accord and equalization payments, which were robbing the two Atlantic provinces of revenues from offshore resources. But instead, this meeting, like the others before it, had collapsed in disarray—not surprising, since it must have been hard for two of the participants to think clearly when all the blood had gone to their clenched fists.

"The PM is really mad," said my federal contact. "He used to like your fellow Danny. He was prepared to go as high as three hundred million right now for your petite province. But after that debacle? Bugger all, pal. ZILCH. You might as well drag your sorry ass back to your benighted rock for good." He concluded with what sounded like a direct quote from the prime minister's office: "Because this thing is EFFIN FINISHED!"

Buddy did have a point. With my main reason for being in Ottawa having just exploded, anyone sensible would shag off home out of it, away from this cold, navel-gazing hell back to our mild, ocean-gazing heaven. But, goddammit—the paltry, miserable sum mentioned at this latest meeting had not gone up by one loonie in weeks. Despite their reasonable rhetoric, and their constant encouragement to meet and discuss amounts, the feds had deliberately stuck the money train in neutral. They kept attaching strings to a deal. Small wonder the premier had nearly come to blows with the prime minister. The federal proposal dangled before us was an absolute insult.

Prime Minister Martin had publicly stated the following in St. John's six months before—on June 5, 2004—during the federal election campaign: "I had a discussion . . . with the premier this morning, and I have made it very clear that the proposal he has put forth is a proposal that we accept." Provincial calculations showed that, based on Premier Williams's proposal, the public commitment made to him by Paul Martin entitled our province to hundreds of millions more than the federal government was offering, and did not include the crippling conditions the feds now kept insisting on.

After the fiasco, I walked away from the Centre Block on Parliament Hill with Premier Williams and his chief of staff, Brian Crawley, and his director of communications, Elizabeth Matthews. I expected Danny's message to the media to be filled with predictions of dire consequences. He stopped for a scrum with national reporters, and then pushed on to an interview at CTV and another with Don Newman on CBC TV. His message was grave all right, but surprisingly upbeat too: Serious difficulties did remain, but progress had been made.

Danny even kept his cool when one senior national reporter, encountering him in the CBC lobby, hoisted her nose high and sniffed, "Premier Williams, how on earth do you expect to get any money from the Department of Finance when you keep insulting their officials?" This was a reference to Danny's well-warranted attacks on the lunacy of the federal equalization formula. I'd noticed before now that some others in the national media shared her condescending attitude. You people down there in the boonies? You need to learn how to brown-nose central Canada properly if you want to get anywhere.

At the CBC building, I spotted the federal minister of Natural Resources, John Efford, scooting into a studio for an interview of his own—no doubt about how ungrateful his native province was in the face of Ottawa's awesome generosity. Efford's director of communications, Tom Ormsby, a long-time acquaintance of mine, strolled up, and we complimented each other on how good at injury prevention we were: his minister and my premier were the full length of the building away from each.

Afterwards, Danny started back to his room at the Château Laurier, where he intended to call *Night Line* on VOCM Radio in Newfoundland and Labrador and give a progress report to the province, after which he would pack his bag for the airport. The man had been up till two o'clock in St. John's the night before—he was a bit of a night owl, one of his young aides had commented to me ruefully—and out of bed before dawn for his flight to Ottawa that morning. Now, after a full day of meetings and media and near fist fights with prime ministers, he was flying home.

He and I talked alone in the lobby before he went up to his room. I half-expected him to be crestfallen and exhausted after today's flop. Before his meeting with the PM, he had talked very frankly to me about his fear that his Accord initiative might fail.

One of the traits I liked about Danny was how honest he was about his feelings, almost to the point of wearing his heart on his sleeve. I considered it a superior feature in a leader, much preferable to the bravado and bluster of some. I'd told him earlier that his anxieties were natural, but, from my vantage point, I couldn't see the Accord negotiations failing in the end: ultimately Paul Martin would have to keep his word in a way that allowed Danny and Hamm to say publicly that he had honoured his commitment.

I knew from talking to close, long-term friends of Martin that he was a "my word is my bond" man, which many credited for his success in business. He would never allow his reputation for honour to be permanently sullied, no matter what the bean counters in Finance or the Privy Council urged him to do.

As Danny and I said goodbye at the hotel, he was, in fact, far from discouraged. He had the air of a man whose round of negotiations had gone extremely well. I asked him how Premier Hamm was holding up; Hamm worried me. When I'd first met him, I'd described him privately to people in the premier's office as a marshmallow compared to Danny, who was a razor blade.

But I discovered it was easy to dismiss Hamm like that, because he was exceedingly courteous and soft-spoken, and although he laughed easily, he did it very quietly. When you got to know him and his history better you realized that, although Danny had forced the commitment out of Martin the previous June, Hamm had started this campaign to ameliorate the inequities of the Atlantic Accords to begin with, nearly four years ago, and he had stuck to his guns ever since. Danny told me that despite serious attempts by the PMO to divide the two provinces and separate Nova Scotia's position from ours during this latest meeting, Hamm had retained his rock-like solidarity.

When we parted with a handshake that evening, Danny said, "We're getting there. But we need to push it ahead. Keep up the networking and the campaigning."

And so, a little later, during a talk with my acquaintance close to the prime minister, I told him, no, it was not finished. That he and his gang had no idea what they were dealing with.

Oh, they had a pretty good idea, he replied—that was to say, from top to bottom on Danny Williams's team, we were all off our goddamned heads.

Well, being crazy was certainly a plus in dealing with the federal government, I responded. It only levelled the playing field. Crazy? He and his chums in the PMO hadn't even glimpsed crazy from our side yet. The two provinces were going to get the money they were entitled to, I told him, or we all might have the pleasure at the next big summit meeting of seeing Danny and Paul rolling about the floor amongst the dust bunnies in their fifteen-hundred-dollar suits, throwing punches at each other's angst-furrowed faces and kneeing each other in the alpha male nuts.

Confronted with that enchanting image, the federal guy couldn't quite squelch his snort. But then he shook his head in dismay at what federal-provincial statesmanship was coming to. We both had to agree on one thing, though: whichever way the battle went in the future, this was one hell of a fascinating time to be adversaries in Ottawa.

— CHAPTER TWO —

Danny's Call to Arms

WHAT WAS I DOING in the nation's capital in the first place, up to my neck in the most vicious federal-provincial battle in Newfoundland and Labrador's history? Not even the clash over the offshore in the early '80s between "the bad boy of Confederation," Brian Peckford, and the haughty Pierre Trudeau, or that conflict over something called Term 29 back in the 1950s between the two egomaniacs Premier Joey Smallwood and Prime Minister John Diefenbaker matched this one in ferocity and nastiness and public entertainment. So, how was I blessed enough to find myself in Ottawa as Danny Williams's representative during his take-no-prisoners combat with Paul Martin which so enraged and amused the gobsmacked Canadian public?

For years, I had inhabited an agreeable niche as a talking head in the provincial and national media. I never harboured the slightest intention of playing any role for the provincial government in Ottawa, and there was no personal or political relationship between Danny and me that would have made my appointment to such position a natural consequence of Danny's election as premier in 2003.

A few months before that election, when he was still leader of the Opposition, Danny had telephoned me at home one day. Could I meet him at his house for a little chat? I was surprised by the call, but it wasn't hard to deduce what he wanted. He thought no doubt that, because I'd been in politics before, I was still daft enough to want to get back into that noble profession/wretched racket.

However, I'd lost all interest in re-entering provincial politics. Elected five times before and defeated twice, I'd had my fill of it. So I could easily have said no to Danny right there on the phone. But instead I agreed to meet with him. How come? Politeness, a desire to hear the man out? Yes, a little of that. Curiosity about his celebrated powers of persuasion? A bit of that too. But mainly, it was pure nosiness on my part: I wanted a gawk at the inside of his big fancy house.

I liked Danny's style. Anyone who would lift a quote from Harold Ballard, former owner of the Toronto Maple Leafs and convicted fraud, and apply it to Mayor Andy Wells—proclaiming that a public argument with His Worship was like "getting into a pissin' contest with a skunk" and adding for good measure that what the mayor of St. John's really needed was a "good shit-knockin'"—well, how could you not like the guy?

But Danny and I had never been buddies. I'd known his father, Tommy, better. When I first started practising law in the late 1960s, Tommy Williams, QC, was already a veteran lawyer, affable, hail-fellow-well-met, and extremely helpful with friendly advice to novices like me. Tommy was a big Tory, and I was an active Liberal, but whenever I ran into him in the court-house or on Duckworth Street, he always had the time to stop and have a chat about law, politics or sports with a youngster like myself, going out of his way to make a greenhorn to the fraternity of the robe feel welcome.

So when I first met the young Danny Williams, I was already predisposed in his favour. And I was glad to find that he was a good bit like his old man—same affable and down-to-earth personality. I first got to know him in the early 1970s when Progressive Conservative Premier Frank Moores appointed him as a deputy law clerk or the like in the House of Assembly. I was then a Liberal MHA and Opposition house leader. Because Danny was a Tory, many of my fellow party members were perplexed at our friendly interaction. They figured we should be natural political enemies. That tone had been set earlier by Joey Smallwood. I well recall Joey shooting glares of disbelief and scorn my way whenever I strolled across the House to have a friendly gab with dirty Tories like Tom Hickey or Ank Murphy or Gerry Ottenheimer, or, worst of all, the "turncoat" John Crosbie. But I tried never to let politics interfere with genial relations with anyone, and I appreciated Danny's similar temperament. During breaks in House proceedings, we often sought each other out for a coffee and a cordial chinwag.

Ten years later, though, I glimpsed a hard-nosed business side of the man which I didn't care for. In the provincial election of 1982, after thirteen years in the House of Assembly, I got kicked out into the political cold with most Liberal candidates by PC Premier Brian Peckford's anti-Ottawa, anti-Trudeau, "it's Newfoundland's oil" juggernaut. I resumed the practice of law and began to do commentaries on public affairs. One of my media appearances was with a weekly panel of pundits on the community affairs channel of Danny's cable TV network.

I loved it. Debating public issues with Patrick O'Flaherty and Gerry Phelan and other skilled commentators every week—who wouldn't love it? But I was struggling with the recession and the stagflation and the 20 percent interest rates then raging. So I told the cable company that, as with all other media I had gigs with—CBC, CTV, VOCM, newspapers—I would have to charge them a fee if they thought my opinion valuable enough to put on the air for their own paying customers. No fee, said the cable company.

I left the show on principle. More mystified than angry, I mentioned to someone I happened to encounter, a higher-up in Danny's company, how strange it was that a cable TV outfit—"a licence to print money," as billionaire media baron Lord Thomson of Fleet, former chancellor of Memorial University, had described it—would not want to pay equitable recompense to professional commentators for their expertise. "But that's how Danny is making his millions," Danny's man replied. "He's as tight as a crab's ass."

A few years later, in 1989, when Tom Rideout ran for leader of the provincial PC Party, Danny appeared on television to complain about party manipulations that had somehow finagled him out of running for leader himself. I was struck by his scowling face and surly tone, and remarked to myself how different he seemed from the days when he was that young official in the House of Assembly, fresh out of law school, all dressed up in his court duds. The sight of Danny then in his bib, tabs and tucker had caused one woman in the gallery—and she a big Liberal—to blurt, "Oh my God, that Danny Williams looks right huggable."

Before he telephoned me in 2003, virtually my only other association with Danny Williams had been during his guest appearances as lawyer for Gregory Parsons on my VOCM phone-in show. His staunch advocacy of Greg's innocence of the charge of murdering his mother, when public opinion was against Parsons, and his tireless public pursuit of compensation for Greg's wrongful conviction impressed me mightily.

Not long after Danny had become leader of the PC Party of Newfoundland and Labrador, I ran into a friend of his in the lounge of an international airport. Over our delayed-flight drinks, this man gave me his theory on Danny's business, legal and political ambitions and successes— a theory that would have done Sigmund Freud proud. My companion believed that the motivation behind Danny's drive had everything to do with a childhood and adolescent sense of inferiority within his extended family, which had led to a secret, heartfelt vow early in his life: "One of these days I'll show those bastards."

Danny's father, my lounge companion said, had married Teresita, one of the celebrated Galway sisters of St. John's. Other Galway sisters had married Jim Chalker, John Mahoney, and Noel Goodridge, all lawyers too.

Jim Chalker became one of the foremost lawyers in the province, heading up his own highly successful firm which represented some of the largest corporate clients in Newfoundland, and the government and agencies thereof. He had fended off many invitations to be elevated to the province's Supreme Court.

John Mahoney, too, was a member of one of the top law firms in the province. He was elected to the House of Assembly, became minister of Justice, and went on to be appointed to the Supreme Court of Newfoundland.

Noel Goodridge was the grandson of a prime minister of the old Dominion of Newfoundland and a partner in a pre-eminent law firm; at a very early age, he was appointed to the Supreme Court of Newfoundland, and later became chief justice of the province.

So these were some of the illustrious uncles by marriage, together with a growing band of first cousins belonging to these elite families, that surrounded our Danny growing up in St. John's. And then, said my barstool psychologist with a smirk, there was Tommy Williams.

Tommy had a modest law practice all his life, he said, including a stint with Danny which didn't last; ultimately, he was appointed by the Tory government to the Public Utilities Board. Tommy was laid-back and extremely sociable, and he enjoyed his drink. His main claim to fame had occurred early in life, when he excelled as a tennis player. But no one would accuse him of being a flaming professional success later in life, especially compared to all those hotshot brothers-in-law. This, said his friend, was the origin of Danny's need to succeed at everything he touched, and not just succeed but to be the best, to be head and shoulders above everyone else. Most of all, he was determined to tower above the progeny of his extended family, those elite-born first cousins in their fancy uptown residences.

"Bullshit. Absolute and unadulterated bullshit." This was the reaction to all that from another St. John's professional, who had gone through school with Danny. From Danny's youngest years, he told me, you could see that he was destined for big things. An admired athlete, top marks all the way through, a natural leader who had an unaffected, down-to-earth relationship with everyone around him. Ashamed of Tommy? Felt inferior to his cousins' families? Total rubbish. In fact, part of Danny's prestige in school was his father's status as a top-rung athlete—sixteen championship titles in tennis—and his reputation as a lawyer who was knowledgeable, approachable and at ease with everyone.

According to the second source, Danny won a Rhodes Scholarship as a young man because of his natural brilliance, his natural athleticism, and his natural leadership, not because he was festering with resentment. You didn't have to dig with a Freudian shovel to discover why he was successful. Given his great intelligence and energy, it would have been surprising if he hadn't been such a success.

Two theories of a man's success. I opted for the latter, myself. But, then, I'm no shrink.

In any event, I trundled along for the palaver with Progressive Conservative Opposition Leader Danny Williams in his big fancy house with mixed feelings.

At the front door, Danny greeted me like a best buddy. I figured we'd go into his study or den where, as a busy party leader preparing for the upcoming election, he and I would get right down to brass tacks. Instead we strolled into the living room. His gracious wife, Maureen, came in for a chat, and to offer refreshments. A daughter and grandchild appeared and said hello, and for a while we all made pleasant small talk. By the time wife, daughter and grandchild departed, I felt like an old family friend on a social visit rather than a virtual stranger come to talk squalid politics.

When Danny invited me to sit down on a sofa in the living room, I asked him if he had an office in the house. No, he said, he'd learned early on that he needed to keep family and work physically separate. If there was any family activity going on in the house, as there ordinarily was, he couldn't concentrate on work. Therefore, he used to do all his after-hours work back at the law office.

Judging by his reputation, there must have been a lot of after-hours work. One colleague, a hard-working lawyer in his own right, told me he felt like a slacker compared to Danny, especially when he drove past his law firm on the way home from a social event in the small hours of the morning and saw Danny's car in the parking lot and a solitary light on in the otherwise dark building.

That regimen of Danny's would come as no surprise to anyone acquainted with his career trajectory—winning a cable television licence from the CRTC while still in law school, and then building a cable company up to the point where he could sell the whole shebang to Rogers (three decades after starting it), for a reported quarter of a billion dollars, while nurturing one of the most successful independent local law firms in the province.

As Danny and I gabbed in his living room, I forgot all about my intended good gawk around the house and became absorbed in the modus operandi of the man's pitch. First he recalled our time in the House of Assembly in the '70s, when, he said, I would invite him into the Opposition common room for a cup of coffee during breaks, while his own gang completely ignored him—he'd never forgotten my small acts of kindness. Then he mentioned how welcoming I'd always been whenever he wanted to talk about his wrongfully convicted client Gregory Parsons on my radio show. He'd never forgotten that generous attitude on my part, either, he said. By now I felt not only like Danny's best friend, but I was starting to wonder when he was going to send my name over to the pope for possible canonization.

Next he talked about his need, after he got elected as premier that coming fall, to surround himself with people of talent and experience, both elected and appointed. He mentioned one man, a scholar of magnificent qualities, who had been on the verge of leaving for an important posting on the mainland: "But how could I let a man of his calibre go, if I'm serious about staving off the disaster facing this province?" Danny had convinced the man to stay in Newfoundland and Labrador by engaging him as a policy adviser.

Then we moved on to the pros and cons of his prospective candidates in the forthcoming election. We went over the PC incumbents in the House of Assembly, plus some new possibilities. One fellow, while bright and amiable, we agreed, was as lazy as a castrated tomcat. Another, though he had impeccable taste in single malt scotch, appreciated a nip of it perhaps a little too often. One laddio, though very intelligent, was led around day and night, not by the big brainy head on his shoulders, but by the little head with no brain lower down on his anatomy.

Some candidates were indeed excellent, but he felt he needed to beef up their number if he was going to be able to form a first-rate Cabinet, and was trying hard to recruit a few more prospects of high quality. He'd asked one prominent man to run, but his wife had put her foot down. If he entered politics, she had promised, it would be over her dead body. Many of Danny's strategists were okay with her funeral scenario, but unfortunately her husband was not.

Finally, he said, "Bill, you and I have over sixty years of vast experience between us. The province needs that."

So there I sat, unmasked and exposed: not only was I a long-time best buddy of saintly qualities, but also utterly my own man as a husband and pos-sessed of indispensable experience. All of which were needed to save the province from ruin. How could I possibly refuse the call to run for him in the upcoming election? Still, I couldn't keep the thought out of my mind that the last two times I'd run in provincial politics I'd made a complete arse of myself.

Back in the mid-eighties, Premier Brian Peckford had shown me a political poll indicating that I would get elected handily under his leader-ship in the district of La Poile. I had only to win the nomination, which was going to be held in a few days' time, but that would be easy. There were lots of party workers there eager to make sure of that. So, out I flew to La Poile, with great fanfare and hoopla. There I discovered that a man whom hardly anyone at head office had heard of, a local gentleman from Grand Bruit, "Big Noise," had been working behind the scenes on the nomination for months. On nomination night he clobbered the rest of us who were running, and I flew back home after just three days, dragging a suitcase full of clean underwear and socks packed for three weeks.

Ten years later and yet another poll, this one presented to me by an enthusiastic group in Mount Pearl district. It showed that I had a good chance of winning there under the inspired leadership of Premier Clyde Wells. The incumbent MHA was not nearly as popular as he used to be, the numbers indicated, and the voters there, like everywhere else in the province, loved our Clyde for his heroic battle against Prime Minister Mulroney on the Meech Lake Accord.

This time I did get the nomination easily, which should have been a dead giveaway of trouble ahead. I started working my butt off going door to door, and that's when I discovered that Clyde's main campaign issue might not be working to my advantage. He had kicked off the election by attacking public employees and their unions for their demands and their threats of job-action. Whom did voters want to govern the province, Clyde demanded publicly right at the beginning of the campaign, those unelected civil servants and their insatiable labour leaders or a Wells gov-ernment elected by and for the people?

Clyde's rhetoric went over well in other districts, and he would go on to win that election handily. There was, however, a slight problem with Mount Pearl. Nearly every door I knocked on was opened by a totally outraged public servant or their equally pissed-off spouse. Mount Pearl must have held the Guinness World Record for number of provincial public servants in one area. And all of them—teachers, nurses, police officers, firefighters, government employees, and their infuriated family members—were straining at the leash, ready to pounce on that ballot come election day and vote against Clyde Wells and me, his henchman from St. John's. At their doors, voters reminded me that the incumbent, my opponent, Neil Windsor, had made Mount Pearl a city in the face of sarcasm from people from St. John's. Sarcasm such as "Shouldn't a real city have at least one building with an elevator?" Neil enjoyed a magnificent victory on election night.

The spectre of running again made me silently say to myself, "Yeah, like hell!" But curiosity got the better of me: I asked Danny which district he had in mind. He named a couple of rural districts, where, he said, I could win handily. What, become a parachute candidate yet again? Thanks, but no thanks. I still had the scars from when my parachute had failed to open twice before. Well, said Danny, how about my own home district of Signal Hill–Quidi Vidi? But we quickly agreed that it was well-nigh impossible for anyone to beat NDP leader Jack Harris there. Nor would I have wanted to, even if I could.

A popular leader like Danny, I mused, shouldn't have too many hotshot candidates running for him. You only needed to look back at Joey Smallwood in the provincial general election of 1966 to see the dangers of recruiting and electing a gang of high-profile candidates. Joey in 1966 was exceedingly popular. He could have won that election handily with forty-one zombies running for him, but instead he went after a dozen eminent new candidates, and he got them: John Crosbie, Alec Hickman, Clyde Wells, John Nolan, Ed Roberts, Bill Callahan, Aidan Maloney, Tom Burgess, John Murphy, John Mahoney. These outstanding recruits were added to a number of highly regarded members already in the House: Jim McGrath, Alain Frecker, Phil Lewis, Fred Rowe, Steve Neary, Eric Dawe, Val Earle. Joey had begun drawing his old-age pension before that election; to add to the youthfulness of his new team, he recruited me as well. Just home from law school and not long out of short pants, I got elected on Joey's coattails at the age of twenty-four.

After one of the greatest election victories in our province's history that September of 1966, with all but three of Joey's candidates elected, I remember looking around the House as we were being sworn in and thinking that there never was, nor could there ever be again, a local legislature full of such dazzling talent. And what was the result? Not two years later, Joey's gifted Liberal caucus, full of egos as big as his own, started to come apart. Crosbie and Wells revolted and crossed the floor, taking others with them. A federal election featuring Joey's choice for national Liberal leader, Pierre Elliot Trudeau, returned only one Liberal from this province, Don Jamieson. The other six MPs were Tory, several of them elected in staunch Liberal seats. (Remember the "Noisy Six"?)

Next, a disastrous leadership convention in the Liberal Party sent Hickman, Earle, and other MHAs across the House as well. In the next election, 1971, the great Joey was all but toppled, and within months he was in fact turfed out of power by his own hand-picked lieutenant-governor. It was a chain of catastrophes, after more than two decades of power, which he knew was of his own making. He would quote, with a shake of his head, the German proverb, "Too clever is dumb," or Lyndon Johnson's mantra, "I never trust a man unless I've got his pecker in my pocket." Joey had neglected to pay attention to both of these. Danny Williams, I figured, should not do the same.

But, reminiscing and philosophizing aside, I had to confess that I was no longer in the least interested in running for provincial politics. The only politics that appealed to me these days was the idea of running for an elected senate in Ottawa, if such a possibility ever came about while I was still compos mentis. I believed that getting elected to represent the province as a whole in the nation's capital, and using that mandate and its real political power to get a better deal for the province in Confederation, would be the ideal political job.

I suggested that Danny should mull over, when he became premier, the idea of appointing someone to represent him and his government right on the ground up there in Ottawa: a permanent provincial office in the nation's capital, his own representative in the federal heartland.

Herb Brett, a former president of the Newfoundland and Labrador Federation of Municipalities, had told me years before that the federation had made a recommendation to the provincial Cabinet back in the '80s that the province should have an office in Ottawa. Quebec had one, and it was the best investment they had ever made, Herb told me. Quebec was hauling in millions from the federal treasury from just being there and in the loop.

Danny jumped at the concept, and it animated our conversation in a way that nothing we'd discussed previously had done. It was clear he had already intuited that, when he became premier, his dealings with the imperious federal government would be the biggest challenge facing our politically tiny and financially weak province. His thought processes had already travelled along that road. He told me that he would begin by using negotiation and logic and reason with Ottawa to obtain a fairer deal for the province, especially with regard to a just and reasonable share of the revenues from the offshore oil. If that approach failed, he was fully pre-pared to resort to "whatever had to be done" to achieve his ends for Newfoundland and Labrador.

As for myself, to make sure that my brilliant political future remained in the past, I nipped in the bud any notion of my political rebirth. Danny had wasted one more hour vainly trying to fill yet another candidate slot. But perhaps our conversation hadn't been entirely for naught. In the lead-up to the election which would make Danny Williams premier, an inter-esting pledge appeared in the PC Blue Book.

Under the heading "Federal-Provincial Relations," a number of federal government practices that seriously impeded this province's economic and social development were listed, including this one: "Through an unjust equalization program and clawback formula, we lose the lion's share of the royalties from our non-renewable resources." Underneath was a "Key Commitment": "We will establish the Newfoundland and Labrador Office of Federal-Provincial Relations in Ottawa."

— CHAPTER THREE —

In the Belly of the Beast

AFTER HIS ELECTION AS premier, Danny Williams was shocked to find that things were just as bad as he'd been saying they were. He appeared on television to warn that the province's financial trajectory was heading straight over the brink of insolvency, and he ordered cutbacks and wage freezes. Public servants, outraged over his throttling of their legitimate bargaining, went on strike. In the middle of all this, Danny asked me to consider helping by taking on the new position, which he had promised in his campaign manifesto, of provincial representative in Ottawa.

I had mixed feelings about it. The idea of tackling the province's problems in the nation's capital, of working to obtain a fairer share of the nation's bounty, was extremely appealing. But I doubted that I had the proper psychological makeup to become a cog in a bureaucratic wheel. Most of my working life, I'd been an independent agent—lawyer, commentator, writer, radio show host—and I liked it that way. Nor did I relish the prospect of being answerable to the whims of a politically powerful boss. I'd already had that experience when Premier Joey Smallwood appointed me, at age twenty-six, to his Cabinet. It was a phenomenal episode in a youngster's life, but that gig had left me with a disinclination to hop to it ever again at the pleasure of a controlling political leader. And Danny

Williams gave every indication of becoming as powerful as Joey Smallwood, and probably more commanding.

None of that struck Danny as a big problem when I mentioned it to him. He pictured this new position, he said, as being virtually autonomous in its operation. And since I myself had promoted the post in Ottawa as necessary to the interests of the province, it would be up to me to carve out an effective sphere of activity in a manner I thought best.

Okay then, I told him, I would consider it on one condition: the position had to be at the level of deputy minister in the premier's office, and I would be answerable to the premier himself, not to some official in another department. That was absolutely imperative if the post were to have any clout with the mandarins and politicos in Ottawa. They had to understand that the holder of this office had the ear of the premier. Otherwise, I would be perceived as just another irrelevant functionary from the regional boonies.

Danny agreed, and ordered a contract to be drawn up. But when the thing came back, the job was at the assistant deputy minister level, and the incumbent was answerable to the deputy minister of Intergovernmental Affairs. Whoever had drafted the contract described this mid-level functionary as being something like the ambassador to Washington. Even Canada's prestigious top diplomat to mighty America reported to the deputy minister of Foreign Affairs. Hence, it was logical that Newfoundland's envoy to Ottawa should hold a similar rank.

The ambassador to Washington could report to the toilet attendant for all I cared. I simply was not interested in a position in Ottawa that I knew wouldn't fly. The job of provincial representative had to be a useful and viable position, and this was not it. So count me out.

Surprisingly, more drafts followed; it was the most tedious process I'd ever been dragged through. The term "glacial slowness" has been used to describe dealings with government bureaucracies, but you could get whiplash watching a glacier move after experiencing the speed of bureaucrats who don't want to go in the indicated direction. That wilful sluggishness seemed to apply even when the instructions came from the newly elected premier himself.

Danny's chief of staff, Brian Crawley, was responsible for getting my new job up and running. Born and raised in Labrador City, Crawley had studied commerce at Memorial University of Newfoundland and journalism at Carleton University before holding communications positions in the oil industry and the health sector. During the two years leading up to the election, he had served as director of communications and senior adviser to Danny. Crawley was a bright guy, a nice guy, and intensely devoted to Danny, but he wasn't much help in advancing the position of representative of the Government of Newfoundland and Labrador in Ottawa.

In the first months with his boss as premier instead of leader of the Opposition, Crawley was either over his head in dealing with canny, veteran bureaucrats, or beleaguered with other crucial problems. After all, it was a new untried government with an empty treasury, facing a strike of its civil service, and I didn't blame him for the growing pains he was experiencing. Still, that didn't mean I was prepared to continue to rely on the assurances of a well-meaning learner who often could not deliver.

Danny, however, was persistent: at least twice more, I was forced to fire letters off to him personally, one in March asking him to please remove my name from any further consideration for the position, and another in June stating that circumstances prevented me from accepting it. And that, from my standpoint, was the end of it. But just as I was starting my summer vacation, I got a call from Danny one weekend morning. He was about to leave for Ireland to meet with the Taoiseach. Could he see me today, before he left?

I had already noticed some elements of Danny's style. However harassed by events, he was never late for any meeting I had with him. And I never saw him looking at his watch during a meeting, or caught him giving the impression that he wanted to get rid of you, even if the matter was completely clued up and you were wasting his time with chit-chat. Plus, he never seemed to differentiate between nighttime and daytime or—as on this particular summer weekend—between workdays and holidays.

I said yes, and he asked me to come to an office downtown. It was the only place, he said, where he could have a completely confidential meeting with someone without their goings and comings being observed. I went down and the first thing he told me was that he'd recently been listening to *Open Line*, the radio call-in show I'd been hosting for years, and he'd heard me talking to a man who had phoned in about his lost dog. I remembered that morning; it had been close to my summer break, and producer Pat Murphy and I relaxed our rule about not allowing lost pooch announcements on the show. We took the poor bereft dog owner's call. "A lost dog!" Danny said, with gut-wrenching pity in his voice. "My God, Bill, a man of your intelligence—a Rhodes Scholar—you can't want to be doing that."

I started to assert self-righteously that the show wasn't all about lost dogs; it was an important democratic institution, blahdy blahdy blah. But before long I had to stop and burst out laughing. This guy was good. Having tried flattery and tedium, he was now taking a crack at intellectually shaming me into accepting the damned job.

I stopped and considered a few things. Here he was, the new premier of a province that was so broke he'd just been forced to legislate his own civil service back to work after an agonizing strike, and who was now facing back-breaking deficits plus mammoth federal-provincial challenges in health, equalization, offshore oil, the fishery, 5 Wing Goose Bay, and a plethora of other issues.

I had recently seen some figures on just one of many continuing disgraces—the laughably inadequate federal presence in Newfoundland and Labrador. Direct federal employment had always been less here than in other provinces, and the situation was made worse when Paul Martin was minister of Finance. From 1992 to 2003, federal government employment in Newfoundland and Labrador decreased by over 37 percent while total federal employment in Canada decreased by less than half that rate. In Ontario the decrease was less than 10 percent. If federal employment here had decreased by the national rate of 17.4 percent, that would have meant more than two hundred million dollars added to our economy in salaries and spinoffs.

To add insult to injury, there were no federal regional headquarters here, except where "regional" meant single province. Nova Scotia had seventeen regional headquarters and New Brunswick had eleven. Even little

PEI had the head office of the Veterans Services Branch of Veterans Affairs Canada. Unbelievably, the Department of Natural Resources, headed by our own minister, John Efford, had no representative here despite our massive offshore resources. Despite all the oil and gas off Newfoundland and Labrador and Nova Scotia, the one representative of the federal Department of Natural Resources in Atlantic Canada was in New Brunswick.

Saving the province from insolvency depended on getting a lot more money from our offshore resources, and Danny was having serious misgivings about being able to hold Prime Minister Paul Martin to his election commitment. Martin had promised to accept the premier's proposal on our offshore revenues under the 1985 Atlantic Accord. Danny's proposal, presented in writing to Efford in March 2004 was that the federal government change the existing offset provisions to provide a payment equal to 100 percent of the net direct provincial offshore revenues; i.e., no clawback of equalization payments.

And here was Danny today, struggling under all those challenges and problems and tribulations, asking me once more to represent him in the nation's capital, where I could perhaps do something to advance the province's cause.

He was aware of the frustrations I'd experienced with Crawley, and he assured me that he'd personally see to it that dealings with him and his office would be to my satisfaction. It was clear that I'd have to be a bastard of the highest order to turn him and our province down in their time of need. I told him I'd let him know quickly.

After the meeting, I went to visit my elderly widowed mother. Increasing physical frailty had forced her in recent months to move from her own apartment to the Chancellor Park nursing home. Of her four sons, my brother Fred and I were the only ones living in St. John's. We felt that she would probably live only another year or so, and I was very reluctant to leave her.

To say that I was absolutely torn between accepting and declining Danny's final offer would be an understatement. But in the end, despite misgivings and conflicting circumstances, I did what I had to do.

* * *

DRIVING TO CONFEDERATION BUILDING on a beautiful, sunny day in July 2004 for the news conference with Premier Danny Williams to announce my appointment as provincial representative in Ottawa, I experienced an almost childlike eagerness. I was extremely enthusiastic about the prospect of tackling new challenges. Danny and I saw eye to eye on what the work entailed, and we were confident, both of us being blessed with blimp-sized egos, that we would make it succeed. And the contract I'd signed incorporated everything I thought necessary to make the new position fly.

During the news conference, Danny mentioned my wife, Penelope Rowe, chief executive officer of the Community Services Council, a charitable organization focusing on social and economic development. Because of her highly praised work in public policy here and across Canada, the provincial government was getting "two representatives in Ottawa for the price of one," he said.

The premier's comment about two for one was said lightly, but his characterization of Penny was well-founded. As a result of her work at the federal, provincial, and community levels, Penny was named to the Order of Canada in 2002. The fact that she would be spending considerable time in Ottawa in connection with her activities while I was there made my decision to take the position far easier. And I would find that almost anywhere I went in official and political circles up there, my wife's reputation helped break the ice and led to fruitful discussions.

At the news conference announcing my appointment, I experienced an adrenaline rush at the thought of the known and unknown responsibilities of the new position, so entirely different from what I'd been used to. It all but reduced me to a twitching heap of nervousness.

But the real impact of what I'd done hit me that night. I was watching the coverage of the press conference on the local CBC television news. At the end, news anchor Debbie Cooper was kind enough to say, "We're going to miss Bill on the panel." She was talking about my weekly appearances on *Here and Now*, CBC's local evening news show, debating public issues with knowledgeable, opinionated commentators such as Peter Fenwick. That activity had been a big element of my cherished independence, together with the feisty exchanges on VOCM's *Open Line*. For years, I'd enjoyed the luxury of making insolent and wisecracking comments on the performance of public figures. Now suddenly my role was reversed: I was the one under the gun. I had ditched the independent good life to go down a one-way street possibly named Disillusion Road. What was I, cracked?

During the next few days, however, I was swept along by the fact that public reaction was pretty positive. I received calls and emails from well-wishers and heard expressions of goodwill on *Open Line* and *Night Line*. I had to laugh when my old political adversary Jim Morgan said some kind words about me, although he did state, in one of his customary whacks at the leader of his party, Premier Williams, that the office of provincial representative itself was a waste of money and I should be heading up a rural secretariat instead. Meanwhile, comments in the *St. John's Telegram* and the *St. John's Independent* and the *St. John's Express* (the latter two newspapers now lamentably extinct) were generally upbeat.

I was well-received on NTV's current affairs show, *Issues and Answers*. And when the premier appeared on the show the following Sunday, the most negative comment was that some Tories were disgruntled at the appointment of a former Liberal. Danny replied that he hadn't been talking to any who were; if there was criticism, it was for political reasons; the appointment itself was non-partisan.

"While the province is well represented by our Members of Parliament, Mr. Rowe will be the *provincial government's* voice in Ottawa," Danny had stated when he announced the position. Asked whether the appointment was a signal to our federal MPs that they were not doing a good job, he replied, "No, not at all." He said, however, that the province could never be overrepresented in Ottawa. "That city is full of politicians, lobbyists, and bureaucrats, and we need a greater presence there from the provincial government's perspective. This new office will create a new and effective identity for Newfoundland and Labrador in Ottawa."

A couple of our MPs in Ottawa announced they liked the idea. The *Express* reported the following during the week of July 28: "Just before making the announcement about Rowe, Williams gave a courtesy call to federal Cabinet minister John Efford who expressed strong support for the move." As we shall see, however, Efford's attitude would take a sharp dip into the dark zone as he found himself caught in the squeeze between Paul Martin and Danny Williams.

A couple of weeks after the appointment, Dr. Christopher Dunn, a professor in Memorial's Department of Political Science, published an interesting article in the "Insight" column of the August 12 edition of MUN's newspaper, the *Gazette*, entitled "Federal Representation: the Persistent Conundrum." In it he wrote, "The choice of . . . Bill Rowe to be the province's representative in the Newfoundland and Labrador Office of Federal-Provincial Relations in Ottawa has had mixed reactions. One view sees it as another layer of unneeded and expensive bureaucracy; another as an indictment of the lack of effectiveness of existing MPs in Parliament; still another, as a development filled with promise."

Dr. Dunn concluded his analysis of the representation regime in our Canadian federation with specific ideas for widespread reform. "Placing the onus for results on a regional minister or the Newfoundland Ottawa Office is bound to disappoint. All must play a role . . . The 'Ottawa Office' opened by the Government of Newfoundland and Labrador should be supported, but its work should be operated according to the principle of transparency."

In the public arena, then, the new position appeared to be off and running. But behind the scenes, out of the public eye, in the bowels of the bureaucracy, I would soon be flabbergasted, and amused, to learn what it was like to have to depend on the civil service to try to lift a job off its blueprint and actually make it work in the real world.

The premier's office may have won out against the "push-back" of reluctant officials in Executive Council and Intergovernmental Affairs, but it had not been easy and it had not been pretty. And in the future I would be squarely in the hands of provincial bureaucrats for the creation, establishment, and operation of this office.

During the contract discussions, I'd already had a taste of the torture that could cause. I was to find out in the coming months of struggling to get things done through the civil service that the sense of misgiving I had felt on that beautiful July day of the premier's news conference was far too feeble an emotion. My reaction should have been shrieks of sheer terror alternating with roars of laughter at the tragicomedy I would encounter. Trying to get the office set up would turn out to be like living in a movie that combined "the horror, the horror" of *Apocalypse Now* and the slapstick absurdities of *The Three Stooges*.

Not everyone I encountered in the civil service was useless. I had dealings with public servants at all levels who were admirable in their efforts and sometimes even in their effectiveness. But there were staggering inefficiencies, unfathomable foot-dragging, and mind-boggling stretches of wasted time as I tried to propel some simple tasks through what felt like a gluey, amorphous bureaucratic mass.

When Danny Williams appointed me, he made it clear, privately and publicly, that getting the office of provincial representative in Ottawa up and running was a matter of top priority. My greatest surprise was to observe how the premier's sense of priority was not reflected in any way in the caverns of officialdom.

Right off, I was placed in the hands of designated officials in the premier's office, the Executive Council, and the Department of Intergovernmental Affairs, and they were instructed to move the thing ahead like a house afire. Brian Crawley; Brian Taylor, director of operations for the premier's office; Dorothy French of the Executive Council, and Renee Tinkov of the treasury board all moved fast within the first days. They fanned out instructions and enquiries. Forms were placed before me for my signature. Conversations took place, by telephone and in person. But then I made the naive mistake of actually endeavouring to accomplish a few things. I soon began to feel as if I were a goat that had been swallowed whole by a giant python—a big lump inching day after day through the belly of a monstrous beast.

Premier Williams stated at the news conference he wanted me to start dealing with the decline of the military operations at 5 Wing Goose Bay in Labrador immediately. The British, Italian, and German air forces were still using the base for low-level flight training, but the Canadian government had done away with thirty-one military jobs there. The Dutch had left Labrador in the fall of 2003, and the Germans were planning to leave within a couple of years.

Upon my appointment, the premier's office directed Intergovernmental Affairs to provide me ("in the next day or so") with briefing notes on 5 Wing Goose Bay and some other key issues. After ten days of asking where the notes were, I had still received nothing. On a Friday night, driving out to take in a movie, I heard on the radio that the British air force had decided to pull out of Goose Bay. I was astounded. It was the first I'd heard of it.

In the washroom at the mall before the movie, a guy I knew congratulated me on the new job, and offered his analysis of the Goose Bay situation: "I see you've had your first failure." We both chuckled, but I was far from chuckling when I called Brian Crawley at home that weekend to describe, in short and pithy Anglo-Saxon words, my reaction.

Early the next week, some two weeks after my appointment, I finally received those "top priority" briefing notes from Intergovernmental Affairs.

Meanwhile, since I had lots to prepare in St. John's before I left for Ottawa, and would be coming back from time to time to confer with the premier and his colleagues, I was to have the use of an office in Confederation Building. There was no space left on the eighth floor in the area of the premier's office itself—they were like sardines up there—so a vacant office in Intergovernmental Affairs, on the floor below, was to be made available quickly. All I needed was a desk, chair, telephone with voice mail, and a computer with access to the Internet and email. While that office was being prepared, I worked out of my home office.

Every now and then, on my way to and from meetings at the premier's office, I would drop into Intergovernmental Affairs to see how they were making out with my office. For three weeks, whenever I looked in, it was an empty space. And no one seemed to know why. All they knew was that they were working on it. All the premier's office knew was that they had issued instructions to get it ready pronto. If someone from the outside had said to me, "Tell me, to save your own life, what is causing the delay in getting your office ready," I would have been forced to reply, "You'll have to shoot me, because I haven't got a clue."

One day an official told me that the office was going to be ready for me to move into first thing the next morning.

I went to my new office at 8:00 a.m. When I got there, however, something about it seemed not quite right. There was no chair, for one thing. A nice woman came out of an adjoining office, and sheepishly told me there were still a few things not entirely geared up.

While I was standing there, briefcase in hand and papers under arms, trying not to laugh out loud at the foolishness of the situation, a woman came into the department and introduced herself. It was Barbara Knight, the deputy minister of Intergovernmental Affairs. She asked if I had a minute to chat. I had heard from the eighth floor that she was not happy about the creation of my new position; this was the first time she'd shown any interest in talking to me, and I was curious to see what she had to say. As we sat down in her office, I noticed how tense she was, and my heart went out to her. The poor woman was not having a good year.

In January, Danny had appointed Doug House deputy minister of Industry, Trade and Rural Development. Doug had written a book a few years earlier, entitled *Against the Tide: Battling for Economic Renewal in Newfoundland and Labrador*, about his time as chair of the Economic Recovery Commission (1989–96). In it, he had pointed the finger at Barbara Knight and others in the civil service, implying they had undermined the commission and helped send it to its death. Doug House's new portfolio was Danny's way of slapping down those naysayers; he held Doug in very high esteem.

Now Knight was faced with a fresh affront to her status—a provincial representative in Ottawa. On the day of my appointment, the premier tried to smooth ruffled feathers. When asked why he needed a deputy minister of Intergovernmental Affairs plus a representative in Ottawa, he said, "The deputy minister of IGA serves an important role in the province—coordinating federal-provincial issues, meetings such as the Council of the Federation, and running the IGA department. Bill's role is completely separate from this position. He will be on the ground, working

our files, and advising me personally on issues in Ottawa . . . He will pro-
mote and aggressively advocate the issues of the province daily. Issues
such as the Atlantic Accord, foreign over-fishing . . ."

Danny's reference to the Atlantic Accord must have stuck in Knight's
craw. I recalled having seen her name under a photograph of the proud
negotiators of the original Atlantic Accord back in 1985. Despite Danny's
efforts to mollify her, she obviously felt that he had done an end run around
her by creating this new position in the first place, and then rubbing her
nose in it by filling it with a rank amateur from outside the establishment
endowed, unbelievably, with the same deputy ministerial status that she
possessed. My present position as deputy minister responsible directly to
the premier, circumventing Knight right in her own bailiwick, no doubt felt
like a terrible insult to her. And it showed in our little chat in her office.

Knight sat in a chair in front of her desk, fairly close and facing me. It was
a gimmick employed by some executives to create an air of comfortable infor-
mality and greater intimacy. But if that was her intent, it didn't work. She was
perched stiffly on her chair, and appeared to be extremely ill at ease.

She opened by stating she was not enthusiastic about my job in
Ottawa or optimistic about its success. Oh? That came as a big surprise.
She said that federal executives in Ottawa were very busy, that our clout
as a province had steadily diminished, that Halifax had become the centre
of the region. I replied that I was well aware that the concept of the
Atlantic Region—one big de facto Atlantic province encompassing all four
of the actual provinces—was alive and well up there in Ottawa. I knew
that political and financial decisions were being made behind closed doors
on that basis, despite the constitutional existence of four individual
Atlantic provinces. Many times on the air I had stated that Newfoundland
and Labrador had become nothing but a pimple on the backside of
Halifax. I told Knight that I assumed those were all good reasons for the
premier to create a position such as mine, and send me up there as a free
agent, unhampered by bureaucratic niceties, to help find ways around that
arrogant federal attitude regarding our province.

I don't think this description of my function as a kind of unfettered freebooter, or hired gun, soothed her much. In the awkward, pregnant pause that ensued, she squirmed a little and then got to the real reason for wanting this belated chat.

"Bill," she asked, "do you know your way around Ottawa? Do you have many contacts there?"

I was about to reply, "Barbara, if you have any doubts about my qualifications for this job that the premier bugged my bloody arse off to accept, you should address your concerns to him." But it sounded like she already had confronted Danny on the matter, and merely wanted to air her skepticism. I didn't know what Danny might have said to her, but I had no intention of inflating my bureaucratic credentials for the job. I gave her a straight answer.

No, I didn't have many contacts there—hardly any at all in the Ottawa civil service. I did know a few political types. The prime minister's principal secretary, Francis Fox, was a friend of mine from university and political days. I was well acquainted with the members of the House of Commons and active senators from here, and some ministers and leading politicians in other parties. The premier of Quebec, Jean Charest, was an acquaintance of mine, which could be helpful in dealing with the Quebec office in Ottawa. Many of the media there I knew personally. But that was about it. I hadn't had any dealings with the federal civil service for many years. (That may have been the premier's whole point in sending someone like me up there, carrying none of the baggage of past relationships with federal officialdom.) Anyway, I said, we'd see how it went.

She nodded gravely, lips pursed. Clearly, my last point had convinced her of nothing except my bureaucratic unfitness for whatever this new job might entail. I had only confirmed her profound suspicion that I was the man who knew no mandarins, that Premier Williams had blundered catastrophically by creating this superfluous position of provincial whatnot in Ottawa, and had then compounded the disaster by appointing a clueless outsider who didn't even know the protocol rulebook, or to whom I was supposed to kowtow in the federal capital. Our conversation dwindled to a close, and I went away with divided feelings: a slight sadness at her sense of having been shuffled aside by the premier, and a slight amusement at her petty reaction to the premier's initiative to improve the province's desperate condition with strenuous, unscripted efforts on the ground in Ottawa.

And that, apart from a later phone call or two, or finding myself now and then in the same meeting rooms in Ottawa, or receiving faxed documents from her office, was the only interaction I had with Knight. I didn't mind because, truly, I had a clear vision of the job I wanted to do in Ottawa, unimpeded by turf wars.

That same afternoon she telephoned me. My office, she said rather tersely, was ready. The next day I took my briefcase to Confederation Building again, intending to spend a couple of days working there before setting out for Ottawa.

Approaching the office, I saw at least four women inside it, from the Department of Intergovernmental Affairs and perhaps elsewhere, all so intent on what they were doing that they didn't even notice my arrival. They were bent over an office chair which was upside down with its legs pointing skyward. Much earnest discussion was going on; they seemed to be trying to fix something on one of the legs. Although they were very serious about whatever they were doing, it would be fair to say that none of them gave the impression of being your typical professional repair person. When I entered the room, they jerked upright in unison. All of us nearly joined the chair in its upside-down position, we laughed so much. I said I should probably come back to my office tomorrow. No argument from them.

The next day, the office looked ready. For example, the problem chair was now standing upright. I walked in and, displaying a courage I did not feel, sat down on it. The chair did not collapse or tip over. Yes! Thus emboldened, I pulled it gingerly up to the desk. Both the chair and I stayed vertical and together, as if we were made for each other. That encouraged me to continue the belated bonding with my new office. I picked up the telephone receiver. My God, I could hear a dial tone, loud and clear. Like an excited child, I turned on the computer. Lo and behold, an image appeared on the screen. I was getting dizzy with success. But now the gods of hubris intervened. Within seconds, I discovered that the phone had no access to voice mail and the computer had no access to the Internet or email. I had to laugh.

This was getting as good as a concert. The date was August 20, 2004—nearly four weeks after my urgent appointment by the premier.

The day after my appointment, the premier's director of operations brought me over to the West Block to have my picture taken and my data registered for the official photo ID card that would allow me access to the Confederation Building without having to go through security in the lobby every time. For the three weeks it took to receive the card, I signed the book in the lobby, and got a sticker at the security desk which allowed me up to the premier's office or to meetings inside the buildings. That was no big inconvenience, but it did provide a comment on the pace of government activity.

I would discover in Ottawa, while setting up the new office there, that I didn't know how lucky I'd been to get something done that fast through the public service. An ID card in three weeks? That was a speed to make your head spin.

The premier told me to make full use of the staff in his office in setting up everything in Ottawa. Brian Crawley's secretary, Judy Wells, and the director of operations, Brian Taylor, were a great support at the beginning. Crawley and the director of communications, Elizabeth Matthews, were always ready to help, and they were the two whom the premier himself seemed to depend on most. They seldom left his side.

Besides his other talents, Crawley had the plus factor of standing well over six feet tall. He was accused in jest sometimes of being called chief of staff purely as window dressing—the joke went that Danny really kept him around as a bodyguard.

Elizabeth Matthews I found intelligent, forthright, knowledgeable, and experienced. A graduate of Memorial University, she had worked in private industry and in communications roles for various provincial departments, including Mines and Energy; Tourism, Culture and Recreation; Fisheries and Aquaculture; and Education. She had played a key role on the Williams team during the election and the transition to government.

Someone in the premier's office mentioned to me that she was the daughter of a former Liberal Cabinet minister in the provincial government.

He wondered if I was surprised that she had become such a major feature in the office of the Progressive Conservative premier. Well, no, I wasn't surprised, I said. I'd been a Liberal Cabinet minister myself and here I was standing in the same Tory office. But my chatty informant insisted on explaining: Elizabeth was the former girlfriend of a young man close to the premier; Danny had been aware of her talents for a long time. And then my gossipy source said, with an uncomprehending shake of the head in tribute to her attractiveness, "But imagine having her as a girlfriend, and letting her get away." This was more commentary than I needed or wanted.

Not only was Elizabeth proficient, I discovered, at distilling complex issues and policies down to their understandable, readable essence, but she was considerate and attentive to little things as well. She relayed valuable contact information regarding Ottawa media people to me, phoning specifically one time, for example, to say she'd run into Mike Duffy of CTV, who had asked about my appointment and given her his cellphone number so that he and I could get together when I arrived in Ottawa. It would be weeks before I noticed the traits that had gained her a whispered nickname, "the Little Princess."

I would remark to Danny as we walked along a hotel corridor between meetings one day in Ottawa that he seemed to be pretty well served by his young staff, from Crawley and Matthews down to his principal assistant, Peter Noel; executive assistant, Stephen Dinn; and various managers and policy advisers—they all seemed to be bright and on the ball and preternaturally devoted to him. He replied that he liked being surrounded by young people: they carried no baggage and were not set in their ways, and they were eager to do things the way he wanted them done.

I responded that when he'd been trying to recruit me for this job, he had emphasized the maturity and the knowledge that he and I both possessed. "Over sixty years of experience between the two of us," he had declared joyfully then. We laughed at the apparent inconsistency, but in reality there was none: the malleable, youthful, no-baggage traits were useful in those who were serving him hourly, day and night, week after week, whereas the more mature attributes of the veteran were beneficial in those he might call upon to provide advice on specific, challenging issues. I had noticed that the deputy minister to the premier, Ross Reid, a canny, experienced veteran if there ever was one, was ensconced in an office away from the premier's premises. But who could fault a middle-aged leader for surrounding himself with eager-to-please young people, and for not surrounding himself with an unlovely gaggle of contrary old codgers?

On my last evening in St. John's, I went up to the premier's office to sign the letters I'd written to federal ministers and officials and our own MPs and senators, explaining what my job entailed. When I arrived on the eighth floor, business hours were long over and the place was virtually empty. But as I was signing, Danny came out of his office with a friend from his business days who was hobbling along on crutches and sporting a cast on his lower leg. We chatted about the man's injury, and then Danny moved quickly to what was currently agitating him—an appearance by our minister in Ottawa, John Efford, on VOCM's *Open Line* that morning. I hadn't heard the show, but Danny thought that Efford had been whittling down and weakening the commitment Paul Martin had made fewer than three months ago to accept Danny's proposal concerning the Atlantic Accord.

An attempt was being made by the feds, it seemed to the premier, to define the commitment as a pledge only, ensuring that Newfoundland and Labrador and Nova Scotia would be, in the vague term that had already caused so much unfairness, the "principal beneficiaries" of their offshore developments. Danny figured that the prime minister's office had probably launched Efford as a trial balloon to see what the reaction might be in the province to an easing away from the PM's obligation. The bastards were attempting to gauge what would be the least amount of money they could get away with.

That commitment by Paul Martin regarding our revenue under the offshore accord—his acceptance of the proposal the premier had put forward—had always been problematical to me. I was hosting *Open Line* myself when it was made, and I had wondered aloud on the show for days afterwards what difficulties, differences of opinion, and outright accusations and battles lay ahead. It had been an oral commitment only; a private commitment, made over the phone. Why, I asked, hadn't Danny Williams gotten a deal in writing?

Of course, I was asking that question partly to provoke discussion, because I knew there was no way Danny could hold a gun to Martin's head and insist on a written contract. In politics, you often have to take whatever you can get under the circumstances and try to make the best of it. A lot of people thought that Danny had the Midas touch when it came to negotiating. One of his fervent admirers had described the premier's bargaining abilities to me as follows: "Listen, my son, when it comes to negotiating, Danny Williams could create a lump of shit out of a fart."

Still, the fact that Paul Martin did not and would not produce his commitment in writing had given some people cause to fear that perhaps Danny had missed the boat on this one. At the very least, it was believed, he was going to have his work cut out for him turning Martin's election fart into a lump of anything substantial. And now we'd had a serious heads-up from Martin's front man, John Efford: any prospective new Atlantic Accord deal between Danny and Paul was heading for a rocky ride. It looked like federal strategists wanted to remind minority PM Paul Martin of a certain maxim. "Remember, Prime Minister: honesty has lost more elections than broken promises have."

That night, loading up my car for the drive to Ottawa, I felt a new thrill of anticipation about this job. The most pressing reason for my appointment, which had been lurking in the wings, was about to explode onto stage, front and centre. And there was no doubt in my mind that the friendly relations between the premier and the prime minister were beginning a long slide toward open hostility. With hundreds of millions, even billions, of dollars at stake for Newfoundland and Labrador under a new Atlantic Accord becoming our top challenge in Ottawa, I couldn't wait to get behind the wheel of the car the next morning and head to the battleground.

Driving across Newfoundland the next day, I recalled some of the commentary in the Canadian media after Danny Williams had won his decisive election victory nine months before. Many national opinion-mongers had nursed the hope that the new guy in Newfoundland would behave himself better than some of our former premiers had in dealing with the federal government.

The *Globe and Mail*, self-proclaimed "Canada's National Newspaper" (with reporters right across Canada, from Halifax to Vancouver), made a pious wish a day after the election that Mr. Williams would be truly prepared to abandon his predecessors' traditional approach of blaming Ottawa for everything, and then demanding more money from the feds. They said this wouldn't be easy for a political novice like Williams, following in the footsteps of demagogic premiers who had made their careers bashing the feds. "But," they encouraged him, "what a legacy it could turn out to be." Everything, it seemed, would be just jim-dandy if Danny was a good boy, tugging his forelock in the presence of the prime minister and kissing his ass every chance he got, like a proper little premier from Newfoundland and Labrador.

I like the *Globe and Mail*, I really do, to paraphrase their columnist Margaret Wente on Newfoundland, but that particular editorial was a masterpiece of utter condescension combined with absolute naïveté. They seemed to be either wholly ignorant of or indifferent to some very basic facts. After more than half a century as part of Canada, Newfoundland and Labrador's per capita debt was more than twice the national average, and the province's fiscal capacity per capita was only 74 percent of the national average. These dismal figures prevailed in a province that possessed massive resources, among the greatest in Canada, including a tremendous wealth of offshore oil and hydroelectrical power. But how the hell could that differential have continued to exist? Why were we so poor and debt-ridden?

The great federal minister John Crosbie, who had brought about the original Atlantic Accord in 1985 in the face of howls of defeatism and dire predictions of fiasco from oil "experts" in Calgary, and who had later, in 1993, persuaded the federal government to acquire ownership of 8.5 percent of Hibernia, thereby rescuing the project from probable death, described clearly why we were, and were destined to remain, poor and debt-ridden under the present federal financial system.

It boiled down to the equalization clawback. And it was not only Newfoundland and Labrador that suffered from such an idiotic policy. In *Atlantic Business Magazine*'s August 2004 issue, Crosbie wrote about the effect equalization was having on a sister province: "In 2001 the equalization system deducted $885 million from Saskatchewan's transfer payments because its oil industry generated $668 million. They'd be further ahead if they shut the whole industry down!"

Then he described the pernicious effect of the equalization clawback on the Atlantic provinces: "This happens in Newfoundland and Nova Scotia with reference to their offshore oil and gas resources despite the provisions of the Atlantic Accord which promised both provinces they would be the 'principal beneficiaries' of the development of their offshore oil and gas. Instead, 86% goes to Canada and only 14% to Newfoundland, [with] 19 cents of the offshore revenue dollar to Nova Scotia, because of equalization clawbacks."

Recalling all this as I drove toward Port aux Basques and that shining jewel of the federal presence in our province, the Marine Atlantic ferry system, I thought of the hopes of some in the national media that Danny Williams would be a nice, polite, well-behaved little premier. And I said to myself, "Oh yeah, that's going to happen—in your shagging editorial boardroom dreams!"

— CHAPTER FOUR —

Where Hell Freezes Over

WHEN I PULLED MY car up to the ticket booth at the terminal in Port aux Basques at seven in the morning, as required, the sour-faced man inside growled, "Reservation number?" Reading from my notes, I gave him the wrong number by mistake. "There's no such number," he barked. "What's your last name?" He processed my ticket in the same churlish manner, and, when I drove on, it was without a single good-natured word from the man. Welcome to Ottawa's major presence in Newfoundland—the ferry service operated by the federal Crown corporation Marine Atlantic.

When tourists make mistakes and get the same reaction, as either their first or last impression of our province, how do they describe the province to their friends at home? Do they say they found the place pleasant and hospitable, and recommend a visit there? Or do they say they found it discourteous and unfriendly, and would not be going back?

On board the ferry, the crew were obliging and helpful, but unfortunately it often takes only one unnecessary negative encounter to undercut all the positive ones. My own reaction that day was that our provincial government could spend all the tax dollars in the treasury putting Technicolor pictures of our lovely scenery in glossy magazines, but it would be to no avail against negative word of mouth from tourists to their friends and neighbours and colleagues back home on the mainland about unpleasant experiences with graceless louts.

A tourist once told me about his nasty first impression of Newfoundland and Labrador. When he and his family arrived in their car at the Marine Atlantic ferry terminal in North Sydney and joined the lineup, they got entangled in some kind of traffic snarl, not of their own making, which delayed their boarding. Fearing they would miss the deadline for checking in and lose their reserved cabin, the man used his cellphone to call the number he'd been given when reserving their passage. He explained how he was being delayed by circumstances beyond his control, and asked that the cabin be held for him.

When, at long last, he and his family made it aboard and went to check in and get their cabin key, the person behind the desk said, "Oh, another no-show. That cabin is gone." The tourist told me he still had a sour taste in his mouth over the heated discussion that ensued, and no, he would never recommend to anyone that they come here on that ferry. In fact, he would advise against it. I wondered whether nice glossy pictures of colourful laundry dancing on a clothesline—even in fresh, clear air with an awe-inspiring scenic background—could compete with negative impressions like that in the minds of a family planning a driving holiday. And in the minds of those to whom they related their stories.

One excellent feature of crossing the Gulf by ferry on a nice day is the opportunity to chat with passengers on the decks in the open air. A fellow Newfoundlander approached me to wish me well in the new position, and to say that he worked in the same department of the provincial government to which Doug House had recently been appointed deputy minister. He was delighted at Doug's appointment, he said. It was a real breath of fresh air. That was encouraging to hear, I told him, because in my short experience, a breath of fresh air in the bureaucracy would do everyone a world of good.

Another passenger came rushing up, to tell us he had just spotted a big sea turtle. That caused a flurry of interest and activity; people hurried over to the rail, to try to see the exotic creature. It was a small example of the serendipitous and fleeting glories of our province, which exist side by side with those more enduring and dependable.

After an agreeable time on deck, I went down to my cabin to study some files. But my concentration was diverted by a faint but pervasive smell of old vomit. I turned on the fan. It rattled and clattered distractingly all the way to North Sydney. The unpleasant aspects of this trip would turn out to be very useful, however: they were good practice for someone about to live and work in the federal capital.

When I arrived in Ottawa I noted that the distance from St. John's, as shown on my car's trip recorder, was 2,583 kilometres or 1,614 miles, not counting the journey across the Cabot Strait. What an unwieldy, impractical distance, I thought, psychologically as well as in miles and time, from my province's capital to the seat of national power. The distance from St. John's to Ottawa was almost as great as the distance from St. John's to Europe. I could well imagine Newfoundland and Labrador's dismal fate in many important matters—fish, offshore oil, access to hydroelectric markets, and so on—if politicians and bureaucrats in, say, the Azores were making all the crucial decisions.

There's nothing wrong with Ottawa, a wag once told me, that half a dozen big state funerals wouldn't cure. But I doubt if the solution to Ottawa would be that easy. It's a beautiful and interesting place, with its waterways, parks, vistas, and national institutions—the Parliament Buildings are among the finest of their kind in the world—and because of this, its off-putting features stand out in stark contrast.

Why was the place so damned noisy? It was the loudest city I'd ever walked around in, and that would include some pretty good rackets heard in the likes of London, Athens, and Calcutta. Maybe I was wrong. Maybe the vehicular noise just sounded louder in comparison to the silence of the cold, taciturn people who inhabited the city. And maybe it just sounded louder at night because much of the city centre was otherwise empty and dead then.

Part of the racket came from those long Ottawa buses (two parts joined in the middle by an accordion device, giving them a faintly reptilian look) which emitted deafening blasts from their air brakes every few seconds. Their headache-inducing din wouldn't be tolerated for one minute in any self-respecting third-world capital.

Plus, there must be more muffler-less vehicles bombing around Ottawa in the middle of the night than anywhere else in the world. And what was going on with the continual sound of police sirens all night long? An anglophone told me that it was all caused by those French guys from Quebec, tearing across the river in their souped-up cars with the mufflers removed. And of course, that commotion, he said, attracted the attention of the police. Hence the night-long wailing of police sirens. I seriously disputed that explanation. I spent some off-time driving and walking in the cities and parks of the Outaouais region on the Quebec side of the Ottawa River. And I found the area peaceful and friendly.

I asked a high-ranking official in the government of Quebec why Gatineau, on the other side of the river, was not part of Ottawa, so that the county's capital would straddle Ontario and Quebec and form an autonomous, integrated, beautiful national capital with a lovely river running through it. He told me that no Quebec government, federalist or separatist, could ever allow that to happen. Even Jean Charest's Liberal Party—the non-separatist, federalist party in power in Quebec—would balk at such an initiative because, to many francophones, it would represent a final surrender to the idea of Canada. A Canadian capital incorporating within it a piece of Quebec would amount to an official consent to Canada's presence in Quebec, a capitulation that no self-respecting Québécois or Québécoise could be expected to stomach.

Some English-speaking people in Ottawa seemed to possess a negative attitude regarding the presence of francophones in the capital. Several told me that the French had completely taken over the city. Oh? Tell that to the elderly woman I heard in a big drugstore on a main street in bilingual Canada's capital city asking an employee in halting English if there was anyone available who could speak to her in French. No, replied the employee, turning hastily away, there was not.

A cold spot, Ottawa. And I'm not even talking about the winter

weather. Long before winter set in, I could see why Ottawa competed with
Moscow for the title of coldest capital in the world. Then I read somewhere that Ulan Bator, the capital of Outer Mongolia, might be even colder
than Ottawa. In degrees of temperature, that might be so; in degrees of
human warmth, I doubted it.

I found that hardly anyone working in an Ottawa store ever met a cus-
tomer's eye. I grew so used to that bizarre phenomenon that I was taken
by surprise one day. I was at Mountain Equipment Co-op, looking at winter
jackets and waiting for someone to notice my existence so that I could buy
one. A young man across the store actually caught my eye and came over.
He didn't know much about the jackets because he worked in another
department, he said with a smile, but he would try to give me a hand.
Where could this obliging fellow possibly have dropped down from—the
planet Jupiter? When I inquired about his origins, he replied, "Labrador
City. That's in Newfoundland and Labrador."

A Newfoundlander in Ottawa told me his preteen daughter and her
friend, also from Newfoundland, would wish a pleasant "good morning"
to adults they passed on Ottawa sidewalks, just to see their startled
expressions. Apparently, they looked as shocked as if they had been threatened. I decided to try it myself. One day, a man walked toward me in the
corridor of my apartment building, his eyes to the side, studiously
avoiding looking at me. "Good morning," I declared, when he got close
enough. He all but jumped out of his skin.

A woman from St. John's who'd worked in Ottawa one summer told me
that she used to walk with her young daughter on the beautiful paths in the
lovely morning weather admiring the sights—the architecture, the birds,
the small animals, the river, the play of sunlight—on her way to work. One
morning her daughter said something that made them both laugh out loud.
Everyone rushing by in their civil service outfits looked at them reprovingly,
she said. She could almost hear them say, "Who's that laughing in Ottawa?
Who did not get the memo that there's no laughing in Ottawa?"

Courtesy is not an Ottawa forte. Once, in a government liquor store, I
wanted to buy some world-famous Ontario ice wine, and I asked an

employee if she could show me where it was. Scowling fixedly at the floor, she waved her hand in an easterly direction and said, "Over there."

On November 11, after the Remembrance Day ceremonies, I went to Ottawa General Hospital to visit Lawrence O'Brien, the Member of Parliament for Labrador, who was seriously ill. I asked a man getting into an elevator if these were the elevators to the patients' rooms. "How should I know?" he said, bristling.

By the time *Reader's Digest* published their survey on politeness in fifteen Canadian cities, I was in a position not to be surprised by Ottawa's ranking. Moncton came in first—the politest city in Canada. St. John's tied for fourth with Victoria and Charlottetown. Toronto was third last. Ottawa sat scowling at the very bottom of the list—dead last in politeness and courtesy. Our nation's capital.

One long-time resident figured that the surliness one encountered in Ottawa was an attempt by the lower orders to imitate the arrogance, haughtiness, and self-importance of those working in government offices. He suggested to me that the official welcome from bureaucratic Ottawa, posted over every government door for arriving taxpayers, should be, "What the hell do you want?"

He also challenged me to find a crease in the brow of any member of the management class of the Ottawa bureaucracy. "They live in a perennially stress-free zone," he said. "No matter how bad a recession or disaster may be elsewhere in Canada, these guys know only their own insulated, silk-lined cocoons; their slow endless meetings; their big salaries, benefits, and perks; and, at the end of the year, a bonus from tax-dollars for remembering to breathe for the past twelve months."

I found the taxi system in Ottawa intriguing. Each of the companies seemed to be dominated by a different ethnic group. I asked drivers a few questions about their countries of origin and their reasons for settling in this expensive city of Ottawa, with its six months of winter. I got the impression from many drivers that they thought it would be easier to get help with bringing family members into Canada if they lived in the capital. But most of them had become disillusioned.

Several times I heard stories from drivers about prejudice—and even corruption—on the part of Canadian immigration officials working in their countries. I found that hard to believe, I told them, but if they really thought that such a thing was, in fact, happening back home, they should give evidence of it to officials or a lawyer here in Canada. Each of them replied that they could never do that because the word would get back to the Canadian officials stationed in their country, and then family members would never get into Canada.

One driver told me that a female relative, who, he claimed, had a Ph.D., couldn't get in because Canadian officials in his country wouldn't accept his affidavit that she was closely related to him; they wanted DNA from both of them. The officials "over there," he said, take bribes, and come back to Canada millionaires. I wondered to myself which alternative was more pathetic—the possibility that those allegations might contain some truth, or the automatic assumption by some immigrants that Canadian officials were just as corrupt as their own officials.

One morning, four of us—a minister and his advisers and I—were returning in a taxi from a federal-provincial meeting when another taxi in the outside lane pulled up abreast of us on the driver's side. The other driver opened his passenger window. Our driver lowered his window, and for a kilometre, while driving at substantial speeds by the Parliament Buildings and those housing the Supreme Court of Canada—our loftiest symbols of Canadian democracy and the rule of law—the two drivers yelled at each other in a foreign language, clearly exchanging insults and threats, accompanied by offensive and menacing hand gestures.

For that minute or so, as far as the two drivers were concerned, neither we nor the passenger in the other taxi existed. We had no idea what the point of contention was, or whether it had arisen recently in Ottawa or was part of a centuries-old grievance between the drivers' ethnic groups back home. At the completion of their discussion, the other driver sped away with an elaborate gesture of fingers and forearm, unfamiliar to us but clearly belligerent. Our driver rolled up his window and turned to us, smiling, to explain the situation. "Asshole. He's from Dystopia." (Not, of course, the real name of the country.) His eyes flared into fury again as he snarled the actual name of the other guy's country.

When I described that episode to a long-time Ottawa resident, he nodded, "Oh yeah," as if it were commonplace. He seemed surprised by my naïveté. "But what I can't fathom," he said, "is how come some immigrants strive so hard to get into this country so that they and their families can have a good and peaceful and prosperous life here, and yet they bring over here with them their goddamned blood feuds and their dark-ages honour systems that they left to get away from."

I thought of that conversation five years later when I read in the *Globe and Mail* that the head of the Ottawa taxi drivers' union was about to be sentenced to a year in jail for threatening and harassing his daughter so severely that the police, fearing for her safety, spirited her out of the city. Yusef Salam Al Mezel had admitted during his trial to pushing her and threatening to break her legs and kill her, and smashing her computer. She had told police he didn't want her to volunteer at a community centre, and that he was negotiating a dowry with a Syrian man. He had written emails about the family sharaf which she'd stained by running away.

From time to time I heard talk in Ottawa about the ethnic gangs that lurked on the shadowy side streets off the main drags. One person told me that serious crime between ethnic minorities—assaults, sexual offences, pitched battles involving gunplay, murder even—in the nether regions of the city was substantially under-reported in the media so as not to detract from the image of the national capital.

Could this be true? I spent a lot of time walking around Ottawa during off hours, away from the main streets, and I must say I never felt a moment's apprehension. What I did see, in this expensive city of double six-figure incomes was a disproportionately large number of ill-clad down-and-out people. The number of bag ladies and men pushing supermarket carts piled high with junk was astounding for such a rich part of Canada. Many of them were obviously challenged physically or mentally.

During a chat about this with a diplomat at a British High Commission function, he told me it was the same in Washington, and every other national capital he'd ever spent time in. It was as if these disoriented and vulnerable people gravitated to the capitals to be near the powerful decision-makers who could give them the help they needed. They were attracted by the democratic theory—not for the first time proved delusory—that those at the centre of political power were there to help.

One afternoon I was driving toward downtown Ottawa with a long-time resident of the city—a university lecturer, very liberal and intelligent. I stopped the car at a red light. While we waited, the front door of a small, rundown house a few feet away across the sidewalk on the passenger side opened, and a large man with dark skin and Middle Eastern features emerged. He bounded down his steps, clutching something in his right hand, heading, it seemed, directly toward the car. My passenger said, "Jesus Christ," threw one arm around his head, and moved frantically away from the window. He would have landed on top of me if his seat belt hadn't restrained him.

The man outside skirted the front of our car and jogged across the intersection while the pedestrian light blinked in warning. He'd been running in order to cross the street before the "Don't Walk" signal came on. When he reached the other side, he stopped and looked back at his house. A woman was standing in the doorway, with a little boy clutching her skirt, and she was calling out something to the man. He nodded, waved, and went into a small shop on the corner. She probably said, "Don't forget the milk." The thing he was clutching in his hand was a wallet.

My passenger grinned at me sheepishly and said, "Sorry about that." Then he said, "Honest to God, for a split second there, I thought the guy had a gun in his hand and that he was about to rob us and probably shoot us in the process." We discussed his reaction. He was no shrinking violet, this fellow, but a big former varsity athlete. And there wasn't a racist bone in his body. He was a liberal, and exceedingly supportive of minorities and immigrants. In previous conversations, he had described how much he appreciated the growing ethnic diversity of Ottawa and Toronto.

Yet, he frankly conceded now, if that man had been a white, mainstream Canadian in a suit, he probably wouldn't have batted an eye. He concluded that all human beings must be hard-wired genetically to feel a spontaneous fear when suddenly confronted by a foreign-looking stranger. Our ancestors who had responded in that way probably had a better chance of surviving an encounter with an invader, he said, and to go on to produce progeny with the same hard-wired reaction. No wonder there were so many unthinking racists and xenophobes in the world. It took rational thinking and a developed culture of tolerance to overcome our genetic phobia. He wondered what I thought.

I told him that if the man had in fact been an invader, I'd be dead, because I'd been staring at the traffic light the whole time, dozily indifferent to danger from all murderous strangers in the vicinity. We laughed, but this experience and his assessment were thought-provoking in a multi-ethnic Canada where prejudice was by no means dead.

I WAS REQUIRED BY my contract with the provincial government to maintain a residence in Newfoundland, and therefore they had agreed to help me find a decent and inexpensive apartment in Ottawa. However, "decent and inexpensive" in one of the most expensive cities in Canada soon proved to be an absolute contradiction in terms.

With the aid of a rental agent, I looked at a dozen furnished apartments all over the city. Considering the rate of rent we were prepared to pay, my choice quickly narrowed down to two. One was in an old house in the Glebe I would be sharing with a delightful couple dressed in horse blanket–like coverings and open sandals over hiking socks, whose own living quarters were separated from the "apartment" by a curtain of swaying beads and fumes you might smell at a rock concert.

The second possibility was in a downtown building with an ancient, faded grandeur; it was nearly as cheap as the first apartment. The relatively low rent of the second place surprised me because I was told that Cabinet ministers and senators had flats in the building. But when I viewed the one on offer, I could understand why its rent was relatively cheap.

As the representative of a province teetering on the brink of insolvency

I had no wish to live in luxury, but I did want to be near government activity. I signed the lease on the downtown apartment. Then I sent the owner's agent a list—the first of several—of repairs: broken toilet, light in bedroom not working, towel rack in bathroom broken, paint badly chipped, window in bedroom stuck open, all lamps too weak to read by, paint cans stored in kitchen cupboard with dishes, aforesaid dishes filthy, oven filthy, fridge filthy, thing in bathtub for turning on shower broken, drain in bathroom clogged, bed in second bedroom in several pieces, scurrying insect spotted heading for cover in bathroom, air conditioner not working despite thirty degrees Celsius outside and inside.

The week I moved in, the refrigerator stopped functioning without warning and spoiled the supermarket cartload of fresh and frozen food I had placed in it. I discovered jagged pieces of broken glass in the oven of the old stove. The landlord's agent dragged in a replacement fridge and stove. On inspection, the new fridge seemed okay, but the "new" stove contained a big splotch all over the inside of the oven, as if a large turkey had exploded in it. I found out from the owner's agent that the landlord was an elderly gentleman who now lived in Toronto; he had issued the agent orders, on pain of certain death, not to spend any of his meagre retirement income on the place.

A person from St. John's who visited my apartment, after it had been fixed up a bit, took one glance around and said, "This is the place Danny's government got for you? Christ, do you think Danny would live here?" We looked at each other and roared with laughter.

A young civil servant from the Atlantic provinces who'd been seconded by the federal government to a mid-level position in Ottawa told me during a chat at a function that the apartment the feds had automatically assigned to her cost nearly double the rent that mine did. The head of a francophone organization funded by the government of Canada, in a province with a minuscule percentage of French speakers, asked me during a meeting how much my budget was. I told him the amount was in our provincial estimates at $300,000, but that that first-year figure was a shot in the dark, and it would probably be less. He looked at me in amazement and exclaimed how pathetic that amount was compared to the federal grant his organization was receiving every year to foster the linguistic aspirations of several thousand francophones. I was starting to see why so many provincial civil servants would abandon their own governments and go over to the dark side—the dark but rich federal side.

THE ONE EXPERIENCE IN Ottawa that would cause me the greatest amount of grief and amusement had nothing to do with my job. In fact, it was totally trivial. After thirty years of comfortable monthly visits to my St. John's barber, Maurice Lahey, to have my locks shorn, it was with some misgivings that I realized it was time for my first Ottawa haircut.

I went into a barbershop near my temporary office. It was in a classy hotel and looked like a nice spot. The barber motioned me wordlessly into a chair and, grunting in reply to my instructions, started snipping. Previous haircuts had always included the satisfaction of knowing that Maurice and I had solved most of the world's problems together. The only words I got out of buddy with the scissors in Ottawa came at the very end, when I said, "That looks like a good job." To which he replied, "Jeez, it's only a haircut."

A few minutes afterwards, I stepped into an elevator containing a woman and her two preteen sons. On our way up, I noticed that the boys were trying not to look at the side of my head, trying not to catch each other's eye, and trying to keep their giggles from erupting into guffaws. Even their sensible-looking mother turned her eyes away from me and smothered a titter.

When they got out, I could hear, as the door closed, their explosion of laughter in the corridor. I ventured a look at myself in the mirror of the elevator. I could see nothing at all laughable about my haircut. But when I turned my head to one side, and then the other, I suddenly discovered the source of their mirth.

It was late summer, and I had spent hours hiking in the sun. My face and neck were deeply tanned, except for those areas covered by hair, which, until an hour ago, had included the skin above my ears. The barber had shaved a wedge shape about an inch long above each of my ears, and these two upside-down V's were gleaming against the tanned background. I looked like *Star Trek*'s Mr. Spock.

Skulking back to my apartment building, I sneaked into the elevator—there was no one else inside, thank God—and furiously pushed the close-door button. Before the door could shut, Deputy Prime Minister Anne McClellan walked in. I couldn't decide whether to turn my back on her or run out. Before I could act, she looked at me as if she recognized me, and said hello. I faced her, mustered a greeting, and introduced myself. She said she'd heard about my coming to Ottawa and graciously suggested that we get together for lunch or dinner sometime. Then she got off at her floor, which was several floors below mine. Still off balance, I wandered out behind her.

She turned and asked me if this was my floor. Realizing my mistake, I said, "No, I'm all confused," and retreated back to the elevator with as much dignity as anyone who had two bright white wedges above each ear could marshal. I shuddered at the prospect of what the most powerful minister in Martin's Cabinet must be thinking: an extraterrestrial alien, claiming to be one Bill Rowe, had tried to follow her. Someone had told me when I first arrived in the capital that in Ottawa you lose a point off your IQ every month. I seemed to be making greater progress than that.

I did take some satisfaction, though, from the public benefit that resulted from my private misfortune. During the long days before sufficient hair grew out to take the glow off my shiny white ear caps, I noticed that, in place of the normal glum look on the faces of people I passed on sidewalks and in buildings, there were frequently grins, exchanged glances of amusement, and outright giggles. I had brought a little joy into their grim Ottawa day.

I FOUND A LOT that was very interesting in Ottawa, especially its fascinating political culture and its fine restaurants, galleries, and museums. A Montreal friend told me that whenever he left Ottawa to drive home to Montreal for the weekend, he always thought: "Happiness is seeing

Ottawa in the rear-view mirror." But I never thought that. I found there were many individual human factors that compensated for the general environment of coldness in Ottawa and warmed our frigid Canadian capital up.

The House of Commons provided much heat, and some light; later in this narrative I'll touch on the ups and downs of my dealings with our Newfoundland and Labrador MPs. What I found most interesting, and droll, was the reaction of some old-hand journalists, who were exposed hourly, day after day, to the goings-on in our central Canadian democracy. One of them said to me that the proof our Ottawa politicians are truthful and fair-minded is that they never speak well of each other.

Terms such as "freak show," "circus," "lunatic asylum," and "zoo" were common currency, but a couple of press gallery veterans I talked to reserved their greatest scorn for the thing that attracted most visitors to Parliament—Question Period. I encountered the two of them in the lobby one day, vying with each other to describe accurately the partisan antics of the Opposition, with their "questions," and the equally partisan antics of the ministers, with their "answers," during the Question Period that had just ended.

"Question Period is by its nature totally self-serving," said the first. "Question Period is to the real world what masturbation is to real sex."

"Moreover," the other stated gravely, "Question Period is to true democracy what porn is to true love."

You had to love those guys. Their commentaries certainly livened up an otherwise pretty dismal and discouraging process.

Later in this book, I'll describe the warm companionship of some of our provincial expatriates in Ottawa, and their contributions to our cause. But right now I want to mention two legendary figures from my past, who had soared exceedingly high before crashing back down to earth in flames. And who, I was delighted to learn, were rising again, phoenix-like, from their ashes.

When I arrived in Ottawa, I spotted media reports on the planned economic resurrection of the once celebrated entrepreneur Rod Bryden. I'd known Rod many years before. We had been in the same class together at law school in the early '60s, and we'd both received Sir James Dunn scholarships. At exam time, Rod always edged past the rest of us to lead the class. We attributed his success to the fact that, alone among us young bucks in our early twenties, he was married. While we were out partying and spending time on the mating dance, he was in his tranquil home, eating well and being looked after, comforted and coddled—and studying his head off as a result of the boredom. But we knew deep in our hearts that he always came first because he was smarter than the rest of us.

Rod Bryden went on to get a Master of Laws in the States and then taught law at the University of Saskatchewan. I didn't see Rod again in person until the late '60s, when Premier Joey Smallwood called down to my office to say an old buddy of mine was in his office—come on up. Federal Minister Otto Lang was visiting Joey, and with him was his assistant Rod Bryden. Lang had been the Dean of Law at the university and Rod had campaigned to get him elected to the House of Commons as the sole Liberal MP from Saskatchewan in the 1968 election, and hence the only choice for minister. It was a pleasure to reconnect with Rod.

Then, in the early '70s, Rod became assistant deputy minister to our own Don Jamieson, who was minister of the Department of Regional Economic Expansion (DREE). Rod became very familiar with Newfoundland and Labrador and its challenges, and I kept hearing about his intelligent ideas. But it was after he'd left government that Rod really proved how much smarter he was than the rest of us.

For the next couple of decades, he used his brains and government connections to accumulate vast wealth. Two companies he founded, Systemhouse Limited and Paperboard Industries Corporation, reportedly enjoyed annual revenues by 1990 of over seven hundred million. He also acquired ownership of the Ottawa Senators. Rod's meteoric business career led to his being named Ottawa's CEO of the Year in 2000, and lauded as the capital's consummate risk-taker. Not long afterwards, he took his precipitous financial tumble. As one of our mutual acquaintances said to me shortly after the new millennium, Rod Bryden's problem was that, as brilliant as he was, his boldness and daring were bigger, regrettably, than his brain.

By 2003, he was no longer the Rod Bryden who had been able to shake off Black Monday in October 1987, as a mere nuisance, easily absorbing his one-day loss of $115 million when the North American stock markets crashed. Now some of his business ventures seemed far too audacious, and had begun to seriously tank.

The year before I arrived in Ottawa, the Ottawa Senators, with debts in the tens of millions, had to petition the courts for temporary bankruptcy protection. The next year, business had gone even more sour for Rod. Disgruntled investors had forced him out of the World Heart Corporation, a company he'd formed a few years before in coalition with the University of Ottawa Heart Institute and some well-known names like Michael Cowpland.

Later in 2004, media reports marvelled at how Bryden had managed to avoid personal bankruptcy through nothing but his negotiating savvy: He'd been able to convince his creditors to accept a mere $600,000 for his almost $100 million of debt. He told reporters, with amazing sang-froid, that he'd been relaxing in Cape Breton over the summer, and was sporting his best tan in years. Now he was going to revive one of his small companies, with just one employee, and he was intent on making millions again in the near future.

I did wonder how his money-losing investors felt about his breezy attitude and cocky self-confidence, but that didn't matter to me personally. I just wanted to get together with him for old times' sake, so I fired off an email saying hello and that I would like to join him for a chat. He replied with an invitation to lunch in a few days, which I accepted with alacrity.

Meanwhile, I asked a mutual acquaintance who knew the business community in Ottawa about Rod's present status there. He told me that Rod still enjoyed a good reputation, and that few if any investors who may have been burned seemed to hold it against him. They had gone in with their eyes open and Rod was an honourable man. I was glad to hear it, for Rod's sake but also because it might be useful to our provincial cause to have a charismatic individual in Ottawa, who was already very knowledgeable about Newfoundland and Labrador, brought up to speed on the Atlantic Accord. Plus he had a brother who was an influential Liberal senator.

A few days later, walking into the Toulouse Restaurant at the Marriott Hotel for lunch with Rod, I ran into a prominent businessman from Newfoundland in the lobby, with his entourage. I told him I was meeting with Rod Bryden inside, and that he should come over and say hello. He said he would like to, although they had meetings that afternoon and were pressured for time. I was curious to see if the businessman would show up at our table. Five years ago he or any other businessperson would have jumped at such an opportunity. But then again, five years ago, Rod might not have been sitting in the restaurant of the Marriott idling away an hour with an old law school chum from the golden long ago.

Rod rose from the table to greet me, exuding fitness and energy and full-throttle enthusiasm. He immediately told me how delighted he was that his proposal to his creditors had been accepted, and would soon be sanctioned by the courts. That meant no one would be able to come after him. He needed space and time if he was to live up to his promise to himself to make $25 million in the next five years.

Talking about promise and potential, we nattered about some of our law school buddies who'd had the world by the tail back then, discussing what had happened to them since. One, a superb student and athlete, a top international scholarship winner, who should have gone to the pinnacle, either politically or as an alpha mandarin, went nowhere near the heights to which his potential should have catapulted him. Why? Sports. Brainy as he was, he also seemed to have a charley horse between those ears. If he had a game of squash booked at three in the afternoon, he wouldn't miss it even if the prime minister himself wanted to see him. As a former squash player myself, I empathized entirely with our friend's priorities.

Another man, who had often led the school in debates over legal issues, and who, I thought at the time, might wind up on the Supreme

Court of Canada, was stuck in neutral at the middle level of the Department of Justice.

As to making Rod savvy to the justice of our position on the Atlantic Accord so that he could get it across to his older brother Senator John Bryden and others, I found that I didn't need to spend much time on background information. Rod's memory of Newfoundland and Labrador's problems from his days as ADM under Don Jamieson remained keen. So, naturally, it wasn't long before we started yakking about our experiences with Jamieson, the literal and figurative political colossus.

How, I wondered, had he found Jamieson to work for, especially with his reputation in those days for drinking a fair amount? Not that his consumption seemed to interfere much. On the government aircraft one day, flying to some meeting, everyone on board had a drink, but Don, over the duration of the two- or three-hour flight, drank a full bottle of scotch. Yet, when he reached his destination he was still able to perform brilliantly. We agreed that his ability in that regard was a blessing and a curse. No matter how much he drank, he still seemed to be able to get up and make a dazzling speech.

I recalled an official function at the Newfoundland Hotel in St. John's, at which Don was the guest speaker. Beforehand, in the reception room where the head table guests were offered a drink, Don lowered several substantial glasses in half an hour. When we arrived at the head table, I noticed Don's eyes swimming about in his head, quite independently of each another. But when he got up to orate, that familiar, unerring pipe-organ voice carried him through with humour and verve and authority.

Sometimes, though, the booze let him down a little. A close friend of mine had been summoned to Don's place in Swift Current; Don had hoped to recruit him as an election candidate. Don was holding court with my friend and two or three others, sitting well back in his easy chair, obviously sozzled, when his wife called out to him from the front door: a group of clergymen—some ministerial delegation or other—had arrived to see him. Attempting to heave himself up out of his chair and grumbling at the interruption, Don tipped the chair, and himself, over backwards, so that he was resting on his neck upside down on the floor with his feet behind his head.

The men around Don, momentarily paralyzed by the catastrophe, started to rush toward him to see if he had injured or killed himself. His wife, knowing nothing about the accident, called out again that the clergy were waiting to see him. A loud pipe-organ bellow emanated from under the overturned chair and resounded throughout the whole house: "TELL THE CLERGY TO GO FUCK THEMSELVES!"

The booze certainly did not hold Jamieson back. He would go on to become Trudeau's leading minister in the late '70s, a man who, as minister of Foreign Affairs, would get off a plane in Russia, bear-hug the fearsome Soviet premier Leonid Brezhnev and kiss him on both cheeks.

I surmised to myself that perhaps Don Jamieson's absolute self-confidence and audacity in any situation had rubbed off on Rod. Now, though, Rod had his work cut out for him in re-establishing his credibility. As we finished our leisurely lunch in the fall of 2004 at the Marriott, I noticed that the prominent Newfoundland businessman out in the lobby had not bothered to come in to be introduced to this former financial titan.

Over the next year or two, Rod became the new chairman of cancer drug developer PharmaGap, Inc., and president and CEO of Plasco Energy Group, an Ottawa firm specializing in developing energy production using "plasma gasification from household waste." If he wasn't on his way to his new $25 million, it was obviously not for want of creative imagination. Meanwhile, in addition to the pleasure of meeting again, I knew he had left our get-together knowlegeable about Newfoundland and Labrador's case in the Atlantic Accord struggle, and willing to convey that knowledge to others when the opportunity arose.

IN ORDER NOT TO waste time when it came to registering at various government offices as a current Ontario resident—health insurance, car registration, and the other hoops I had to jump through—I asked an Ottawa orientation agency to advise me on what I needed to do and to help me get to the correct offices fast. On the day designated for our rounds, I waited in my car at the appointed time and meeting place for Margaret, my assigned guide, to come by.

At 1:00 p.m. on the dot, a Chrysler PT Cruiser slowed down next to me and the driver opened her window. "Are you Bill?" she asked. I answered, "Yes," and then I asked, rather insincerely, "Are you Margaret?" Like anyone else in Canada, I would have recognized Margaret Trudeau in a throng in a packed stadium. "Yes," she replied. "Follow me." Whereupon I was led across town by the former first lady of Canada to a garage where my car would be inspected.

Margaret Trudeau seemed to be well acquainted with the garage, and exchanged pleasantries with the employees. In turn, they bantered with me, answering my serious questions with smartass replies, showing off shamelessly in front of her like adolescent boys. While we waited for the tests to be performed, Margaret took me to a nearby coffee shop. Inside, people's heads swivelled as she preceded me to our seats. (At the time, she was awaiting trial on impaired driving charges.) She didn't seem to notice the attention.

Over our coffees, she said the garage was where she and Pierre used to get their cars serviced when they were together. I told her that she and I had met twice before. Once during a federal election in the '70s—God, nearly thirty years before—when she was in St. John's campaigning on her husband's behalf and, incidentally, outshining him mightily. The second meeting was at a reception hosted by her and Pierre in Ottawa; she was the attentive and charming hostess whom every man there was in love with. What I didn't tell her about was a dinner meeting I'd had with Trudeau at the Château Laurier in Ottawa in 1978 after his and Margaret's scandal-filled split.

I was there as a provincial Liberal Party leader, and I was seated next to the PM. During dinner, he told me that federal Liberal Party strategists were trying to use his sympathy-inspiring status as a betrayed husband and martyred father to persuade him to call an election. Do it now while he was the injured party, they were advising; if he waited too long, Margaret's antics and all the other negative aspects of the very public marriage breakdown might damage his chances for victory. But Trudeau had serious doubts about allowing that experience to be employed as a political tactic. I said he was right to have doubts, both generally and in this particular case. There was no way he was going to lose to Progressive Conservative leader Joe Clark anyway, so why should he sully himself by trying to benefit politically from the behaviour of the mother of his children?

Trudeau waited another year, until 1979, to call an election. On the eve of that election, photos of Margaret somewhat scantily clad about the nether regions enjoying herself at Studio 54 nightclub in New York, together with detailed accounts of her shenanigans, were featured on front pages across Canada. The query on everyone's lips was what the hell was the prime minister's wife and the mother of his children going to do next to embarrass Canada? Trudeau lost the election to Joe Clark.

Now, twenty-five years later, Margaret Trudeau and I were sitting in a coffee shop talking about her life. She was open and frank, as she has been in public, about the undiagnosed bipolar illness that had been the cause of much of the early turmoil. She spoke of how proud she was of the children of both her first and second marriage. The latter had broken up not long after her son Michel's death. "They say that often happens in these cases," she remarked; after her son's death she thought she'd never do anything again. But she went on to say that "time does heal"; this part-time job, orienting people like me coming to Ottawa to live, was her first emergence after years of staying home. She was being paid eleven dollars an hour.

When we went back to the garage, the top guy there reminisced about the old days when they used to service Trudeau's notorious Mercedes convertible. I paid the hefty bill for the unnecessary inspection of my two-year-old car. It was an obvious rip-off by the Ontario government and an insult to a sister province. Why couldn't you simply transfer your registration from Newfoundland and Labrador to Ontario?

I followed Margaret Trudeau to another garage for an emission test. The person performing the test asked me if my car, a well-known model, was front-wheel drive. That certainly gave me confidence in his expertise. He drove the front wheels onto rollers and revved the car up to a frightening speed for an inordinate length of time. It caused one godawful racket, but Margaret and I had to stay in the same room since they did not provide a waiting room we could escape to. We sat on old dusty metal chairs, trying to chat politely over the din as the test went on and on. My two-year-old car—I was told it had been manufactured in Ontario— passed the Ontario emission test. I paid that hefty bill with a strong feeling that this test was even more of a total rip-off of car owners moving to Ontario from another province, and that it existed solely for the financial benefit of garages and government. A service department manager at a garage where I later went for grease and oil told me that it would have taken thirty seconds to look in a specifications book on cars to see if my model and year had acceptable Ontario emission standards.

Then Margaret took me to register for OHIP, the Ontario Medicare plan.

With those momentous transactions out of the way, Margaret Trudeau and I parted company, me with renewed, nostalgic recollections of federal-provincial politics involving her husband in the '60s and '70s, and she—I hoped—with a fair understanding of our position on the Atlantic Accord. She had shown a sharp curiosity about it, and said she would be sure to convey, where possible, her heightened appreciation of where we stood. I hoped that by making use of such one-on-one opportunities, wherever I went and whomever I talked to, I could further our cause incrementally. Certainly I took merciless advantage of every chance and every person I spent time with to do so.

I followed Margaret's course in the media after that, especially her candid public discussion about her long undiagnosed manic depression. And I have to confess that, as disapproving as I may feel about any leniency toward drinking and driving, I was not unhappy months later when the charges against her were thrown out by the judge for police violation of her constitutional rights under the Charter of Rights. That was the document brought in by her estranged husband after he won his next election against Joe Clark less than a year after the first and became prime minister again, quipping, "Welcome to the eighties."

If Trudeau hadn't been defeated in 1979, at least partly as a result of

Margaret's frolics, and hadn't received the unexpected chance to become PM again months later, he would never have brought in the Charter of Rights. Traumatic defeat and surprising victory gave him the impetus to create a solid legacy as prime minister, after several years of drift. The result was the Charter of Rights. Margaret Trudeau had indirectly influenced its conception, and would benefit from it.

MEANWHILE, ON A FAR lower plane than constitutional philosophy and human rights, I was struggling to get a mundane little Ottawa office set up. As before in dealing with the bureaucracy, the process produced moments that alternated between utter stupefaction and gut-busting hilarity.

My needs in Ottawa were not numerous or complicated: a cellphone, a laptop, an assistant, and an office space with some standard furniture and equipment. Until a permanent office could be established, I had made arrangements to rent a provisional office, a small, one-person room at the Minto Business Centre.

When I first arrived in Ottawa at the end of August, I marched right over to the business centre to put my files in a temporary office and get down to work. The manager came out to greet me in the lobby. She looked embarrassed at my eagerness. She had thought things were going well with her contact in my government in St. John's, she said, but after sending them the lease for signature many days ago, she still hadn't received a signed copy back from the official she'd been dealing with in the Department of Transportation and Works. And, regrettably, the centre's corporate policy was that I couldn't be permitted to occupy an office until she had the signed lease in hand. I skulked over to a corner of the lobby and called the premier's office. They tracked down the lease, gathering dust in a pile on the responsible official's desk, and finally got the thing signed and faxed back.

One problem with entering the civil service after a professional or business career is how naive you are about the way government operates. In a law office, the need to meet a payroll and other overhead expenses week after week meant that you had to produce at a fairly fast clip or you simply went belly up. Arriving from that world with the innocence of a babe in arms, I actually believed that three months was enough lead time, guided by an Ottawa rental agent, to locate and set up a permanent office, and I had negotiated the temporary lease for that period. "Lord, what fools these mortals be!"

Meanwhile, I shouldered the equally Herculean task of trying to acquire the two basic tools I needed to function—a cellphone and a laptop. I was told upon my appointment that these items would be provided forthwith. But afterwards, they seemed to be beyond the wit of humankind to obtain. Apparently the delay in getting a cellphone was caused by some insurmountable difficulty in obtaining a phone number from Bell Telephone in Ontario, a difficulty I could never learn the nature of from start to finish. Whatever the problem was, the cellphone with a government number did not arrive for twelve weeks.

When it did arrive, out of the blue, with no information accompanying it, I sent an email to the responsible official in the premier's office, asking if there was anything I needed to do to get it up and running. I received an email back from him with no greeting, no salutation, no vestige of human courtesy. Nothing but a one-word message: "No." Evidently he had gone sooky on me. I had noticed earlier his tendency to do that.

For long periods, messages to my operations man in the premier's office went unanswered. My work diary is full of entries about emails and telephone calls that received no reply. The poor fellow had gone underground, incommunicado; apparently he couldn't cope. Judging from his monosyllabic reply when he did emerge from his shell for an instant, he was angry because I'd had the temerity to ask him occasionally over the past twelve weeks how the acquisition of my cellphone was coming along down there.

And a laptop? It would take sixteen weeks of asking him and, in the end, my (reluctant) going over his head to complain to his boss, before I received a computer. Honest to God, I could only marvel at the genius-level procrastination involved.

And how were the officials back in St. John's, who were responsible for setting in motion, on an urgent basis, a competitive process for hiring my administrative assistant, making out? Here's what they had to do: place an ad in the newspapers, cull the applicants, and then get together with me for the interviews some morning or afternoon. My original estimate was that the whole process would take six weeks, tops, even if someone were trying to break the *Guinness Book of World Records* for the world's most sluggish bureaucratic pace. But it turned out to be more entertaining than that.

I emailed and phoned my contact in the premier's office every week for a status report; after firm assurances that all was in hand, I waited and called again, waited and called again. Between the day of my appointment and the day my administrative assistant was hired on the aforementioned urgent basis, seventeen weeks—four and a half months—had inserted themselves.

The assistant we chose was Christie Meadus, and she was a treasure. On the very day I'd been appointed back in July she had fired off an email to the premier's office from Ottawa, where she was living and working, expressing her keen interest in becoming involved with the new provincial representative's office. Months later, when we interviewed her along with the other applicants on the short list, she shone.

Christie was representative of many other young people from Newfoundland and Labrador living on the mainland who are such positive forces for our province. Hailing from Labrador West, she had attended Carleton University; as a first-year undergraduate, she represented Newfoundland and Labrador in the House of Commons Page Program. Graduating with an honours degree, she subsequently worked as a research assistant for several Members of Parliament.

It pained me to think that, with a little efficiency in the hiring process, the province's new office in Ottawa could have been benefiting for weeks from the expertise of this eager, earnest, and knowledgeable young person. Christie dealt with most of the day-to-day challenges of setting up the permanent office while I pursued outstanding matters, especially the Atlantic Accord, along with 5 Wing Goose Bay. The Labrador air force base was being woefully underutilized. The town of Happy Valley–Goose Bay, the Government of Newfoundland and Labrador, and Labrador MPs had been carrying on a campaign for quite some time, trying to pressure the Government of Canada into increasing the activities of its own air force there, and those of its international allies.

After seventeen weeks, the responsible officials in St. John's had finally obtained the required number of lease proposals for a permanent office and we quickly decided on the most appropriate one. A month after that, the end of December—five months after my appointment—a formal lease was still not in place. Whenever I ventured onto the chosen premises of our permanent office to have a look at the renovations being done (at the landlord's cost), said landlord would lunge out of wherever he was lurking and ambush me in the corridor to ask, reasonably enough, when he was going to finally receive that signed lease from my government.

I could only tell him what I'd been told: the lease for the office had to go to Cabinet for formal approval and then the appropriate minister had to sign his or her name to it. I kept asking the premier's office to try to accomplish those massive undertakings as soon as possible, since my painful encounters with the frustrated landlord were straining our relationship.

Christie was great. Every day she conferred with authorized officials in St. John's in an attempt to acquire furniture and equipment for the office. I asked her to keep, for the record, a detailed list of each and every difficulty she was encountering. I wasn't interested in ratting anyone out. I was only interested in giving our relatively new premier an overview of how, in my experience, the civil service functioned. The list of foot-dragging by officials grew as long as my arm. It included the fact that the official responsible for paying the rent for our temporary office had neglected to do so for the month of December, and the representative of the premier of Newfoundland and Labrador in Ottawa was being threatened with eviction.

Acting on the absolute assurance from St. John's that we would have delivery at the start of the new year of the required furniture and equip-

ment, and that we'd be able to move into the permanent office right after
the Christmas break, I gave notice to quit the temporary quarters for the
end of December.

From St. John's, where I'd gone for year-end meetings with the premier's office, I telephoned Christie in Ottawa first thing in January for a
status report. We both broke out in laughter over the absurdity of her news:
the responsible officials had waited until Christmas Eve to place the order
for furniture; the supplier closed down between Christmas Day and New
Year's. Nothing would arrive at the office until well into January. We would
both be working out of our apartments for the next month. Between the
day the premier appointed me and the day we managed to obtain and
make functional a small office space in Ottawa, six months would elapse.

A few weeks before that happened, I had recounted some of the problems I was having getting any action from people in various departments,
including one in the premier's office itself, to Brian Crawley. I told him that
officials did not seem to take requests or orders from the premier's chief
of staff very seriously.

He seemed surprised, and then said dismissively that he didn't like
administration; it was not his strong point. I could understand that, I said,
but surely that kind of administration wasn't his job. Surely his role was
to oversee administrators, ensuring that administration moved along effi-
ciently and professionally, especially when specific problems were brought
to his attention. I wondered if his lack of consciousness of my problems
might have been part of the problem itself. In fairness, the premier relied
on Crawley heavily during every crisis, and this was most obvious during
much of this period, when the dire Atlantic Accord situation was preoccu-
pying everyone.

At the end of 2004, five months into the job, I felt it necessary to give
the premier's chief of staff—and, through him, the premier himself—a full
report, chapter and verse, on how the directives from the premier's office
had been met by various government departments. This kind of report is
a tedious exercise, of course. Compiling it wasn't primarily for my own
benefit; I had already come through the worst. But I was so appalled and

disgusted at the wasteful ineptitude of various government services—indeed, I considered it dangerous—that I felt obliged to report to the premier what I had experienced. And so I laid it on the line in writing.

I wrote that the logistics of setting up the office in Ottawa were handled with staggering inefficiency and a complete lack of priority. And it wasn't for lack of carping on my part. I pitied my liaisons in the premier's office and the Executive Council office who were on the receiving end of my constant badgering. I had no idea what problems existed in the bureaucracy to cause incessant delays and outright inaction when I tried to make the stogged-up system percolate. Was it lack of resources? A breakdown in the chain of command? Lack of clear accountability? Pure vindictiveness? Crawley's guess was as good as mine.

Whatever caused it, the importance the premier had attached, both publicly and privately, to getting this office up and running simply had not flowed through the system. Although I had received expressions of co-operation and can-do-ism at the start, in practice I encountered lethargy, roadblocks, and unaccountable delays.

I told the premier's office how hard it was to disengage oneself from such day-to-day frustrations and operate at a productive level. The success of the office to date had been in spite of rather than because of the level of logistical support. To say that the situation was tolerable, however, would be false. Only the thought of the huge challenges facing the province and Danny Williams as its premier, a novice premier in his first year in office, had kept me involved in this administrative quagmire.

This time, when I met with Brian Crawley in St. John's at year's end to discuss the fact that I'd never experienced anything so constipated, apathetic, and sluggish to the point of complete incompetence in my life, he agreed. He'd already made calls about the situation, and he said the premier himself was going to make heads roll at high levels. Why, I wondered, did it require a French Revolution solution for the premier's representative in Ottawa to obtain a small office with some basic equipment and a few sticks of furniture?

One comical matter sticks out in my mind as symbolic of the total malaise. Because I drove up to Ottawa in my own car, and would be using my car for work there, the government undertook to have my snow tires sent from St. John's to Ottawa. No problem with that, my logistics liaison said: "Done." But as time went by, I realized that sending my tires must be a challenge beyond the wit of man—bureaucratic man, anyway. Every time I called him about it, they were looking for someone to do it. They needed three quotes on the job. That meant having the representatives of three different trucking companies traipse down into my basement in St. John's to look at four tires so that they could bid on the project. "Oh for the love of God," I said. "Just get some trucker who is coming this way to throw them aboard and I'll pay for it myself."

"Right on," replied my liaison. "Guaranteed, sir." Do I need to add that my car would plough through the snow and ice of the Ottawa winter without snow tires, which remained in my basement in St. John's?

Maddening at the time, it was amusing for a while in retrospect. But I stopped laughing in July 2007, when the Williams government was forced to set up Justice Margaret Cameron's Commission of Inquiry on Hormone Receptor Testing, to investigate hundreds of botched breast cancer tests. I am not for a second comparing the trivial problems I encountered with the gravity of that inquiry, but the victims' experiences struck a resonant chord with me as I listened to the delays and ineptness and lack of professionalism described at the Cameron Inquiry with respect to the operations of the provincial Department of Health and the Eastern Health Corporation.

I can't claim to predict the future, but a remark in my notes after five months of wading through the administrative swamp strikes me now as sadly prophetic. I told Brian Crawley toward the end of 2004 that a person more knowledgeable than myself about these unfathomable bureaucratic practices should advise the premier on whether my experiences reflected a breakdown peculiar to the setting up of this new office in Ottawa, or whether, more alarmingly, they were symptomatic of very serious problems throughout the entire government system.

I used to make the following remark to people about the delays in getting my office set up: "The only thing that saves us from a tyranny by the bureaucracy is its absolute incompetence and inefficiency." As I write this in the wake of the Cameron Inquiry, that doesn't sound as amusing to me as it used to. Tragically, incompetence doesn't always stop at the level of someone like me not receiving a phone or a desk or an office in a timely, efficient fashion. Since the Cameron Inquiry, there have been more indications that the health care system in this province is foundering, and that other government departments are also suffering from dysfunction.

SPEAKING OF INADEQUACIES IN the health care system, a summit of the first ministers of Canada on health took place in Ottawa a few weeks after my arrival. It was designed to address the problems in health care across Canada. It was there that I would see clearly the huge obstacles that Danny Williams was up against in making some headway on finances with the prime minister and his henchmen. At that top-level meeting, I would watch Quebec premier Jean Charest leave everyone in his dust as he ran circles around the prime minister and the other premiers. Newfoundland and Labrador would lag far behind, struggling for breath.

— CHAPTER FIVE —

To Danny and Paul's Good Health

IN MID-SEPTEMBER 2004, Prime Minister Paul Martin and the premiers met in Ottawa to discuss the crisis in Canadian health care. The event would contain elements of high drama and low comedy. More money for health care was important to Danny Williams, of course, but the role of equalization was also on the agenda, and just as urgent a matter. This would be Danny's first opportunity for a face-to-face public confrontation with the prime minister since Martin made his commitment to the premier the previous June for a better deal on the Atlantic Accord.

The media were skeptical about the summit's chances of success. The always astute Chantal Hébert of the *Toronto Star* wrote on September 10 about the horse-trading that would begin at the commencement of the summit. She was right, especially when it came to the provinces of Quebec and Newfoundland and Labrador, with their separate agendas that had little to do with health. Paul Martin, she said, was walking into a political minefield, and he'd better be armed with enough cash and political acumen to get across it.

Enough cash? No problem. Cash was coming out of federal ears all of a sudden. Now that Martin was prime minister of a minority government, loot was miraculously available—in stark contrast to when he'd been the Finance minister, proudly bringing down budgets year after year that cut the guts out of provincial health care systems and caused most of the problems he was now so eager to solve.

Political acumen? There would be divided views on that. Some would argue that Martin's behaviour at the health summit indicated total political collapse in the face of Quebec's demands. Others would say, no, Martin pulled off a work of political genius that would save the federation. (Still others would respond that if that was genius, then the fine line between genius and insanity had been erased.)

Well, whatever part Martin played at this summit, I believe that street-smart Jean Charest, the canny premier of Quebec, emerged the clear winner. And we shall see what Danny Williams was up against in trying to compete with Quebec for a little attention, and how he walked away with yet more rhetorical bullshit from Martin which would blow up in everyone's face a month later.

Danny had made me a delegate at the summit. I possessed no expertise in the area of health care or its delivery, but I was delighted to be involved as a critical observer and networker for the province. On Sunday, September 12, the day before the summit began, Brian Crawley asked me if I could meet him at five that afternoon in his room at the Westin Hotel to discuss our strategies.

When I entered his room, Crawley and other officials were preoccupied with composing some speaking notes for Williams for the opening of the summit. Crawley's room was not a suite but a simple bedroom filled mostly by the bed, leaving only cramped space for the steady stream of officials coming in for briefings and discussions. There wasn't even a real desk to work on. Big tall Crawley looked rather comical sitting there on the side of the bed hunched over and typing unsteadily into his laptop. The fruits of his creativity were supposed to emerge from a small portable printer on the bedside table. It looked like the kind of printer that you

might have given your ten-year-old to fiddle around with in the early days
of computers. It didn't work very well. In between the spasmodic typing
and the printer breakdowns, we began to talk about health care, but
within minutes we got diverted by what was really on everyone's mind—
Danny's problems with achieving a new Atlantic Accord.

Danny and Elizabeth Matthews came into the room while we were discussing the Accord. Danny said he had never been so frustrated by anything in his life. The federal position on the Accord was purely oral, and it
kept changing constantly. The feds had put absolutely nothing on paper,
and evidently refused to do so. Danny looked and sounded like he was
really spoiling for a fight with Martin at this health meeting. Crawley and
Matthews and I interjected some remarks about the feds playing their shell
game: how their performance was a complete sham and a charade and an
exercise in bad faith. All of which had the effect, not that he needed it, of
egging Danny on even more.

I said that if only Paul Martin could have seen the premier's chief of
staff a few minutes ago, sitting there on the side of his bed in this little
room crowded with advisers, trying to pump out some words on a hopelessly inadequate Mickey Mouse printer, the sight would have made the
PM pony up all the Accord money we wanted, right then and there, no
questions asked. We laughed, but the underlying issue couldn't have been
more serious. Without big changes in the way equalization and clawback
were handled under the Accord, the wealthy federal government would
continue to reap the lion's share of our offshore revenues while our
province, so resource-rich yet so cash-poor, faced insolvency, as deficits on
current account continued to balloon. When I parted company with Danny
and his entourage that evening, he had built up a pretty good head of
steam, and I could see that he was going to let off a powerful blast at our
federal tormentors during the next couple of days.

This drastic deterioration in fellowship, just three months after Paul
Martin's commitment to Danny in June, was an indication of how the
growing animosity between them over the Atlantic Accord would domi-
nate all their relations, impairing progress on other federal-provincial pro-

grams and causing serious strains, as we shall see, in Danny's own government.

The first morning of the three-day health summit, according to the proposed agenda, was to be devoted to Aboriginal health. The second and third days of the conference were to be given over to, among other things, reforming health care. There was an action plan for waiting times, a national pharmacare program, home care, improving the delivery of health care in the territories and Labrador, and for funding the package, which included, ominously, the thorny issue of equalization. In true form, Martin had thrown into the mix everything that the federal ministers and the provincial premiers could dream up, plus, some wag said, whatever the receptionist at Martin's own private health clinic in Montreal might have groused about during his latest visit.

When I arrived at the conference centre for the beginning of the summit, I ran into a large, loud, placard-waving demonstration of nurses outside the main door. They were in the nation's capital from across Canada to din their health care messages into the ears of the first ministers. I was thinking to myself that nurses were about the best demonstrators I'd ever encountered, when I heard my name called above the racket. Turning, I saw, wearing a slogan-bearing T-shirt and waving a placard bigger than herself, the president of the Newfoundland and Labrador Nurses' Union, Debbie Forward.

She and I had a little gab before I went inside. I had always admired her front-line activism and unremitting advocacy for nurses. The demonstrations she'd led during their strike against the government of Brian Tobin in the '90s drove poor Brian and his government off their heads with its slogan-shouting, loud singing, and wooden-placard-handle-pounding on the floor just outside the House of Assembly. Their constant in-your-face presence in the media had put a big dent in Tobin's popular vote during the provincial election. It was probably the trauma of that strike more than anything else, some Liberal Party members mused, that made Tobin vamoose as premier of Newfoundland and Labrador a year or two later, and escape back to the mainland.

Inside the conference hall, the premiers would make many references to the nurses outside and to their colleagues back home on the front lines of health care. Even if the remarks were mealy-mouthed and insincere and meant purely for the occasion, at least the first ministers were impressed enough to make them. Not every demonstration outside a first ministers' summit has caused a similar reaction inside.

Before heading up to our provincial caucus room, I encountered a female reporter who used to be posted to St. John's. Her stint in Ottawa had not increased her esteem for the federal civil service. As we talked, she pointed out to me a gaggle of young male federal bureaucrats, congregated in a corner and continually fishing their BlackBerrys out of their pockets. "The junior mandarin class looks a lot more content these days," she said. "With all those BlackBerrys in their pockets on 'vibrate,' all of a sudden they have a sex life."

Upstairs in our provincial room most of the members of our delegation of ministers and officials were milling or sitting around. Williams and Minister of Finance Loyola Sullivan were not present yet, but those that were there already comprised a high-powered group: Minister of Health Elizabeth Marshall; Clerk of the Executive Council Robert Thompson; Ross Reid; Brian Crawley; Deputy Minister of Finance Terry Paddon; Deputy Minister of Health Deborah Fry; Barbara Knight; Elizabeth Matthews; and other members of the departments of Health and Intergovernmental Affairs. The presence of some of these top officials, I heard later from the PMO, signalled to the prime minister that Danny Williams's agenda here went well beyond concerns with health.

The First Nations' delegates made impressive speeches about the health problems affecting their people, which were responded to in high-flown terms by first ministers. It was sad to contemplate that, if history were any guide, those responses would again turn out to be just so much empty puffery. But so it went. After this latest immense show of recognition and concern expressed in the most sympathetic political rhetoric at the highest levels of all governments in Canada, nothing would change on the ground. Hundreds more millions of dollars would be spent on the various empires at all levels, and many Aboriginals would still be left without decent water or sewerage or shelter. When I expressed my doubts to a mid-level official of Indian Affairs I met in the common room, he thought I was being much too cynical. I was starting to see where the main impediments to progress might lie.

For a good while that afternoon, I watched the proceedings of the first ministers on our TV screen, trying to get a grip on the various provincial positions. "Good luck with that," said one of our delegates. "That's like trying to get a grip on a St. John's fog bank." What was it, I wondered, about the makeup of the premiers—McGuinty of Ontario and Campbell of British Columbia in particular—that made them so rambling and long-winded? Was it Paul Martin's chairmanship that made them that boring? I tried to hearken back to the federal-provincial conferences I'd attended as a minister with Joey Smallwood when Pierre Trudeau was prime minister. Could our discussions have possibly been as soporific? They hadn't seemed to be. But that might have been because I was a participant. Someone back then who was in my position now—a captive audience of one—might have said that listening to us was the dreariest afternoon they had ever punched in. A journalist summed it all up for me. "I've come to the conclusion after all these years," he sighed, "that the only way to examine statements by first ministers at these things is not with a microscope but with a proctoscope."

Meanwhile, we officials in our provincial room were analyzing the input of the premiers as the proceedings droned on. I take pride in my major contribution to the analysis that day. When Ontario Premier Dalton McGuinty's face appeared on the TV screen and stayed on—and on and on—I noted for my colleagues his unnerving resemblance to Norman Bates of Hitchcock's *Psycho*. No one disagreed.

One of our officials seemed to have the right idea. He kept pecking at the keys on his laptop, occasionally glancing at the TV screen. I wished I'd had the wit to bring my own laptop with me so that I too could be working on some files, productively multi-tasking like him. When I was leaving the room at one point, I happened to glance down at his computer. He was multi-tasking all right. Big time. The screen was filled with a half-completed game of solitaire.

That evening I went to the official reception for delegates at the West Block. I was the only one there from the Newfoundland and Labrador delegation. That was too bad because there were federal ministers and officials present whom it might have been valuable for the others to talk to. I was told, however, that members of our delegation with line functions had important issues besides health sprung on them that evening, and would be discussing them among themselves.

I was delighted to meet at the reception, though, some young people from Newfoundland and Labrador who were working with the Canadian departments of Foreign Affairs and Intergovernmental Affairs. Every federal government official I talked to during my entire stay in Ottawa invariably brought up, spontaneously, the names of bright, creative Newfoundlanders and Labradorians in their departments, and the admirable contributions they were making to work and morale.

I also had a chat with federal Intergovernmental Affairs Minister Lucienne Robillard. Had she perceived at this summit, she wondered, a growing truculence on the part of my premier, Danny Williams? When I smiled and said she was very perceptive but that she "ain't seen nothin' yet," she laughed and signified that she was far less perturbed about Danny's belligerence than some others on the federal side. Being from Quebec, she was pretty used to hearing rants at prime ministers in that conference centre. Then she brought me over and introduced me to my counterpart from Quebec, the newly appointed provincial representative in Ottawa, André Bachand. Talking to André that night was an eye-opener for the future.

To learn how other provinces and territories conducted the affairs of their Ottawa offices, I had already sought out and met with most of their representatives, and had sized up their operations. Yukon, Nunavut, the Northwest Territories, Manitoba, New Brunswick, and Quebec maintained offices in the federal capital. Harley Trudeau, a distant cousin of Pierre's and Yukon's senior government representative, was especially helpful and keen on a relationship, an alliance even, in Ottawa with the Atlantic provinces. Gilles Verret, New Brunswick's representative, was always obliging and full of suggestions for progress.

Upon my arrival in the capital, I had gone looking for André Bachand; he was, after all, head of the biggest provincial operation there, one of four Quebec offices in Canada. But he'd been away. Meeting him at this first ministers' reception, I found the man immediately likeable and we hit it off. He had a great sense of humour, an immense knowledge of the Ottawa scene which he wore very lightly, and a refreshing bluntness, expressed through an excellent and easy command of French and English.

Though just into his forties, André Bachand had already had a full political life. Elected mayor of Asbestos in Quebec in 1986 at the age of twenty-four, he ran federally in 1997 as a Progressive Conservative and won, amazingly, in Richmond-Arthabaska, a riding that the Bloc Québécois had taken by a landslide in the previous election.

In 2003, he was the sole Progressive Conservative MP from Quebec in the fourteen-member caucus in Ottawa when he ran against six other contenders, including Nova Scotian MPs Peter MacKay and Scott Brison and Saskatchewan environmentalist David Orchard, for the leadership of the PC Party of Canada. He wanted, he said, to unite all people, francophones and anglophones from all regions of the country and all backgrounds, who wished to turn the page on a decade of drift, adding, rather presciently, that the Progressive Conservative Party risked becoming a regional party like the Canadian Alliance.

When Peter MacKay won the leadership and began discussions to unite the PC Party of Canada and the Canadian Alliance Party, led by Stephen Harper, Bachand made no secret of his dislike of Harper's policies. After the two parties fused to create the Conservative Party, André declared himself uncomfortable with the principles of the new party and sat as an independent MP. Then, in the federal election of 2004, with Harper newly elected as leader of the Conservative Party, André announced that he would not be running himself but would support the Liberal candidate in his former riding to try to defeat the Bloc Québécois. Soon afterwards, Premier Jean Charest appointed him head of the Quebec office in Ottawa.

I joked to André that Premier Williams had created the new post I was in because he wanted an ambassador to Ottawa just as Quebec had had for so many years, with such uncanny success. The more I talked to Bachand about his office the more I realized that my use of the term "ambassador" was not far off the mark. Successive Quebec governments for decades had taken their Ottawa office very seriously. It had been in existence for nearly a century, having been established, André told me, in 1908; currently, there were some nine officials working there. André impressed me as being more of the calibre of an ambassador of a country than a parochial provincial functionary. The very best job in Ottawa was being an MP, he said, but this—his position now—was the second best job in Ottawa.

He appeared to be pleasantly surprised when I said I thought the idea of asymmetrical federalism, then being bandied about, made a lot of sense for Quebec. From the beginning, most of the provinces had never had arrangements identical to one another's with the central federal government, I remarked, so why should we be trying to force them now, based on some misguided federal dogma, into a Procrustean bed?

We agreed to get together again soon, and regularly thereafter. One of the first things he was going to do, he said, was host a working reception of all the provincial representatives in Ottawa. Not long after our first meeting, André would invite me to a late afternoon get-together at the Quebec office, with his staff and other provincial and territorial representatives, including a woman from a trade office representing Ontario. Ontario had no full provincial representative in Ottawa, which was not at all surprising. Why would they need to bother with that?

The capital of the country, containing the Canadian Parliament, was right on their provincial territory. The vast majority of federal civil servants had offices there. Billions of dollars in rent and other federal expenditures poured straight into Ontario's provincial economy, not to mention billions in provincial income taxes paid by federal employees resident in the province. And every time Premier McGuinty whined about how ill-done-by his poor old province was in Canada, it was captured by the Ottawa and Toronto media for the federal brass to read and hear and see. So Ontario needed no hired guns in Ottawa to get more attention or money. I was surprised, though, that neither Nova Scotia nor the western provinces beyond Manitoba had a provincial representative in the capital.

At the meeting at the Quebec office with André Bachand and the others, various kinds of cheese, wine, beer, fruit and other delectable produce were served—all originating in Quebec. No wonder, I said to myself, digging into the delicious bounty of *La belle province*, that the Québécois were so proud of their great homeland, and that so many of them believed it had the right stuff to be its own separate country. My experience with Quebec and the Québécois has invariably contributed to this conviction: if I were not a Newfoundlander I'd want to be a Quebecer.

After André Bachand and I parted company at the health summit, I spotted Francis Fox, principal secretary to Prime Minister Martin. He was surrounded by a sizable group, all speaking animated French. I butted in, said hello and that I hoped we'd get a chance to talk later in the evening. Then I went over to a group of young Newfoundlanders working with federal Intergovernmental Affairs, whom I'd already met briefly at the summit. As usual with Newfoundlanders who run into each other outside the province, we immediately became as friendly as if we were old buddies from way back. Listening to them, I contemplated again what an asset to our province it was to have such bright young citizens occupying influential posts across Canada.

Francis Fox appeared, and one of the bright young Newfoundlanders splashed his drink all over Francis's jacket while shaking hands with him. It was terribly embarrassing for the young fellow, but Francis was as cordial and relaxed as I'd always found him. Brushing the liquid off the front and arm of his jacket, he quipped that he didn't think there was any need for such violence this soon from Newfoundland—it was still possible that we might be able to settle the Atlantic Accord through peaceful negotiations. Even the drink-tosser laughed.

I had gotten to know Francis as a fellow student at Oxford University in the '60s when we were both Rhodes Scholars. A graduate of Collège Jean-de-Brébeuf, the University of Montréal and Harvard Law School, he was also very much down-to-earth and street-smart, with a sense of humour and a broad-minded philosophy. He would need all those personal strengths to survive the disaster in store for him in politics.

Trudeau tapped him as his special assistant in the late '60s. Then, in 1972, Francis got elected as a Liberal MP from Montreal and was soon appointed to ministerial portfolios, including solicitor general of Canada, secretary of state, minister of Communications and minister of International Trade. He was responsible for the first access-to-information legislation in Canada, for building the new National Gallery and the Museum of Civilization, and for setting up Telefilm Canada. He was often described in the media as a "star minister," and it was taken for granted that he'd ultimately become prime minister of Canada.

When I was leader of the Liberal Party of Newfoundland and Labrador in official Opposition during the late '70s, I looked forward to productive dealings with Francis if my party ever formed the provincial government. But at the end of January 1978, after Trudeau had appointed him solicitor general, Francis caught everyone in the country off guard with a dramatic personal disclosure.

The solicitor general is Canada's top law-enforcement officer, and Fox was put in the unenviable position of having to publicly acknowledge that he had obtained an abortion for a woman by forging her husband's name on hospital documents. Trudeau accepted Francis's resignation, stating to the media, "Naturally I'm very sad about the events which have just taken place. I just hope people will understand that this is a human failing and that he will not be lost to political life forever."

He wasn't. Francis got re-elected and became a minister again under John Turner until he was defeated by the Mulroney juggernaut of 1984. Brian Mulroney had earlier told me in St. John's, when he himself was a star contender for the Progressive Conservative leadership, that he held Francis Fox in such high esteem, even though they were on opposite sides, that he had tracked him down when he was recuperating out of the country after his resignation, to offer his support.

Some years later, when we were both out of politics and Francis was in

St. John's on business, he and I got together. I told him the word was going around that there was a movement afoot to make him leader of the Liberal Party of Canada, and prime minister. If he decided to go for it, I said, I would certainly do everything I could for his campaign, in Newfoundland and Labrador and anywhere else. He replied that he would not be running. He felt that, as soon as he got in the limelight again as a leadership candidate, the scandal from 1978 would come back to haunt him. I told him I was disappointed, that I thought he could win the leadership despite that one mistake. But he said he would not subject his family to it.

And now, in 2004, after successful years practising law with a leading Montreal firm and holding senior management positions with Rogers Communications, he was principal secretary to the prime minister, at whom my own chief, Danny Williams, was starting to take some serious potshots.

Francis and I left the reception in the West Block together, and walked along the street talking. I brought up the Atlantic Accord, and he said Danny Williams stood to do well on it. Paul Martin liked Williams, he said, despite the fact they'd had another public set-to a couple of weeks previously, during which unkind words flew from Danny. Francis said Paul still admired Danny, respected his position on behalf of his province and wanted to do right by him. But, I asked, just what did the feds think was right? I hoped they didn't have in mind the paltry amount with no guarantees and a skein of strings and conditions attached, which, I'd heard from confidential sources, was the federal idea of an improved Accord in keeping with Martin's pledge.

As I gave some specifics, Francis looked at me sharply—perhaps I'd hit the nail on the head—but, naturally, he would not confirm or deny. Because if that was the case, I continued, there would be no deal, and any hostilities lurking in the wings were sure to escalate. Francis didn't quiver in his boots at my bravado. We shook hands cordially and made plans to get together again soon. But he did indicate that he'd got the point.

Francis would leave his position in the PMO later that fall, and be appointed to the Senate the following summer. I would hear that Martin continued to seek his advice on troublesome issues like the Atlantic

Accord. Knowing how reasonable and sensible he was, especially compared to some of the yobs around the prime minister, I could tell that his
moderating influence and wisdom was helping the federal side navigate
the bumpy road.

After Francis and I said goodbye, I fell in with a First Nations delegate
heading back to his hotel. We'd seen each other that morning at the session on Aboriginal health care. He invited me into the Marriott Hotel
lounge for a beer. There we met another First Nations delegate from
Atlantic Canada. We had a great hour together, extremely enlightening for
me as we talked about the defects in the structure of Canadian politics and
the bureaucracy that kept Aboriginals from thriving in this country. I told
them that I believed that problem to be the greatest Canadian challenge
of this new century.

With that, one of the men asked me about Williams's attitude regarding
the First Nations people of Newfoundland and Labrador. I replied that I
hadn't had detailed discussions with him on it yet, but what I'd found generally was a very liberal and progressive attitude. Whereupon I was "hoist
with my own petard." The Aboriginal representative from Atlantic Canada
told me he'd tried twice that morning to arrange a meeting with Williams,
but the premier had bolted away after each session in the Grand Hall. The
Aboriginal leader was leaving the next day, but he said he'd stay if I could
line up a meeting for him with my premier. I said I'd mention it to Williams
in the morning if I got a chance, I'd certainly make his request known to
the premier's chief of staff. But knowing how preoccupied Danny was with
the health conference, equalization and the Accord, I had to be honest. I
told the Aboriginal leader he shouldn't delay his departure.

I did pass on his request next morning and, as I'd suspected, there was no
way for the premier to fit in a meeting with him that day. When it came to the
issue at hand, the Accord, our premier was nothing if not focused, to the point
where, as we shall see, it caused strained relations in his own Cabinet.

That same morning, the first ministers and Aboriginal leaders put out
a communiqué called "Improving Aboriginal Health." In it they expressed
the need for an action plan to improve health services for all Aboriginal

peoples, and gave specific measures to close the gap between the health status of Aboriginals and the rest of the Canadian public. As I write these words, several years later, another big uproar has just erupted in the media over the urgent need for drinkable water on First Nation reserves.

On this second morning of the summit, Danny asked me to go into the Grand Hall where the first ministers were seated, and sit behind him as an adviser. Someone gave me the proper admittance tag to sling around my neck, and in I went, parking myself between Finance Minister Loyola Sullivan and provincial Health Minister Beth Marshall. There the three of us advised the premier by staring silently at the back of his head, getting a good look from behind at that Roaring Twenties hairdo with the crease down the middle. Occasionally, Marshall and Sullivan and I conferred by rolling our eyes at one another in excruciating boredom. Too many speeches by premiers, finished too long after their end. Premier Campbell of British Columbia vied with Premier McGuinty for the worst case of Wreckhouse Speech Syndrome—sustained, gale-force, life-threatening windiness.

I did only one more stint in the Grand Hall behind Danny; there were only so many admittance tags to go around. But my brief appearances there were glimpsed on television by some quick-sighted representatives from other provincial offices in Ottawa, who told me later that they couldn't get over the dizzying heights to which I had risen. I told them they were the lucky ones, to have escaped the torment, but they deemed me guilty of false modesty.

During one session in the Grand Hall, Martin halted the proceedings for something called a "nutrition break." It turned out to be identical to a coffee break, and I had an opportunity to talk to Jean Charest during it.

Years before, when he had been a minister in the Mulroney government, he used to come to St. John's frequently; usually, he would appear as a guest on my call-in show. As I approached him, I said, "Premier Charest, I see from your eloquence today that you learned a lot from going on *Open Line* in Newfoundland." We hadn't seen each other since he'd converted to Liberalism, to become leader of the Liberal Party of Quebec in 1998. He looked at me piercingly for five seconds and burst out laughing.

"Bill Rowe!" He turned to an aide beside him and said he used to love going on that show in St. John's, more than on any other show in Canada, because the questions and comments from the callers were so feisty. It prepared you for anything in politics, he said—you'd never be caught off guard in the House of Commons again.

I replied that he was invited on my show so much because of the overwhelming popular demand from listeners. We were uninhibited in our flattery, and it was amusing afterwards to hear from one of the other provincial representatives, who'd seen our exchange on closed-circuit TV, that some federal and provincial delegates keeping an eye on Charest were astonished at the joking between the prime minister of Quebec and some functionary from Newfoundland and Labrador who was so inconsequential that he normally walked around the conference centre with only one access card hanging from his neck.

They were right about the access card. There were several coloured cards on chains or strings given out to delegates and advisers, depending on their status, for access to different areas of the building, including the Grand Hall where the first ministers held forth. The colour of the dangling cards showed security guards where you were allowed to go. Me, I toted just the one general card, which allowed me access to the main building and common areas only.

A few of the top functionaries had several cards hanging from their necks, so that they looked like walking file-card indexes in living colour. They had access to various mysterious inner sanctums. You could tell even before you saw their multicoloured necklaces that these personages were of exceedingly great consequence. Their officious swagger, peculiar to self-important clerks, clearly demonstrated that, even from a distance.

On Wednesday, the third day of the conference, I went to my office at 7:30 a.m. for an hour. Then I walked to the conference centre, and went up to our provincial office. To my surprise, a big meeting of our entire Newfoundland and Labrador delegation was well under way, presided over by Danny Williams. No one had notified me of this unscheduled get-together. Everyone turned to look at the latecomer; Danny stopped talking in mid-sentence and asked me cordially to come on in. I sat there trying to piece together what I might have missed.

Because I wasn't staying at the hotel with the rest of them, it was easy to fall out of the loop with this gang. Brian Crawley later apologized—he'd been preoccupied by a crisis last night. It had really hit the fan, and he was still trying to scrape gobs of it off. He looked wasted. It must have been a doozy. I looked forward to a full report.

After our meeting broke up, a woman poked her head in to say there was an urgent call for all the premiers to meet immediately to iron out a serious problem. Could someone get the message to Premier Williams as quickly as possible? But Danny was nowhere to be seen, and no one knew where he was. One of our delegates, who was on his way into the room, said he'd just seen Danny go into the washroom. Brian Crawley rose to his full height and muttered, "I'll go in and get him." As Brian headed to the toilets, Ross Reid shouted after him, "Well, you were the one who wanted the big fancy job!"

A while after the premier and his communications director left, the half-dozen people remaining in the room started to find the air hot and stuffy. Somebody checked the thermostat and discovered that the air conditioner had been turned off. Everyone growled—who the hell had done that? A top insider in the premier's office said it had to have been the Little Princess. Everyone grinned at the reference to Elizabeth Matthews. The incident reminded me of something a friend had told me a while ago.

Matthews and Williams and Crawley happened to be on the same flight as my friend, a woman from St. John's. The premier and Matthews, she said, were sitting side by side in the plane, with Crawley a few rows away. It perturbed my friend that during the flight Matthews was curled up in the seat beside the premier, with her shoes off and her feet drawn up under her, just like a daughter or a wife might do next to a father or husband, she said. She suggested I should quietly advise Danny that the impression presented was not a very professional one for a premier and a staff member in public.

I'd laughed, and asked my friend if she was mistaking me for Miss

Manners. If two smart, educated adults didn't comport themselves in public in a manner satisfactory to her or anybody else, it wasn't my role to correct their behaviour. I had observed nothing but professional conduct between Danny and all his staff members.

Waiting around with the others in our provincial room, in a conference centre which had once been the old train station, I concluded that the building had been chosen for summits such as this because it was designed to allow underutilized delegates—i.e., most of them—to kill idle time without going nuts from boredom. Many advisers at these functions found themselves with a great number of hours on their hands as their political leaders talked the morning away and proceeded to annihilate the afternoon. Luckily, the conference building was so hopelessly inefficient that a delegate's day could be swallowed up by just two of its wonderful time-consuming features.

It possessed the slowest elevators in Canada, which were often so crowded that when they finally reached your floor you had to wait for another one to inch along many minutes later. That exercise could easily massacre a good part of an hour. Also, an incredibly long and meandering hike was required to get from the provincial rooms to the delegates' lounge. That slog, two or three times a day back and forth, could easily break the back of any adviser's working day.

Downstairs in the delegates' lounge, a young Newfoundlander introduced me to some of his colleagues and superiors in the federal Department of Intergovernmental Affairs, including the deputy minister, Madame Marie Fortier. She happened to be married to a Newfoundlander, Ambrose Hearn, a well-known health care administrator and CEO, whose career had included serving as deputy minister of Health for Newfoundland and Labrador during the 1980s. Madame Fortier and I had the first of what would be several frank and informative chats. She was refreshingly forthright, and later in the day she approached me again to ask if I could enlighten her on why my premier was so angry.

I asked her if she meant generally, or was she referring to something specific? She meant, she said, Danny's loud, public criticism of Martin's health proposals. "I don't know what's wrong with this fellow's [Martin's] attitude," he had proclaimed to the media. "We're not even getting crumbs, let alone the scraps."

In fact, I hadn't been told precisely why the premier was so angry. Danny's outburst had come to me, if not as a surprise, without warning; Brian Crawley had not gotten around to briefing me on it. But I could take a shrewd guess. Danny was angry at Martin for dragging his feet on his Atlantic Accord commitment, and I told Madame Fortier so. But, she replied reasonably enough, this was a health conference. Yes, I rejoined, except that equalization was part of the agenda at this conference, which made royalties from our offshore resources very pertinent indeed at the table. Then she staggered me. But the prime minister's Atlantic Accord commitment, she said, was a done deal.

Suddenly, I saw why our province was having such a hard time making federal ministers and their top public servants see the seriousness of the Atlantic Accord crisis. The deputy minister of the federal Department of Intergovernmental Affairs, the department responsible for dealing with our provincial government, was obviously being fed a full load of malarkey by someone on the federal side about the Accord being all sewn up, when in fact it was right on the verge of total collapse.

Back on the fifth floor, in our provincial room, Danny had returned from a meeting, and briefed us on his strategy for any further meetings with the prime minister. A health pact, he said, would be absolutely conditional on a written commitment that an Atlantic Accord deal was to be concluded by the end of September. I told him that top federal bureaucrats were seemingly labouring under a false impression about the status and likely success of the Atlantic Accord negotiations. We asked ourselves where the false optimism was coming from. We agreed that most likely it was being stimulated by morons or mischief-makers in the PMO.

I went down to the washroom. One of the premiers was urinating there, and we exchanged hellos. He walked out of the washroom without washing his hands, and I made a mental note to avoid any of that premier's social events if finger food was involved. In came John Charest, and we ended up at adjoining urinals. I mentioned that Howard Hughes used to make his multi-million dollar deals at urinals like this—maybe we should drag Paul Martin down here for a leak and make him stand at the middle urinal with Charest on one side and Danny Williams on the other. We could conclude a health deal for Quebec and an Accord deal for Newfoundland and Labrador. We had a chuckle, but I was soon to see that Jean Charest needed no Howard Hughes props at this summit in order to squeeze a uniquely favourable deal for his province out of Paul Martin.

Back down in the delegates' lounge I saw Brian Crawley sitting by himself on a couch by the wall. I started to walk over for a chat. I wanted to remind him to keep me briefed so that I would be able to respond to our best advantage when federal officials, such as the deputy minister of IGA, approached me about the premier. I also wanted to probe the implications for us of the PMO apparently misleading senior mandarins with unwarranted optimism regarding the Accord negotiations. But halfway over to him I stopped. Crawley looked semi-catatonic slumped there, staring off into space and exuding misery. Danny must have worked the poor bastard to death during the night. I decided I'd talk to him when he was a little fresher, find out later about the "crisis" which had caused his state.

Turning around, I saw Stephen Harper, then leader of the Opposition. He was staring at me, probably trying to place me. We'd talked on *Open Line* several times, and I thought I'd remembered he'd been on in person. I moved toward him to reintroduce myself and have a chat. At my sudden approach, his eyes looked panic-stricken, and then they went as cold as if they had been frosted over with a sheen of ice. He moved closer to the two aides standing near him. When I told him who I was, he said he remembered our earlier encounters and was glad to see me. But our short chat was a bit like pulling teeth.

I'd heard that the guy was not what you'd call a people person. But till now I'd thought the allegation was just partisan propaganda. I had to wonder why anyone would go into politics if the thought of having to talk to someone who wasn't your wife or a flunky gave you the horrors. In my notes that night, I wrote that Harper might fluke into a minority government by default in the next election because the Liberals would probably defeat themselves with their scandals, but he would never be able to gain enough support, saddled with that personality, to form a majority government.

Next, a federal official I'd met before came up to me to talk about Danny Williams's public irritation with Paul Martin. As we bantered a little, he said he "admired" the high-and-mighty attitude of the premier of such a small province. "Too bad he wasn't present at the Creation," he said. "He could have given God some useful hints." I told him that if he was impressed now, he should wait a few weeks, when his prime minister would be forced to fork over a couple of billion dollars to Danny. Buddy's smirk indicated he thought this was pure bravado on my part. And it was. But that smirk motivated me; I wanted to see it wiped right off his mug in the near future.

When I went back to the Newfoundland and Labrador room on that last day of the health summit, Beth Marshall and Loyola Sullivan were having an animated tête-à-tête. She seemed agitated and out of sorts, and he appeared to be trying to explain something to her, or placate her. I remained across the room till they were finished.

After Loyola had left the room, Beth showed no inclination to leave herself, which I thought unusual for a Health minister at a health conference, with talks going on in the Grand Hall. She and I had a long chat on a variety of matters, including how her mother had told her that she and my father were close blood relations. It was lighthearted and interesting, but I could sense, without her saying so, that she wasn't pleased with how things were going at this summit, and her dissatisfaction had nothing to do with the feds.

Later that day, I learned that the night before she had been excluded from the dinner meeting at 24 Sussex Drive, for the premiers and the prime minister and their ministers of Health. Apparently, Danny figured that the Accord was more important than health care, even at a health summit, and he had taken Sullivan to the dinner meeting instead of Marshall.

No wonder Brian Crawley had looked semi-comatose in the lounge earlier. There must have been some pretty intense conversations in the small hours of the previous night. I wrote a note in my journal that this new Atlantic Accord, if and when it was ever signed, had better be darned good. Because Danny wasn't going to have colleagues of the calibre and independence of Beth Marshall in his Cabinet much longer if he continued to conduct himself in such a hard-nosed and insensitive manner.

You didn't have to be Nostradamus to see what was coming. Less than two weeks after the health conference, Brian Crawley would phone me from St. John's to let me know that Beth Marshall was resigning as minister of Health. The immediate reason was a dispute with Danny over his handling of a Victorian Order of Nurses strike in Corner Brook while Marshall was on holidays in Alberta. Danny said that he had kept her officials informed of what he was doing, and had seen no need to keep her personally informed.

According to a friend of mine who'd talked to Marshall's deputy minister, Deborah Fry, on a plane coming back from one of the territories, Fry had been up north during much of the period. Whatever role Fry had or had not played in the whole debacle, Danny soon let her go as deputy minister. Someone in the provincial civil service told me that Danny's attitude reminded him of Hollywood movie producer Sam Goldwyn's, who once said, "I don't want any yes-men around me. I want everyone to tell me the truth even if it costs them their jobs." Those two women, he said, were definitely not yes-persons.

Danny's handling of the VON strike, on top of the affront of being squeezed out of the dinner meeting at the health summit, was the last straw for Beth Marshall. As for her fired deputy minister, Deborah Fry— less than three years later, in May of 2007, recently elected Prime Minister Stephen Harper, by then Danny Williams's new worst enemy, would appoint her as a judge of the Supreme Court of Newfoundland and Labrador. And Beth Marshall, who would stay in Danny Williams's caucus in the House of Assembly although she would not play his game of "Anything But Conservative" (ABC) against Stephen Harper in the October 2008 federal election, would be appointed by Harper to the Senate in 2010. Obviously, when it came to Danny Williams, Harper would play his own game: "My enemy's enemies are my friends."

On the last night of the health summit, at about ten o'clock, Danny came into our provincial room and said that there would be no deal between the federal government and the provinces on health care. The main reason for the failure, in the opinion of most premiers, was that Dalton McGuinty was weak and vacillating. He hadn't been able to persuade the prime minister to accept the counter-proposal of the premiers, which demanded more money for general health costs and specific programs, and—just as important, or more so, for Danny—an improvement in equalization.

It soon turned out, however, that the premiers were wrong. It must have been a measure of Paul Martin's desperate need to achieve success that, despite Danny's strong certainty of failure at ten o'clock that night, a deal was, in fact, slapped together over the next two hours. Exactly how it was achieved was unknown to the media, since the final meeting was held in camera. But reporters had a pretty good idea: to save face, Martin had caved in to the premiers. Lyndon Johnson once said, "While you're saving your face, you're losing your ass." And so, at twenty-four minutes after midnight on Thursday, September 16, 2004, the prime minister led the premiers in a big announcement on health care spending.

Martin started this public conclusion of the summit with "bonsoir," even though it was early morning, and stated that Canada's first ministers had just signed a ten-year plan, "a deal for a decade," that would lead to better health care for all Canadians. This deal, he said, would kick-start a reduction in waiting times right across the country, "except for reporters at federal-provincial meetings." (The guy was a card.) It would improve access to health care professionals so that Canadians could see a doctor when they needed to, where they needed to. It would result in the expansion of home care services across the country, better pharmaceutical coverage and management and, above all else, real accountability to Canadians.

During their discussions, Martin noted, "there was passion and forthrightness and, yes, there were tensions forcefully expressed." That was a polite way of describing Danny's public attack on him. But in the end, said Martin, there was steadfast political will among the first ministers, who had stood up for health care and for Canadians.

As part of the agreement, Canada's premiers had agreed to provide information to Canadians on the progress they would be making in the use of federal money to reduce waiting times. That meant, said the prime minister, multi-year targets set by each province, which would be reported nationally. Martin must have forgotten that Quebec was still part of Canada, because any reporting to the people of Canada on Quebec's use of federal health funds was exactly what Jean Charest would say he would not be doing.

To help the provinces and territories produce measurable results, Martin went on, the federal government would increase by some $41 billion its contribution to health care in Canada over the next decade. That money exceeded, he said, the financial recommendations of the Romanow Commission.

Then he mentioned the federal concession that had made this health agreement possible: the first ministers were also agreed on the necessity of improving the predictability of equalization, and would be discussing that important question at the next meeting of first ministers on October 26, just over a month away. This concession was part of the price of Danny Williams's support for the health deal. In reality, it became a carrot dangled tantalizingly over his head. Combined with federal foot-dragging on Martin's Accord commitment, it would set the stage for some true drama on Danny's part in less than six weeks.

Then up spoke the premiers, with Dalton McGuinty of Ontario providing the best unintentional humour of the night. "Regional differences," he intoned, "had been put aside." That statement must have made it hard for Danny Williams and Jean Charest to keep a straight face.

Next came Premier Jean Charest of Quebec. The agreement was made, he asserted, with the superior interests of Quebec in mind, and with a modern vision of Canadian federalism that recognized and developed Quebec's differences. An understanding had been concluded that brought in a new era in the functioning of the Canadian federation. It ratified important progress in the acceptance of a federalism that respected Quebec's differences.

Charest said he was following in the footsteps of other premiers of Quebec who had frequented this conference room, René Lévesque and Robert Bourassa. But he had gone far beyond what those other two premiers had been able to achieve, thanks to the recognition of "asymmetry" by all partners in the federation. They had dared to make a gesture that had never been made before, recognizing the difference which was so dear to "us Quebecers," and which, above all, defined all of Canada. He thanked the first ministers in the name of the population of Quebec, telling them, "We will mark on our calendar forever this day of 15 September, 2004, as being an important day in the history of our people."

What exactly was it that Charest got for Quebec that he considered so epoch-making? A mind-blowing amount was what he got.

The notion of asymmetrical federalism agreed to by the first ministers seemed to come right out of the blue for many observers. It had not appeared to be on any agenda leading up to the summit. But how much it changed the nature of federalism in Canada was obvious from the separate statement put out by the Quebec government following the general announcement of the agreement on health.

The Quebec communiqué was entitled, in big capital letters, "ASYMMETRICAL FEDERALISM THAT RESPECTS QUEBEC'S JURISDICTION." It stated that Quebec supported the overall health care objectives set out by the first ministers in their announcement of September 15, 2004, and intended to co-operate with other governments regarding health care standards. But the prime minister of Canada and the premier of Quebec had agreed that Quebec would apply its own wait time reduction plan, in accordance with the objectives, standards and criteria established by the relevant Quebec authorities. The government of Quebec would report to Quebecers, but not the rest of Canada, about progress in achieving its objectives. "Nothing in this communiqué shall be construed as derogating from Quebec's jurisdiction. This communiqué shall be interpreted as fully respecting its jurisdiction."

According to this astonishing document, not only had the prime minister of Canada recognized Quebec's de facto sovereignty vis-à-vis the rest of Canada, but Quebec would be entitled to receive billions of dollars from the federal treasury with absolutely no accountability to Canadian tax-payers. Quebec had been given the right to have its cake and to eat it too. A separate nation when it came to accountability, a province of Canada when it came to receiving Canadian benefits.

At the close of the summit, Danny Williams also spoke approvingly of the first ministers' deal. But he didn't want to raise expectations in Newfoundland and Labrador, he said. It was a great plan to strengthen health care, and he was proud of it. It was a great start. But his province still had a ways to go from a financial perspective. "We have a lot to do, a lot of hard work to do, and we do need some more funding."

He thanked Premier McGuinty for his leadership role; as head of the premiers' organization, the Council of the Federation, McGuinty had done a wonderful job on everyone's behalf, Williams said. (A couple of hours is a long time in federal-provincial politics. At ten o'clock that same night McGuinty had been weak and vacillating.)

Danny then thanked Martin, saying he'd always respected him, but now he had even more respect for the prime minister. Martin was a tough negotiator, he said, but he was also prepared to compromise. He thanked Martin for his patience, for his commitment to health care for Canadians and for his willingness to achieve an agreement for Canadians from St. John's to Vancouver. He congratulated him on a job well done.

Positive remarks after the shots he'd taken at Martin during the course of the conference. We were hearing a little conviviality now, which sounded promising for the equalization meeting in just a few weeks. Jean Charest had walked quietly and carried a big stick, and had come away the clear winner. Danny had to satisfy himself with continued promises. No jam today, Danny boy, but you be a good little fella, now, and we'll give you jam for your bread tomorrow. Little wonder that Danny's new attitude didn't last long beyond the conference.

Every now and then at the closing of the summit, some inadvertent comedy broke out. For example, the minister of Health for Alberta told the conference that he had been in constant contact with his absent premier,

Ralph Klein, during the course of the last two and a half days of the three-day conference. This drew audible sniggers. Premier Klein had been spending, it was alleged, much of his conference time enjoying himself at the casino in Gatineau. Nevertheless, Alberta's Health minister wanted to advise the other first ministers that, like them, Premier Klein would be signing the agreement. Someone stage-whispered, "If he can hold a pen."

Paul Martin's attempts at humour were intentional, and he leavened nearly every exchange with his trademark one-liners. The premiers, perhaps feeling over-jolly at barely escaping the complete collapse that had threatened the summit just two hours ago, laughed uproariously at them. When Premier Lord of New Brunswick said he looked forward to the coming summit on equalization on October 26, Martin said that he too looked forward to that meeting, but he wasn't sure it would be the unalloyed joy for him that it might well be for Lord and the other premiers. The premiers guffawed.

Regarding the references by the premiers to late-night meetings at 24 Sussex Drive, Martin said there was one point when there wasn't a room in the house where federal officials and provincial officials weren't collected in corners—in fact, when he'd woken up that morning, there were still two provincial officials walking around looking for the door. The premiers roared.

As for the heat generated at those meetings, Martin said, it had been his intention to install air conditioning at 24 Sussex, and he'd had the money up until today. But now it was all gone. The premiers howled.

In his efforts to be amusing, Paul Martin let the cat out of the bag over how he'd behaved as Finance minister when he'd been angling for Chrétien's job as leader and PM. He said he wanted to thank Alex Himelfarb for the work he'd done at the conference. Himelfarb had been clerk of the Privy Council under Chrétien as he was now under Martin, a position equivalent to deputy minister to the prime minister. Martin now joked to the premiers, "Let me tell you that I, as minister of Finance, spent a lot of time saying very nasty things about the Privy Council office [i.e., Alex Himelfarb]. I take some of it back. I've got to say to Alex, he did a tremendous job." Sometimes there's a symmetrical irony (as well as asymmetrical federalism) in Canadian politics. Paul Martin, who had undermined majority Prime Minister Jean Chrétien's advisers, such as Himelfarb, to grab the PM's crown for himself, was now forced to rely on Chrétien's top adviser to help keep his own weak minority government alive.

Martin seemed understandably reluctant to say anything in plain English about the radical separate deal he'd made with Quebec. Only when Premier Gary Doer of Manitoba raised it did Martin respond, and even then in a most inarticulate fashion, passing the responsibility on to the premiers. "I also want to add my voice to what Premier Doer said in terms of the agreement with Quebec, in terms of the nature of the agreement with Quebec, in terms of the recognition by all of the premiers, and I think it is very important to understand the leadership that the premiers took in understanding that in fact the great strength of our country is the diversity of our population and our ability to approach things in different ways and yet with common purposes. So I think, Premier Charest, this was a historic agreement, and I want to thank all of the premiers for their leadership as well as you, Premier Charest."

It might not have been Shakespearean, but its buck-passing drift was clear. Speaking in French for the Quebec audience, however, Martin appeared to be much happier about the separate Quebec deal. "Je pense que ça a été vraiment quelque chose de très, très important qui s'est passé aujourd'hui." ("I think that it was truly something very, very important that happened today.")

I talked later to a highly placed Quebec civil servant about the difference in Martin's tone and content, depending on whether he was speaking in English or French, regarding the concessions to Quebec. The Quebec civil servant was always amazed, he told me, at how easily such radical, even revolutionary side-deals with Quebec could slip by with little or no reaction in English Canada as long as their true nature was fudged or understated in English. It was as if Martin and other federal politicians had learned that anything granted to Quebec would be tolerated in the rest of Canada as long as the truth was not baldly stated in plain English.

The health summit concluded at 1:35 in the morning of September 16 and a press conference began two minutes later, after Martin begged the premiers to sit down again. "Could I ask the premiers to come back. The press is here and if you don't come back to the table I think my career is over. We will do the press conference now and then we are going to do a group photo after. A group hug, yes."

A reporter asked Martin in French why a particular, specific agreement was signed with Quebec. Martin replied in French that it was because they recognized that Quebec had obligations that were completely specific. The process had been truly an evolution in the way of seeing, he said, that there were different ways of attaining common aims and objectives.

Charest jumped in, recalling that the subject had been debated well before the start of the health conference, since the premiers had already tackled it at a meeting of the Council of the Federation at Niagara-on-the-Lake, when the possibility of a national program of pharmacare had been raised. Quebec had its own program of pharmacare. That example, he believed, permitted the Council of the Federation to see that there was a justification for such an approach. They recognized that asymmetry applied elsewhere, he said. It was not something which prevented other provinces from having themselves recognized, but one which permitted Quebec in any case to assume and to assert its difference. It was something that Quebec held very much to its heart, because historically Canada would not have existed had it not been for the ability of the Quebec people to have this difference recognized.

A reporter asked Charest in English what precedent he thought the Quebec clause would have on future agreements between Quebec and the federal government. Charest replied that it would establish the common will of both the federal government and the government of Quebec to operate within the framework of our constitutional arrangements. The agreement clearly said that this was part of what Canada was about. It was not a contradiction, he said; quite the contrary. It was something we should value, something that we should identify more clearly as being part of our Canadian federalism. In that respect, rather than trying to diminish federalism, we had celebrated it through the agreement. Charest concluded by saying he had no doubt in his mind that there would be plenty of other opportunities to celebrate that difference in the future.

No kidding. The accommodation of Quebec at the health care summit was obviously a long way beyond the Meech Lake Accord and the pathetic controversy spurred by it over whether Quebec could be referred to as a "distinct society." Listening to Charest and Martin at this health conference talking about their special deal with Quebec, I wondered what Newfoundland and Labrador under Premier Clyde Wells had lost by resisting the Meech Lake Accord. What gains might we have been able to negotiate on the Upper Churchill, the Lower Churchill, the offshore, and the fishery with the Mulroney government as a quid pro quo for agreeing to Meech Lake's comparatively tame recognition-seeking?

Just how far the country as a whole had changed since the Meech Lake fiasco would be demonstrated just over a year after the health summit, when the new government of Conservative Prime Minister Stephen Harper, in its scramble to keep up with the constitutional "advances" made at that first ministers' gathering, would grant the people of Quebec the status of "nation," with scarcely any fuss whatsoever from the rest of Canada.

Yes, le Premier Ministre Charest and his nation, Quebec, walked away the clear winners at that historic health conference, with hardly a ripple of protest from anyone, excluding the weakly expressed opinion by a few in the media and in politics that Martin's asymmetrical federalism was a betrayal of Canada. Others, more reasonably, said that it was hard to criticize Martin for Quebec's separate health deal with the federal government when it had been other premiers, notably Premier Bernard Lord of New Brunswick and Premier Gary Doer of Manitoba, who had lobbied hard to make it happen. Many experts in Canadian constitutional history could find no fault at all with this "new" brand of Canadian federalism. Nor did they fear for the future of the country.

Here, for example, is L. Ian MacDonald, editor of *Policy Options* magazine, three years later, giving the F.R. Scott Lecture at McGill University on November 6, 2007:

"As for asymmetrical federalism, it was not created with the Health Accord of 2004. It's found in section 93 of the BNA Act, enabling confessional schools in Quebec and, later, Newfoundland. And in section 133, recognizing French and English as the languages of the courts and legislature in Quebec.

This is the fundamental bargain of Confederation. The bilingual character of our country has its very origins in the duality of our legal heritage. Long before there was a Charter of Rights, this duality was reflected in the Constitution Act of 1867.

This is classical federalism, federalism as it was intended by the fathers of Confederation. Without the division of powers, without the asymmetrical features to accommodate Quebec's religion and its English-language minority, Sir John A. Macdonald would not have been the father of our country."

Asymmetrical federalism may not have been created by the health care accord of 2004, but it certainly grew large there, with scarcely a squawk from any source in English Canada. It makes one grieve for all the wasted time and jettisoned opportunities of previous eras in federal-provincial politics.

But how did Newfoundland and Labrador fare at this famous health summit? A reporter at that early morning press conference wondered the same thing: "A question for Mr. Williams. The first day you described what the prime minister put on the table as scraps . . . you said he had offered crumbs. Can you make a meal out of what you have now? Is it enough to keep up with talk of national standards, benchmarks and accountability?"

It wasn't a bad appetizer, Danny said, and there was a bit of dessert in there as well. "Newfoundland and Labrador has a very, very serious fiscal situation . . . We are really at the bottom of the heap here, so funding is a huge issue for us." The prime minister's initial offers on a stand-alone basis, involving just health care funding, were simply not enough to make a difference in Newfoundland and Labrador if there wasn't equalization money and other commitments, he continued. He'd come up here looking for a full package, and as a result of the last day's negotiations, the prime minister had increased his offer by 30 percent on health care funding.

And then came, what was for Danny, the deal clincher. "As well, the Prime Minister very graciously gave us a commitment this evening that the Atlantic Accord would be resolved before the fiscal imbalance [equalization] meeting on October 26th. That is the full meal deal for me." So Danny Williams had received yet another commitment from Paul Martin on the Atlantic Accord to go with the first unfulfilled one.

As the press conference wrapped up at quarter to two in the morning, with the prime minister and the premiers scurrying over to stand in front of the Canadian and provincial flags for some triumphant group snapshots, Jean Charest was carrying away from the table some de facto constitutional progress for Quebec more revolutionary than anything Premier Bourassa and Premier Lévesque would have dared dream about, let alone actually try to obtain from Canada.

Danny was walking away with another earful of Ottawa rhetoric. Within weeks, this would lead to a greater political uproar than perhaps any prime minister-premier duo had ever experienced in Canada's history.

— CHAPTER SIX —

Blowing the Top Off
the Equalization Summit

MANY POLITICOS AND PLAYERS in Ottawa, from all parties and at all levels of government, wanted to dive in and help resolve the Accord problems. They included the seven MPs from our province, and I'll detail their contributions, both useful and destructive, later.

Newfoundland Senator George Baker, a big Liberal, contacted me as soon as he arrived back in Ottawa for the fall session of Parliament. He enthusiastically invited me to testify on the Atlantic Accord before a senate committee he chaired and to appear before the Atlantic caucus to present our provincial position. (Ever the true politician, George urged me not to forget to tell the media I'd been invited to speak to these two important groups.) I replied, like the true bureaucrat I had now turned into, that I would take his kind invitations "under advisement."

When I visited André Bachand at the Quebec office in Ottawa one day, I noticed that there seemed to be a lot of office staff on the premises. I was told that, in addition to the head, there were four policy advisers, two administrative assistants and other support staff. I asked one of them if they were very busy, and received the surprising response, "No, not very."

Perhaps they were not very busy in the paper-pushing sense, but they certainly seemed to be on top of everything. During our chats, André showed considerable inside knowledge of our growing battle with the federal government on the Atlantic Accord. One time, apropos of nothing we were talking about, he leaned close to whisper, "And by the way, don't worry, you're going to get your Accord money. But you must keep plugging."

It would not be the last time that the Quebec representative in Ottawa displayed an excellent awareness of what other provinces were involved with vis-à-vis the federal government, how we were making out behind the scenes and what the ultimate outcome was likely to be. I knew he would never violate confidences from any source, but he and his office did receive a lot of information through the grapevine. Throughout my stay in the capital, I would find André genuinely helpful and always eager to make sure we clearly understood our respective premiers' positions on issues. We talked about the future of these provincial positions in Ottawa, and even the idea of bringing all provinces under one roof, with offices in one building, as a symbol of provincial power in the federal capital.

Once, when Danny announced an initiative on the development of the Lower Churchill—a call for proposals—André met me to say that my premier should really get together with his premier and talk informally about a possible joint development. He was concerned over Danny's comments about a possible deal with Ontario or someone else. He thought that Danny Williams and Jean Charest, the two best and brightest premiers in Canada, could come up with a win-win deal that was there for the making. I passed this on to the premier's office, with the appropriate warnings, of course, about Quebec's shrewdness.

One day André mentioned that he'd just arranged a meeting at short notice with a senior deputy minister in the federal government. His implication was hard to miss—his office could command high-level attention from federal officialdom more or less at will. I'd heard from other provincial offices that their access was normally neither fast nor smooth. I was interested to see how our province stood, now that we'd developed some political heat.

At the health summit, I'd suggested to Marie Fortier, the deputy minister of the federal Department of Intergovernmental Affairs, that we should get together before the upcoming equalization summit scheduled for October 26. Before long, she called to invite me to her office for a coffee and a chat on a certain day. Could I make it at 10:30 a.m.? Yes, I said. Our phone conversation wasn't long, but during the course of it, she asked if we could change the time to 10:45. Just before we hung up, she changed it again, to 11:00. I asked her if she kept changing times to find out if I spent all day sitting on my hands doing nothing. We laughed, but a little while later she called back to change the time of our meeting to 8:30 a.m., because of a "crisis on Parliament Hill"; she needed to brief her minister for a Cabinet meeting.

I didn't joke this time. I might have said no on principle, if getting our position across weren't so important. Deputy ministers in Ottawa, I mused—that famous federal mandarin class—were, in truth, often reduced to dancing attendance on ministers whose gargantuan egos were only matched in size by their paranoid insecurities.

On the day of our meeting, I walked into Fortier's waiting room just before 8:30 a.m. The receptionist welcomed me with a smile, and led me immediately to the anteroom outside her office. Several staff members were standing there in a cluster; when I entered, a whispered but highly audible conversation in French broke out, containing a flurry of accusations directed at the receptionist. I gathered that the deputy minister had not given instructions that she was ready to receive me just yet. I was hustled unceremoniously back out to the waiting room.

The receptionist told me she was new to the job and wasn't *au courant* on all the proper protocol. Ah yes, the proper protocol. It was more important, I was learning, that proper protocol be maintained even if it meant that officials made fools of themselves, or that a receptionist was humiliated, or that a guest was embarrassed.

About thirty seconds later, a staff member came out of the anteroom, saying that the deputy minister was now ready to see me. She preceded me into Fortier's office, where the DM of Intergovernmental Affairs welcomed me most cordially.

She and I touched on our current federal-provincial issues, and I was delighted at how frank, though pleasantly so, she was throughout most of the meeting. The only time the air became a little frosty was after we agreed that any time either of us suspected that the other was labouring under an error about the other side's position, we would bring it to the other's attention immediately. For example, I went on, her approach to me at the health summit, where she'd been perplexed by Danny's attack on the prime minister, was a very useful case in point because it showed that senior bureaucrats in Ottawa were being fed incorrect information by the prime minister's office on the rate of progress regarding the new Atlantic Accord.

She didn't appear to like that allegation very much; it lowered the mild temperature of the discussion to a much cooler level for a while. Notwithstanding some blunt, off-the-record, statements on both our parts, though, and despite her minister's crisis, our meeting lasted for fifty minutes and ended as cordially as it started.

In the future, she and I conferred by telephone to useful ends. But over time, the fear grew that nothing anyone said or did, outside of the PMO and the federal Department of Finance, where the problems were being created, seemed capable of forestalling the blow-up between Williams and Martin at the upcoming equalization summit.

MARTIN HAD SOLEMNLY UNDERTAKEN at the health summit to come to an agreement with premiers Hamm and Williams on new Atlantic accords before the equalization summit on October 26. Part of the prime minister's problem was that, as the summit drew closer, some provinces were making it clear to him publicly—and even more forcefully in private—that they didn't like what Hamm and Williams were trying to achieve.

A line from the *St. John's Telegram* of October 13 showed the tip of the iceberg. "A Canadian Press report . . . quoted Manitoba's finance minister . . . as saying Newfoundland and Nova Scotia's campaign to garner more offshore revenues could hurt other provinces receiving equalization payments." That minister's rather mild public statement was nowhere near the level of ferocity being expressed by New Brunswick and Ontario, as well as Manitoba, to Martin and Finance Minister Goodale and their top advisers behind closed doors and in private phone calls. Rob Antle's October 14 *Telegram* article gave the reason for their sound and fury. "Soaring oil prices potentially increase the benefits the province could reap from a deal with the federal government . . . Oil has skyrocketed to more than $54 US a barrel in recent days . . . That's roughly 75 percent higher than a year ago."

In the face of all that, the provincial Finance minister and the federal Finance minister were trying to achieve something. After the health summit, Loyola Sullivan spoke to Ralph Goodale a number of times, and sent him a document describing precisely what the province insisted the prime minister's commitment to a new Atlantic Accord must include.

On October 14, less than two weeks before the equalization summit deadline, Sullivan came to Ottawa for direct talks with Goodale and others. He is quoted in Antle's *Telegram* article of the same day as hoping to have the federal government put on paper a confirmation of what the province was looking for. It also quoted him as saying "A sustained price bump [in oil] could increase benefits [to the province] into the $2-billion range over the next eight years . . ." The talks between Loyola and Ralph went nowhere.

Then Danny Williams jumped in. But four days before the summit, Danny telephoned me to say he had made no progress with Martin or Goodale on the Accord. His deadline for a deal on the Accord, Danny said, which he had clearly stated as his condition for putting his name to the health agreement, and which he had confirmed since, was the opening of the equalization summit. He said he would boycott the summit if there was no agreement between him and Martin by then. That was the last thing he wanted to do, Danny told me, but he would definitely do it if necessary. He wanted me to get that message across to people of influence with the prime minister's office, to avoid a big public blow-up. I gave Danny some names to contact, including those of Liberal MPs and senators who had indicated their sympathy for the province's position on the issue.

I called around. All the Liberal MPs and senators I reached were very worried, and they promised to try to remove the stumbling blocks in the PMO, the Finance department and the Privy Council office to the full implementation of Paul Martin's election pledge. Senator George Baker and MP Gerry Byrne told me they were gravely concerned by the escalating crisis and would do what they could to prevent the coming uproar. George Baker stated flat out that he was on the province's side on the issue, and would get that across to the PM and his Cabinet. Gerry Byrne stated he was ready to take a similar stand with the prime minister's office, even if it meant losing his parliamentary secretary's job and its $14,000 a year salary.

I also called Melissa McInnis again. She was the new Atlantic provinces contact in the prime minister's office, having taken over from Newfoundlander Mark Watton. She wasn't available when I called this time either. I left another message, knowing it was futile. She had not returned any of my earlier calls, and had called me exactly once, to say she'd been out of the picture with a strep throat. On the day I'd been appointed provincial representative for Newfoundland and Labrador, Mark Watton had left a message for me saying he wanted to touch base soon. At that time he was still in the PMO. From what I could gather from everyone in the premier's office, it was too bad he had left—too bad not because he was a Newfoundlander, but because everyone thought his keen analytical and creative mind carried extensive clout with those around the prime minister. In any event, there was a lot of pressure on the PM to move substantially in the direction of the two provinces over the next four days.

On Sunday, two days before the equalization summit, I walked across town to the Lester B. Pearson Building at 125 Sussex Drive. This was where the first ministers would be meeting on Tuesday. The impressive, award-winning edifice housed the Department of Foreign Affairs and International Trade, and fronted on Ottawa's most important route, the one linking Parliament Hill with the residences of the governor general and the prime minister.

The area was maggoty with swanky embassies and high commissions. I was, however, headed for a less impressive structure, not unworthy of an appearance in *Trailer Park Boys*, at the back of the Lester B. Pearson Building. The trailer had been hauled in there to register delegates to the equalization summit and to provide them with their photo ID.

When I opened the door, the woman and man inside were visibly startled. I said I was sorry if I had taken them by surprise, but didn't the literature say registration was beginning here today? They conceded that it did, but I got the distinct impression that the very last thing they expected on this earth, or in the entire solar system, was a public servant, federal or provincial, actually using his or her Sunday to register for a conference. But they were nice about it.

On the way back to my apartment, I stopped at the Nicholas Hoare bookstore and bought Rex Murphy's *Points of View*. I strolled on, contemplating a delightful evening reading Rex's collection of commentaries from CBC's *The National* and the *Globe and Mail* while I was waiting for return calls on my cell. Suddenly, as I was crossing a quiet street with the walk signal, I was halted in my tracks by the abrupt appearance of a regiment of police officers. They were there to let a cavalcade of big black limos, accompanied by an overkill of police cars with sirens howling and lights flashing, into the Château Laurier. I recalled hearing on the news that the president of Mexico, Vicente Fox, was arriving in Ottawa today.

I couldn't help thinking as I was being held up by the procession of speeding vehicles, and deafened by the racket, that El Presidente would have been a lot safer if he had arrived quietly by himself in a Volkswagen Beetle. Nobody would have noticed him.

That Sunday, just a couple of days before the conference, Finance Minister Ralph Goodale sent a letter to Premier Danny Williams "to follow up on discussions I have had with your Minister of Finance with regard to the commitment made by the Prime Minister to ensure that Newfoundland and Labrador receives greater financial benefits from its offshore petroleum activities." He confirmed that our own federal minister, John Efford, had been dumped—although his wording was more polite—as lead minister. "While the Prime Minister has asked me to lead the Government of Canada's work in regards to this matter, I want to stress the important contribution made by the Honourable R. John Efford, Minister of Natural Resources Canada, in advancing this file in recent months."

Then Goodale came to the point. "This letter will serve to confirm how the Government of Canada intends to meet its commitment . . . The Government of Canada is prepared to propose legislation to Parliament to provide additional annual payments that will ensure the province effectively retains 100 percent of its offshore revenues for an eight-year period covering 2004-05 through 2011-12, *subject to the provision that no such additional payments result in the fiscal capacity of the province exceeding that of the province of Ontario in any given year* . . ." (Italics added.)

Despite our much greater per capita debt, Newfoundland and Labrador would not be allowed to surpass Ontario as a result of our offshore resources during their relatively short lifespan. We would not even be allowed to play catch-up with the rest of Canada.

Goodale's letter ended with the following: "The Prime Minister is willing to sign an agreement in principle reflecting this approach before the First Ministers' Meeting of October 26." That gave Premier Williams less than one working day, a day in which he would have to travel to Ottawa. The arrogant contempt of the feds was blatant.

The next day, Monday, Brian Crawley called me from the Sheraton Hotel in Ottawa. Not surprisingly, he said that the feds and the province were not in agreement on the Accord; the federal proposals were just not acceptable to Danny. I told him I'd heard from some Liberal politicians that they were not making much headway cracking through the walls erected by the prime minister's office and the Department of Finance.

Just as disquieting was the media's lack of interest. They were extremely low-key about the equalization summit, and even more indifferent to the Accord controversy. There was little mention of the summit in the *Globe and Mail* or the *Ottawa Citizen* or the *National Post*. And if there'd been any mention of it at all in the *Hill Times* weekly schedule of events for Ottawa, it was so obscure I missed it. Danny's battle with Paul Martin seemed to have slipped below the media's line of sight altogether. If he wanted to keep the pressure on the prime minister, he'd have to come up with something dramatic.

Brian invited me over to his room at the Sheraton to meet with the other advisers. As before, Crawley's hotel accommodation was not a suite with a sitting room, but one bedroom, with much of the space again taken up by the bed itself. Crammed into this bedroom talking over the Accord problems were Robert Thompson, the top civil servant of our province, Ross Reid, Barbara Knight, and Terry Paddon, and a couple of other advisers and me.

Robert Thompson was manfully struggling to print out something on what looked like the same Mickey Mouse printer he and Crawley had been using at the health summit. If it was a different one, it was equally dysfunctional. Elizabeth Matthews popped in and out of the room, delivering word from on high—the premier's suite across the hall. Every now and then Crawley would come back from the premier's suite too, looking a bit overcome.

I have never suffered from claustrophobia, but the press of the crowd in that little room was giving me serious insight into what the Black Hole of Calcutta must have felt like. As I backed out of the way of all these highly skilled professional advisers, jam-packed together exchanging expert financial opinions, I hit the side of the bed with the backs of my knees and was forced to sit down. I put my hands behind me to steady myself. My fingers dug into something softer than the bedspread. I looked over my shoulder and saw that my hands were resting on a soiled pair of Brian Crawley's socks.

After what seemed like a very long time in Crawley's room, though it was probably no more than half an hour, we all trooped over to the Lord

Elgin Hotel, where a meeting of the Council of the Federation was to take place. That was the elegant name for the premiers hunting as a pack. In December 2003, the premiers had entered into an agreement to create the Council of the Federation as part of their plan "to play a leadership role in revitalizing the Canadian federation and building a more constructive and co-operative federal system."

This was the group that had laid the groundwork for Quebec's being able, for all practical purposes, to opt out of Confederation at the health summit. It was not surprising, therefore, that the premiers' get-together before tomorrow's big summit with the hapless prime minister was sparking every manner of conspiracy theory among the journalists. As each provincial leader filed into the hotel lobby, media scrums erupted.

I hung around with our delegation in the lobby; after a while, pure ennui made some of us drag our lethargic butts into the dining room for a coffee. Everywhere in the dining room, as was the case in the lobby, scores of provincial advisers were twiddling their thumbs, with or without BlackBerrys, or gabbing casually. I mentioned to a couple of our delegates how much the sight still continued to astonish me: such a wealth of talent, intelligence, knowledge, and experience standing, or sitting around or loitering aimlessly at these meetings of political leaders, waiting for the call from their masters that never seemed to come. I wondered if Samuel Beckett had ever been a government delegate. It would explain where the inspiration for absurdist dialogue and static, inert plots in plays such as *Waiting for Godot* had come from.

Meanwhile, word was percolating through the waiting advisers that the atmosphere inside was surly and getting worse. Some premiers were expressing their extreme discomfort with Danny's demands, and most of them were not happy about the possibility of the summit being hijacked by his histrionics. Danny argued his points strenuously, but some of the other premiers were singularly unsympathetic. He got back from them as good as he gave.

The summit of first ministers on equalization was scheduled to begin at 10:00 a.m. on Tuesday, October 26, at the Lester B. Pearson Building.

Early that morning, Brian Crawley called me to say that there had been no further progress on the Accord talks, and our delegation was getting together at the Sheraton Hotel before going with the premier to the summit.

At the Sheraton, Crawley told me that Danny wanted to speak with me privately. He brought me to the premier's suite; Danny and Elizabeth Matthews were standing in the sitting room earnestly exchanging points and lines. I had noticed many times before how she hovered near the premier with her notes in hand, citing facts and arguments, or walked quickly beside him, briefing him as he headed for the next scrum or news conference.

Danny confirmed to me that Goodale's letter utterly betrayed Paul Martin's commitment, and would mean a loss to the province of more than $1 billion over the years left in the Atlantic Accord. He asked me what I was hearing. I mentioned the political gossip around town—that this equalization summit, like the health summit, had been concocted by the feds to funnel more billions by the bushel into Quebec. And that the feds were encouraging resource-poor provinces to allege that the demands of Premiers Williams and Hamm were threatening to destroy Confederation.

Danny turned to Crawley and Matthews and said that was exactly what he'd been saying. It was not so much a matter of what I was hearing, I continued, as what I was not hearing. Despite the activity of reporters at the scrums with the premiers yesterday, there was very little media interest in this summit, and even the idea that Danny might blast the prime minister before the summit started was evoking, not interest, but a semi-exasperated reaction from the pundits. A kind of "Yeah, yeah, more fed-bashing from Williams, so what else is new?"

I suggested, therefore, that Danny should tone it down this time, because I didn't think it would be helpful to his cause. When he took on Martin at the microphone, coming on too strong might give the impression he was just a wearisome rant artist. His blast at the prime minister at the health summit about not even getting crumbs, let alone the scraps, had gotten the media's attention, but a repeat performance would be viewed by them as the same old same old. A boycott of the summit would send a big message, and his reasons for boycotting it should be along the lines of "more in sorrow than in anger."

Danny responded between coughs and sneezes. He had a very bad cold.

Our delegation left the Sheraton for the summit in a cavalcade of cars, a chauffeured limousine provided by the feds for the premier and Loyola Sullivan and a couple of taxis for the rest of us. As we turned left on Sussex, a large contingent of police on foot, in vehicles, and on motorcycles stopped us to let a motorcade of limos turn into Wellington against the red light, and then into Château Laurier. It was the President of Mexico again. I thought the incident said a lot about priorities in our country. The leader of a foreign country took precedence over the premier of a Canadian province and his delegation who were trying to arrive on time at a summit of our country's top leaders on matters critical to the nation.

At the Pearson Building, Danny Williams and Loyola Sullivan stayed outside in their car while Brian Crawley, Ross Reid, Robert Thompson, Terry Paddon, Elizabeth Matthews and I walked into the lobby. The media saw us, and congregated near the door to wait for Danny's grand entrance. Meanwhile, the prime minister had also arrived, in his limousine. A journalist whom I knew leaned toward me and whispered, "An empty limo stopped and Paul Martin got out." Saucy bugger.

Danny kept everyone lingering for a while longer, and then strode in with Loyola and went to a microphone already mysteriously set up only a few feet away from where the prime minister and the rest of the premiers were assembled.

Danny started by saying he should be angry, but that he was speaking this morning more in sorrow than in anger. (Hey, that was good, I thought.) He went on to describe how Martin had breached his commitment to Newfoundland and Labrador on the Atlantic Accord, and how the PM would not even respond to his phone calls, including a call he'd made on Sunday, two days before the summit. The prime minister's conduct, he said, had rendered it impossible for him to attend this equalization summit.

He sounded impressive: very reasonable and level-headed. But when he solicited questions from the media, the reporters seemed to alternate between hostility and condescension. Many gave the impression they thought Danny was too big for his britches. My suggestion that he should appear more sorrowful than angry certainly wasn't working with this lot. Why, they demanded, was he walking out? Why not stay? Why not, they bawled, try to work it out here? It was as if he had not just painstakingly informed them of why. They seemed to regard our premier's boycott as a parochial action by a provincial—literally and figuratively—premier. And that was the beginning, middle, and end of the damned story.

Danny was interviewed for CBC television by Don Newman on the spot, and even Don, who ordinarily looked like he was bearing the tom-foolery of politicians with amused tolerance, appeared to be exasperated. After that, another TV news team made Danny climb up on some sort of platform where they hooked him up to wires. They had him stand there like a detainee in a terrorist prison photograph, no doubt dying from his cold as he waited for the remote interview to begin.

Meanwhile, twenty feet away, Paul Martin had left the other first ministers to speak to the media as well. A reporter asked him why, since he and Premier Williams were here in the same room a few feet apart, they didn't just talk to each other right now. The perpetually sidetracked prime minister replied that he would not be sidetracked from his agenda by Premier Williams's shenanigans.

Martin emphatically denied Danny's allegation that he had called Martin for a discussion on Sunday. "When the premier calls me, I certainly return his calls and I never fail to do so," he told Don Newman. "I did not receive a call from Mr. Williams. I looked into it, no call has been received from Mr. Williams." Then he blamed Danny for being the uncommunicative one, by not meeting with him and the President of Mexico over drinks: "I expected to meet with Premier Williams last night during the reception with the President of Mexico. I met with the other premiers who were there and I was waiting for Premier Williams to appear . . . I did not receive a phone call from Premier Williams . . . There was a reception, he

knew I was going to be there for the Mexican president. All the other premiers were there. I did have an opportunity in a private room to talk to
them along with the president of Mexico. Premier Williams was expected,
but he did not come . . ." Observers of this performance by Paul Martin
looked at each other in amazement: No doubt a meaningful discussion of
the Atlantic Accord with the Newfoundland premier over drinks and hors
d'oeuvres at a reception for the president of Mexico had been high on
Vicente Fox's agenda during his visit to Ottawa.

Brian Crawley and I were standing next to each other during all this
nonsense. Brian took out his cellphone, went into his voice mail and
played a message he'd saved in my ear. I heard the voice of a staff member
in the prime minister's office acknowledging Danny's call to the prime
minister on Sunday. Either Paul Martin's own staff had misled him, or he
had just deliberately misled the media.

Naturally, the message was immediately released to reporters. It
looked like the prime minister of Canada had been caught telling a big, fat
whopper. The message got extensive media play, and seriously undermined the prime minister's position. I was struck once again by how badly
served Martin seemed to be by many members of that gang in the PMO.

After that, the entire delegation from the province of Newfoundland
and Labrador, led by their premier, left the building. The equalization
summit had been boycotted. Back in my office, telephone messages were
waiting from MP Gerry Byrne and Senator George Baker. Both Liberal parliamentarians said that Danny's position on the Atlantic Accord was the
right one, and that they would work to try to change the federal attitude.

As soon as the equalization summit concluded, Martin put out a news
release announcing the Government of Canada's new approach to equalization. There was a new framework, he said, which, subject to approval
by Parliament, would increase the support provided to provinces and territories by $33 billion over ten years.

This was, Martin claimed, the most significant improvement in the
program's history. By providing predictability, stability and increased
funding, the framework would play an essential role in ensuring that all

Canadians, no matter where they lived, would have access to comparable public services. The increased funding would assist Canada's less prosperous provinces and territories in meeting their commitments under the ten-year health care plan, and others. The new $33 billion framework, when combined with the $41 billion of health enrichments through the Canada Health Transfer, would result in a cumulative increase of $74 billion more over ten years than estimated at the time of the February 2004 budget.

Then Martin concluded the summit with his second fib of the day. The implementation of the new equalization framework, he said, "underlines the goodwill and spirit of co-operation shown by everyone involved." He uttered not a word about the racket with Danny Williams.

You had to pity Paul Martin. As well-intentioned and determined to do the right thing as he was, no matter how hard he tried, he couldn't seem to win for losing. At the beginning of the day, the unanimity of the first ministers' summit was ruined as the media spotlight shifted from Martin's proud equalization program to Danny Williams's accusations and raucous exit. At the end of the day, the credibility of Martin's new equalization initiatives was undermined by renewed muttering among political observers and many in the media that the whole deal was contrived and executed solely for Quebec's benefit. Extrapolations from current equalization figures showed it clearly, they said.

With Newfoundland and Labrador, and perhaps Nova Scotia and Saskatchewan, coming off equalization soon, the only substantial "have-not" province left would be Quebec, which meant that *La belle province* would be receiving by far the lion's share of the huge equalization increases.

In the financial year 2003–2004, the year the equalization summit took place, seven provinces received equalization payments from the federal government, to the tune of some $8.69 billion: Quebec, Manitoba, British Columbia, Newfoundland and Labrador, and the three Maritime provinces. Because of its large population, Quebec got the biggest cut, approximately $3.8 billion.

As a result of the new increases in funding announced by Martin, equalization payments received by Quebec would, according to an estimate released later by the federal Finance department, rise phenomenally. Federal government figures indicated that in 2007–08, just three years after the summit, Quebec's share of the $11.7 billion equalization money available would increase to $6.5 billion. Manitoba, with the second largest share, would be far below Quebec, at $1.7 billion. Newfoundland and Labrador would receive only $477 million by way of equalization that year, and we were heading toward zero.

You didn't need to pity Premier Jean Charest of Quebec, though. He was one shrewd cookie. To my mind, he was the pre-eminent political leader of the era, and probably the best that Quebec had ever produced. At the health summit, he'd received huge amounts of federal funds without having to account to the federal government or anyone else. And while Premier Danny Williams had been busy boycotting the equalization summit, Jean Charest of perennially discontented Quebec had been sitting at the table with the prime minister and the other premiers quietly making a deal with the federal government which would amount to increases of billions and billions of federal dollars for his province.

Charest negotiated changes to equalization that would see his province receive more than half the expanded equalization moneys available during the coming years. He had pulled off two extraordinary coups in the space of one month. Clearly, Danny Williams had his work cut out for him if he had any hope of rising to the level of Charest's elite status when it came to fleecing the federal government.

I might have been a bit discouraged during the days following the equalization summit if it hadn't been for the indications I was picking up that the feds, despite their unfazed public facade, were in fact in a state of near panic behind the scenes at the blow-up between Danny Williams and Paul Martin.

The very next morning after the summit—Wednesday, October 27—I was going down in the elevator in my apartment building at seven-thirty when it stopped and a parliamentarian got in, fuming. In reply to my "good morning" came a growled, "I'll kill that Gerry Byrne. He told me our meeting was at eight o'clock and George Baker called up wondering where I was—the meeting was at seven-thirty." At the ground floor, the parliamentarian bounded out of the elevator and down the corridor. Evidently, an early morning caucus meeting of Liberal MPs and senators had been called in a hurry, and judging by this member's words and actions, it was an extremely important one.

A Liberal caucus member faxed me a copy of an "Info Flash," a list of "facts" and quotes put out by the National Liberal Caucus Research Bureau, and circulated at that caucus meeting. Among other contentions, it stated that "Premier Williams is walking away from a historic deal that would give Newfoundlanders more than twice what he had asked for— $1.4 billion over eight years." Conveniently left out of the document was the fact that, since the time of the premier's ballpark estimates back in February 27, 2004, which they were selectively using in their "Info Flash," oil prices had skyrocketed.

The Liberal caucus document proposed a cute little sound bite for federal Liberals to use: "It falls to Premier Williams to explain why he won't take 'yes' for an answer."

I was told that no decision had been made in the Liberal caucus to attack Danny Williams personally. A decision as stupid as that, my informant said, could only have been made in the prime minister's office. The following excerpts from a *Toronto Star* story on October 28, 2004, by Ottawa Bureau Chief Susan Delacourt provide an example of media coverage of that decision.

> Prime Minister Paul Martin's office is warning that Newfoundlanders will be the real casualties in the anti-Ottawa crusade that Premier Danny Williams launched this week when he walked away from a first ministers' meeting and accused Martin of lying.
>
> "He's making a mistake of historic proportions and he's doing it on the backs of his own citizens," Martin's

spokesperson Scott Reid said yesterday. "He may get some short-term gains but he'll pay for it in the long run."

"The problem that the premier will have eventually is that the truth will get out," Reid said. "And $1.4-billion or twice that perhaps will not end up in the pockets of Newfoundlanders for the sake of his ego and his political ploy."

Meanwhile, all five Newfoundland Liberal MPs have been swamped with calls and emails from back home, including many imploring them to sit as Independents or cross the floor to the opposition.

"It's the first time in my 22 years in public life I've seen this," said Bill Matthews, the Liberal MP for Random-Burin-St. Georges.

I sat in the gallery of the House of Commons soon after the summit boycott, and heard leader of the Opposition Stephen Harper lambaste Martin for "flagrantly" breaking his 100 percent promise. Harper stated that Bill Matthews had said he was reconsidering his future over the broken promise, and that the Liberal member for Humber–St. Barbe–Baie Verte, Gerry Byrne, had said he was now concerned that conditions and strings were being attached to his own leader's promise.

"If members of the Prime Minister's own party do not believe him," Harper asked, "why should anyone else believe him?" Then, in a conclusion to his attack (which I consider to have been nothing but a political ploy now, considering Harper's own deliberate and conscious breach of his commitment to Newfoundland and Labrador on natural resources after the election in which he became prime minister), he stated, "Newfoundlanders and Labradorians have heard enough [from Martin] of 'I feel your pain.' They want the prime minister to fulfill his commitments."

Meanwhile, Danny told a news conference in St. John's, "We are not prepared to have Ottawa keep the loaf and give us the crumbs."

The attack by the PMO on Danny Williams blew up in their own faces.

Scott Reid, the prime minister's director of communications, was accused of being a political bully, pitting the powerful federal government against a vulnerable and struggling province.

In federal-provincial politics, one politico told me, "Nobody roots for Goliath." Martin had to stand in the House of Commons and apologize for the ill-chosen words and sentiments of his communications director. A Liberal MP, one of Paul Martin's own, said to me afterwards that, "If you ever need a brain transplant, choose Scott Reid's, because you'd have a brain that's never been used."

On November 5 in the *Halifax Chronicle Herald*, Stephen Maher of the newspaper's Ottawa bureau referred to a speech in the House of Commons that Ralph Goodale had made a couple of days earlier. The Finance minister had stated that the proposal from Newfoundland which Martin publicly accepted during the election campaign in June included placing a cap on what the province could receive—the Ontario clause. Stephen Maher refuted Goodale's claim. "The proposal Newfoundland Premier Danny Williams made public before Mr. Martin's June 5 commitment did not include such a clause," he wrote, "and Mr. Martin did not mention a cap on June 27, the day before the election, when he told this newspaper he would end the clawback, giving both provinces 100 percent of royalties."

On November 5 as well, a story by Rob Antle on the front page of the *St. John's Telegram* quoted Walter Noel, a Liberal candidate in the federal riding of St. John's North in the June election, as saying that the prime minister had put no conditions or qualifications on his commitment. Noel had heard him make it during a stop on the campaign bus atop Signal Hill. "Martin made no mention of either condition [time limit or Ontario cap] on that June 5 bus ride," Noel said. "It was an unconditional commitment for the life of the resource." Needless to say, I made sure that this discrediting of Goodale's statement was disseminated widely.

One day during this period, I got a call from Newfoundlander Mark Watton, the former Atlantic representative in the PMO, now chief of staff for one of Martin's ministers. He said he was heading out of town, but when he arrived back in Ottawa the following week he'd call me for a get-together on the Accord. His approach to me was a signal that the prime minister's office felt an urgent need to bring this knowledgeable native Newfoundland son—someone on the ball—into the Accord discussions, even though his new minister had absolutely no connection with it.

Marie Fortier soon called as well to discuss all the kafuffle. We thought out loud to each other for twenty minutes about possible procedures for finding a solution to the Martin-Williams problem. We were very frank. I told her there was no way that anyone but the two principals, Danny and Paul, was going to solve this. Certainly no one in federal Finance or the PMO had the clout to make any satisfactory final decisions. She said she would talk to Alex Himelfarb. That was a good idea, I replied. It might get the two top guns to come together themselves.

That night I had a long telephone conversation with Brian Crawley on the impasse between the two governments on the Accord. I suggested to him, as I had done with Marie Fortier earlier in the day, that Paul Martin and Danny Williams had to personally solve the Accord problems. Maybe some groundwork could be done at the official and ministerial levels, but the final decisions—and not just in a token or figurehead or formal way, but in substance—were in the hands of the two leaders themselves. They had to meet behind closed doors, without any bureaucrats or political advisers whispering inhibitions over their shoulders, and come to an agreement. Crawley said he was arriving at much the same conclusion himself and would certainly convey my strong feelings on the subject to Danny at their next meeting. Danny would no doubt be calling me about it.

That was another brilliant brainwave beamed by me into the premier's office—within a couple of weeks, the meeting took place in Ottawa. Danny and Paul got together behind closed doors and, instead of resolving their problems, all but got into a bare-knuckled brawl.

We had a long way to sink in this quagmire yet before we touched bottom.

— CHAPTER SEVEN —

Our "Magnificent" Seven
Part 1: The Private Members

OUR PROVINCE'S SEVEN MPs tried to play key roles during the Atlantic Accord battles. They made their own choices and decided on certain statements and actions, which was their right. During the federal-provincial warfare, six of our MPs were mostly helpful to the province and one was mostly harmful.

MPs Norm Doyle and Loyola Hearn were in the Conservative caucus. MPs Lawrence O'Brien, Gerry Byrne, Scott Simms, Bill Matthews and federal Minister of Natural Resources John Efford were in the Liberal caucus. The decisions they made and the actions they took on difficult issues provided a fascinating insight into how conflicts between their provinces and their political parties affect a Member of Parliament. I discovered that our seven MPs were not all created equal.

The very first political player in Ottawa to telephone me upon my arrival in the capital city in the late summer of 2004 was the MP for Labrador, Lawrence O'Brien. He called from Happy Valley–Goose Bay, saying he wanted to help me in my work in Ottawa as soon as he got back from Labrador himself. Now Lawrence was a staunch Liberal MP and a loyal friend of Martin's, and made no bones about it, while I was the representative of the Tory premier, who was about to go to war with the prime minister. But none of that bothered Lawrence or me at all, and I told him I'd be delighted to work with him.

At the time—heartbreaking in retrospect—he wanted to make long-term plans on the basis of friendship, and invited my wife, Penny, and me to join him and his wife, Alice, at a fishing lodge in Labrador the following summer. But Lawrence and I would not be able to spend much time together in Ottawa, let alone in Labrador. His life that autumn would become consumed with battling the recurrence of cancer.

Some MPs whom I talked to during the Atlantic Accord dispute thought that Lawrence wasn't very interested in the Accord because it didn't directly affect Labrador. I told the MPs they were wrong. In fact, he was very interested in the Accord, and was trying to use his considerable influence with Paul Martin to help get it solved. But it had to be remembered, I said, that he was Martin's good friend and loyal supporter, and would react solidly against any attempt to politically hurt the prime minister. (Lawrence flew to Ottawa by charter flight from Labrador, where he'd been undergoing cancer treatment, so that he could vote to keep Martin's minority government from being defeated. The state of his health at the time was such that it was of no consequence to him personally whether the government stood or fell.)

But to say he was primarily interested in his Labrador riding was no lie. He worked hard on 5 Wing Goose Bay, which was like pounding on a brick wall with your fist every day. And that September, less than three months before the end he knew was imminent, he talked delightedly to me about his success in helping to obtain nearly 400,000 dollars from ACOA to upgrade the not-for-profit Smokey Mountain ski facility in Labrador City.

On a day in November, a day on which I had planned to visit Lawrence at the Ottawa General Hospital, a meeting came together suddenly in Ottawa between Danny Williams, Paul Martin and John Hamm on the Accord, so I postponed my visit to Lawrence by one day. When I got to the hospital the next day, Lawrence told me that I'd missed seeing the prime minister in the hospital room the day before. Martin had dropped by to say hello after his meeting with Danny Williams.

Lawrence said Paul had described the get-together as rather rough. I mentally concurred; the prime minister and the premier had all but come to blows. Lawrence laughed and told me I was lucky I hadn't shown up at the hospital a day earlier, as planned. If the prime minister's bodyguards had seen me after that meeting—one of Danny Williams's gang lurking around the PM—I might be receiving visitors in my own hospital room right now.

Martin had mentioned Liberal MP Gerry Byrne's recent comment on *Open Line* in St. John's—he'd said he wanted to "smack the prime minister" for the federal government's position on the Atlantic Accord. The PMO was aghast at a remark like that coming from one of their own MPs, and not just any member of the Liberal caucus, but a parliamentary secretary appointed by the prime minister himself. Apparently, the PMO wanted to lower the boom on Byrne.

I told Lawrence that any such action by the PMO would be a total overreaction to Gerry's remarks. I had seen a transcript of that show, and this is what had happened: VOCM's *Open Line* host, Randy Simms, and Gerry Byrne were talking about a statement by Scott Reid, communications director in the PMO. He'd said that there was absolutely no possibility of a deal at the upcoming meeting between Premier Williams, Premier Hamm, and Prime Minister Martin. Reid's negativity, not to mention his inappropriateness, had caused great consternation in the two provinces, and among Atlantic Liberal MPs and senators. On *Open Line*, Randy Simms asked Gerry Byrne, "Are you going to go smack Scott Reid in the nose?"

Byrne had replied, "No, I'm not. I'm going to smack the prime minister. Quite frankly . . . he's the employer in this particular situation."

I said to Lawrence that if there was a culprit in the piece, it was Scott Reid. Gerry Byrne had only been stating the simple truth: the PM was ultimately responsible for the crap coming out of his own spokesman. Martin

would be crazy to discipline Byrne and perhaps weaken his support in the
House. If anyone needed disciplining, it was Reid.

Lawrence nodded. He had already gathered from Martin that he was
loath to do anything about Gerry's statement. The PM wanted to consider
it one of those quaint Newfoundland phrases, which made Gerry's true
feelings sound exaggerated. He felt that Gerry hadn't really meant it the
way it was being interpreted by the media.

I replied that it would be to everyone's benefit to maintain that attitude. Good old Paul, I said, he had his work cut out for him, not only in
dealing with the provinces' demands but also in trying to overcome with
his own wisdom and decency the thuggishness of a couple of actors in
his office. Lawrence shook his head over the counterproductive, aggressive words that often came from Martin's people. We agreed that "communications director," in the case of Scott Reid, was a complete mis-
nomer.

Lawrence's wife, Alice, was in the hospital room during my visit, and
I was delighted to renew my acquaintance with her. I'd met her in West
Ste. Modeste in Labrador some thirty years before, back in the early '70s.
At the time, I was campaigning in a by-election in the provincial district of
Labrador South with our candidate Joe Harvey (father of writer Kenneth
J. Harvey). The days of that Labrador summer, many spent in a trap skiff
travelling with Joe from place to place to meet with fishermen and their
families, were among the most pleasant and enlightening of my life. One
of the pleasures had been meeting the McDonald sisters of West Ste.
Modeste, all lovely, intelligent and accomplished "fisherpersons" (before
that word was invented), working with their father. I told Lawrence that
when I learned, years later, before I'd even met him, that he'd had the
intelligence and good taste to marry one of those McDonald sisters, I knew
he was destined to go far.

The three of us talked the afternoon away, Lawrence and Alice reminiscing with razor-sharp humour about the challenges at the beginning of
Lawrence's political career. In 1996 he had contested the Liberal nomination in a by-election caused by MP Bill Rompkey's elevation to the Senate.

There was a crowded field in that nomination battle, including heavy-weights such as former Fish, Food and Allied Workers Union President Richard Cashin, and a serious effort was made by the top brass in the Liberal Party—Brian Tobin, Mel Woodward, and Ed Roberts, among others—to keep Lawrence out of the nomination and make sure someone more "suitable" got it. They seemed to regard him, Lawrence said, laughing, as a loose cannon.

From his hospital bed, Lawrence told me how he'd managed to beat the powerful forces arrayed against him in that hard-fought campaign. It was largely because of the fair and even-handed management of that nomination, he said, by the Liberal Party's executive director at the time—my own brother Fred. Lawrence had been an MP for nine years as a result, he said, and he asked me to tell Fred again how much he still appreciated the fair procedures at the beginning that had made his political career possible.

During our chat, John Efford's name came up, and Lawrence was kind to him. John was sincerely interested in doing the right thing for the province, and he kept in touch with the Newfoundland and Labrador members of the caucus better than any other minister he'd ever known, Lawrence said. But he thought there was a disconnect sometimes between what John really believed and the bravado he spouted publicly, such as his boast that he was so popular he could get elected with the Green Party, or his ultimatum to Danny Williams that the prime minister's latest offer on the Accord was final and the premier could take it or leave it—an absolutely unnecessary declaration of war in his own home province; a war he couldn't possibly win.

Lawrence's highest praise, however, was reserved for George Baker. George, now a senator, had been an MP for years when Lawrence was first elected, and the senior man had gone far out of his way to give him lots of good tips and solid advice when he'd first come to Ottawa as a novice MP.

We parted, agreeing to get together again soon. A day or so later when I called the hospital to arrange another visit, Lawrence had been discharged. When I talked to him at home, he told me that, based on the medical information he'd received, he felt there was no point in staying in hospital; he wanted to free up the bed for someone else. Going by Lawrence's spirited conversation during my last visit, it would have been easy to take this the wrong way, to think that he meant he wasn't sick enough to be in hospital. But, in fact, he was going home to die.

We talked several more times about the Accord; I know he tried to bridge the differences and bring the two sides closer together. I sincerely believe that if he had been well, and had lived longer, the battles would not have been so vicious.

It would turn out to be a sad irony that on the evening of Thursday, December 16, 2004, I was at a meeting in Ottawa with a delegation from Happy Valley–Goose Bay about the future of 5 Wing Goose Bay. Present were Perry Trimper, head of the citizens' coalition in the town; Brian Fowlow, head of the chamber of commerce there; and Jamie Innis, an adviser to the associate minister of the Department of National Defence. At the start, around seven-thirty, Perry Trimper confirmed that Lawrence O'Brien was at the Health Sciences Centre in St. John's and had only a short time to live. That thought hovered over our discussions; we waited for the inevitable, which turned out to be a call from the hospital to Perry's cellphone at around nine-thirty. Lawrence had just died. He was fifty-three years old.

Few people knew that his battle with cancer was so far advanced, because he had resolutely gone about his business. For example, when Newfoundland journalist Craig Westcott came to Ottawa in November to do interviews for the *St. John's Express* during the Accord battle, he wanted to confirm, after his interview with me, his arrangement to meet with MP O'Brien. I called Lawrence on his cellphone; he was at his office in the Justice Building working away, and Craig Westcott went off to interview him there. This was weeks before his death.

The long and fierce nature of his fight was indicated by the thank yous in his obituary to the doctors and staff of so many hospitals: the Health Sciences Centre in St. John's, the Blanc Sablon hospital, the Labrador

Health Centre in Happy Valley–Goose Bay, the Ottawa General Hospital and the St. Clare's Mercy Hospital in St. John's.

The morning after Lawrence's death, I telephoned Gertie Mullins at the front desk at Steele Communications in St. John's, and Pat Murphy, the producer of VOCM's *Open Line*, to tell them that Lawrence O'Brien had always spoken very highly of both of them; he wanted them to know how much he had appreciated the courtesy and affability they'd always shown him whenever he had called in.

The same day, the premier issued a statement of condolence to Alice and the O'Brien family, mentioning Lawrence's "instrumental role in having the constitutional name change of the province to Newfoundland and Labrador."

Paul Martin was vacationing in Morocco when Lawrence O'Brien died, but he flew back across the Atlantic to Happy Valley–Goose Bay to attend the Roman Catholic funeral Mass at Bethel Pentecostal Tabernacle on December 20. The next day in the *Globe and Mail*, columnist Margaret Wente criticized Paul Martin for his frenetic travel schedule; she was of the opinion he flitted about the world to escape from the demands of his job. Wente described one of Martin's unproductive, escapist journeys: "After his midnight meeting in the desert, he was compelled to race back to Goose Bay, Nfld., for the funeral of an obscure Liberal politician."

I received a Christmas card from Lawrence after his death. His aide had written on it that Lawrence had said to him before he died, "Whatever you do, don't forget to send a card to Bill Rowe." It was one of the most moving messages I'd ever received.

AS A LEADING MEMBER of Stephen Harper's Conservative Opposition, Loyola Hearn was a great help to the province in the House of Commons on the Accord. He deserved a lot of credit for his efforts. I, however, would experience an incident in Ottawa that undermined my own fondness for the man.

Judging by his constituents, though, my diminished affection was an exception: the more they got to know him, the more they seemed to love him. Having been first elected with moderate returns in 1982 to the House of Assembly as the member for St. Mary's–The Capes, the next time he ran there, three years later, he was re-elected with the biggest majority in the province. In the election of 1989, he held on to his top margin of victory personally, even though his Progressive Conservative Party lost the government to the Liberals under Clyde Wells.

When Loyola entered federal politics in a by-election in May 2000, he had a rough time getting himself elected as a PC in the former riding of St. John's West. But mere months later when Liberal Prime Minister Jean Chrétien called a general election, Loyola was re-elected with the highest percentage of votes of any Progressive Conservative in the country.

I was hosting *Open Line* during his early federal career, and he used to call now and then, in his role as an Opposition MP. I would often rebuke him and his Progressive Conservative Party for giving the Grits a free ride into government every election. The Liberals' percentage of the popular vote was only in the mid-thirties, but because the Opposition parties were fractured and divided, they were allowing the Liberals to rule the country as if by divine right. So I would badger Hearn: Why didn't the PCs and the Canadian Alliance get their damned act together? Join forces, unite the right and restore a competitive environment to Canadian politics? Such a union could replace the Liberals as the new natural governing party of Canada.

Hearn would always respond that he was working on such a union, and, of course, I would always greet this with skeptical kidding. But the shagger was in fact working on a union, and before long he helped engineer a deal between Peter MacKay, then-leader of the Progressive Conservative Party, and Stephen Harper, leader of the Canadian Alliance, to form the Conservative Party of Canada. Hearn considered that accomplishment to be his greatest contribution to public life in Canada, and he was right. Stephen Harper recognized it by appointing him the first House Leader for the new Conservative Party as well as critic for Fisheries and Oceans.

In September 2004, soon after I'd arrived in Ottawa, Loyola Hearn and I had had a long, frank and friendly chat by telephone. This was just over two months after the federal election that saw Paul Martin's Liberals come back with a minority government. Already, Loyola was worried about the leadership and policies of his new Conservative Party. He was "half happy," he told me, that they hadn't formed the government after the June election because Harper had a lot to learn. I got the distinct impression that Hearn, as a middle-of-the-road PC—a red Tory on some issues—was dismayed by the ultra-conservative doctrines of the new political gang he'd worked so hard to get his Progressive Conservative Party joined up with.

What surprised me most in Ottawa, though, was his attitude toward Danny Williams. I had assumed that the federal Conservatives would be Danny's natural political allies. In my naïveté, I thought that Conservative Party MPs from Newfoundland and Labrador and the provincial PC government under Williams, while experiencing the normal bickering and jealousies within any political family, would pull together against their real enemies, the Liberals and the NDP.

An old-time federal Tory political operative in St. John's, who'd known Williams for years, said to me once with a laugh, "One thing about Danny—you can't say his financial success spoiled him. He's always been insufferable." But I'd considered that an individual disgruntlement.

Imagine my astonishment, then, when I discovered that the federal Conservative MPs from this province and the Newfoundland and Labrador Progressive Conservative leadership seemed to despise one another more than they did the dirty Grits and the socialists. The rapport between what many people consider the federal and provincial wings of the party was worse than non-existent; it was actually negative. I found the relationship between Danny Williams and Conservative MP Norm Doyle cooler than I'd expected, but the one between Loyola Hearn and Danny was positively hostile.

I would learn later—long before Stephen Harper formed a government and became prime minister—that Danny had never had any time for Harper and his political doctrines. "I don't like Harper very much," Danny said to me during a tête-à-tête in Ottawa one day. "In fact, I don't like him at all."

But the animosity between Hearn and Williams predated the uniting of the federal PCs and the Alliance.

Hearn told me that he had not had one single call from Danny Williams for advice or information or even a chat since Danny had become the provincial PC Party leader. "The premier wants to do absolutely everything himself," Hearn groused, "with no involvement by anyone else." Danny had given old-time Tory operatives the distinct impression that there was absolutely nothing that couldn't be solved if they would simply do as he said.

I was frankly taken aback by the level of irritation—outright animosity, actually—displayed by Hearn, but he assured me sincerely during our first conversation that he really wanted to co-operate, to help me achieve some objectives up here. A few weeks later, he called me one morning out of the blue, inviting me for lunch that very day in the parliamentary restaurant. To accept, I would have to cancel a longstanding appointment. But Hearn made our need to get together sound urgent.

This was during the time the Opposition was pummelling Martin in Question Period over his broken promise on the Atlantic Accord. For days on end, from the gallery of the House of Commons, I had gotten a good view of the Opposition in action. Stephen Harper, Norm Doyle, Loyola Hearn, and NDP Leader Jack Layton questioned Prime Minister Martin ferociously. The organization of the questions from the Opposition, spearheaded by MPs Loyola Hearn and Norm Doyle, was very effective and damaging. I honestly couldn't see Martin allowing himself to go on being subjected to it day after day.

So that was the atmosphere in which I received Hearn's invitation to meet him for lunch immediately. Once I joined him in the restaurant, though, his conversation turned out to be merely general, even trivial— not at all urgent. Hearn said he was sad about being obliged to make a savage onslaught on the prime minister of our country every day, but it was absolutely necessary. A big part of the problem, he thought, was John Efford.

Hearn then moved on to some kind remarks about my new position and its importance to the province. And thus ended our lunch, during which I was fed nothing but general comments, gossip, and flattery. I left the restaurant feeling that Loyola Hearn was a great lunch companion for an idle day. But I was still wondering why he had rushed a get-together, which, in effect, had turned out to be a courtesy meeting. I soon found out.

What Hearn had not mentioned during our lunch was the fact that he had been interviewed that same morning by Doug Letto of the CBC, up from St. John's to do a story on the Accord. During that interview, which was aired a few days later, Letto said, "Loyola Hearn [is] a Conservative, a supporter of Danny Williams on the Atlantic Accord, but ask him about having Williams appoint a provincial representative in Ottawa."

I watched Hearn on TV dismissing my post; apparently, he considered my existence in Ottawa an insult to his position as an MP. "I challenge anybody," he declared, "to say we're not doing what we came here to do." Then, with staggering inconsistency, he criticized the province for not having had Bill Rowe herd all our MPs and senators together—Liberal and Conservative alike—the week before, in the midst of the debate about the Atlantic Accord. That way, he said, we could have presented a united Newfoundland and Labrador front. "That person has to be the coordinator for major events," Loyola Hearn pronounced. "In this past week, it didn't happen. Whose fault, I don't know, but I believe we should have seen a Newfoundland effort."

Then he veered off into Danny's "hidden agenda" regarding my appointment, which was what really had Hearn's knickers in a knot. "I don't know whether somebody wants to, you know, take all the credit or whatever for this, but look, this is not something that one individual . . . a lot of people have been heavily involved in this issue for a long time. The offshore revenues have been raised in this House, you know, a longer period than since the last election."

It was right after this interview with Letto that Hearn felt the urgent need to invite me to lunch.

Brian Crawley called me early in the morning to talk over developments, including the upcoming Tory resolution in the House of Commons condemning Martin's position on the Accord. He mentioned the CBC TV story on my job in Ottawa. Letto had interviewed John Efford about my appointment as well; Crawley said he wasn't surprised that Efford had been petty enough to attack my position, but he was certainly surprised that Loyola Hearn had taken a serious smack at me.

Christ, I said, laughing, I was surprised too. At the big lunch he'd pushed on me in the parliamentary restaurant right after the interview, he couldn't have been more complimentary and eager to help. Crawley replied that Hearn's nose must be still out of joint because Danny hadn't helped him during the federal election the previous June. Apparently he'd made a public swipe at me because his fragile ego was smarting from Danny's neglect.

After realizing what he'd said about me on tape, Hearn must have been trying to do some pre-emptive damage control, I replied. If so, the tactic failed. All it had done was make me lose trust in Hearn. I told Crawley I was flattered, though: after all the years John Efford and Loyola Hearn had spent at each other's throats in politics, the only thing they'd ever agreed on was slamming my appointment as provincial representative in Ottawa.

Unfortunately, however, as bizarrely amusing as the little episode was, lost trust is hard to regain. Years after my experience with Hearn, St. John's Mayor Andy Wells got into a very public scrap with him. Andy claimed that Hearn, who by then had become minister of Fisheries and our regional minister in Harper's government, had assured him of one thing privately regarding a position for Andy on the Canada-Newfoundland and Labrador Offshore Petroleum Board, and then turned around and denied it publicly. Andy called Hearn a two-faced liar. This episode would ring a familiar bell for me; I had no difficulty accepting Andy's side of the story.

CONSERVATIVE MP NORM DOYLE also played an important role in the House of Commons in undermining Martin's public posturing on the Atlantic Accord. Loyola Hearn played the leading Opposition role as an MP from this province, and his pre-eminence was shown by his seat in the House in the front row, just a few seats away from Harper. But Doyle was very effective during Question Period from his seat in the second row, just across the aisle from Paul Martin. Norm is one of nature's gentlemen; he told me how desperately hard he found it, in the name of partisan politics, to have to hurl insults across the aisle—double-dealer, forked tongue, liar—right into the face of a decent individual "and a man who is the prime minister, after all, of the whole country."

I don't know if Norm Doyle felt similar qualms about attacking John Efford over the Accord, but, if so, he must have concluded later that fate had punished him more than enough for his nastiness. He told me that, during the worst period of his verbal abuse of Efford in the House, he was returning to Ottawa after a brief, rushed visit to St. John's and he'd managed to get the very last seat on the plane. As he walked toward his row, a horrifying awareness dawned on him: The only empty seat—his assigned seat—was situated between John Efford and his wife, Madonna. When Norm indicated it was his seat, Efford became hostile. "You should move. Why don't you move?" Norm told him there were no other seats, and asked John if he'd like to move over one seat and sit next to Madonna. The minister growled "No." So Norm had to climb over Efford, and endure the unnerving experience of having to sit for hours on end, hip by flank, cheek by jowl, between a husband and wife who said absolutely nothing to him throughout the long flight.

At a meeting with Norm to discuss the Atlantic Accord debates a few days after my lunch with Hearn, he said he was astonished that his colleague had taken a run at my job on television. I said I was too, but only because he'd said the exact opposite to my face on the very same day. I told Norm I was glad he'd brought it up, because I was going to find it difficult to rely on anything Hearn might tell me in the future.

For example, take the potential conflict of interest that was brewing inside the Conservative Party regarding the Accord: whereas Norm and Hearn, as Newfoundland and Labrador MPs, were trying to settle the thing as soon as possible in the province's favour, Harper and the rest of the

Conservative Party would like to keep the dispute going right up to the next election, so they could go on saying Paul Martin had broken a promise. My problem with future dealings with Hearn was that even if he assured me he would get the party to pull back in their attacks at a strategic point so that Martin could come to an agreement with the province, I wouldn't feel comfortable relying on Hearn's word. He would just as likely say one thing privately and do the opposite publicly the same day.

Norm told me not to worry about that happening. He would make sure that any conflict would be resolved absolutely in the best interests of the province, and he was certain that Loyola Hearn would do the same. I felt less anxious after Norm's assurance. And I would find, in fact, that both he and Hearn acted accordingly.

GERRY BYRNE WAS A Liberal MP from Newfoundland and, political partisanship being what it is, some might have thought that Gerry wouldn't go out of his way to lend a hand to a Tory appointee like me. I had heard from a reliable source in the Liberal caucus that there had been a big discussion among the Newfoundland and Labrador Liberal MPs and senators over what their relationship should be with Bill Rowe. One of them suggested that they should all shun Williams's hired gun, but if they were forced to have any dealings with him, they should be on their guard. The other Liberal parliamentarians dismissed that suggestion as absurd, and said they intended to have as positive and helpful relationship with the premier's representative as possible, to further the interests of the province.

Gerry Byrne was certainly not the federal Liberal MP who had suggested shunning me. As soon as he arrived in Ottawa, late that summer, he called me to say he was back in action, following his young son's serious surgery in Newfoundland, and he wanted to get together right away to chat about the lie of the land. After that, Gerry and I talked by phone or in person nearly every day about how to resolve federal-provincial difficulties with the Accord negotiations. He was genuinely helpful to the province, even when, from time to time, his enthusiasm caused him to put his foot in it. I used to remind Gerry on occasion of that profoundest of political maxims: "A closed mouth gathers no feet."

Gerry and I had something else in common besides a desire to help Newfoundland and Labrador gain a better Accord deal. This was a knowledge and love of his riding of Humber–St. Barbe–Baie Verte, which included Bonne Bay. That's where my mother had grown up, and where I'd spent every boyhood summer. It also included White Bay South, which I'd represented in the House of Assembly for eight proud years. And we had something else in common, too: former Newfoundland and Labrador premier Brian Tobin.

Tobin was my executive assistant when I was leader of the Opposition back in the late '70s. Some years later, after I was out of politics, Gerry Byrne had been Tobin's assistant in his federal riding. When I got to Ottawa, I'd wondered to myself if Tobin might still have any influence with the Liberal government, if he could be of some use to his native province on the Atlantic Accord.

When Tobin had been premier of Newfoundland and Labrador in the '90s, he'd put me on his list for one of the Christmas parties he held each year at his house on Waterford Bridge Road. Over time, as I criticized his policies on radio and TV, I descended from his A-list party to his B-list party, and was finally dropped altogether.

Nevertheless, after he left the premiership to become a federal minister again, and announced he was running for the leadership of the national Liberal Party, I called him to say that, as a Newfoundlander, I would do everything I could to help him become leader and prime minister. But before I could act on that, he dropped out of the race in the face of the Paul Martin juggernaut, and I lost contact again.

Brian Tobin was living in Toronto, having raked in millions from a severance package from one of Belinda Stronach's daddy's businesses. I asked Gerry Byrne if he ever saw or talked to him. Gerry said, rather emphatically, that he did not. Then he described to me Tobin's reaction back in 1996 when Gerry told him he'd decided to run in the by-election in Tobin's former riding on the west coast of Newfoundland, after Tobin had resigned to become premier of the province. Tobin had gone completely cold. How dare Gerry Byrne, his former lackey, take such a step without Tobin's prior approval? That was bad enough, but worse was to come.

When the next federal general election was called, Brian Tobin as premier and provincial Liberal Party leader, launched a blitz to keep Gerry from being renominated as Liberal candidate in Humber–St. Barbe–Baie Verte. I remembered the vicious nomination battle. I was host of *Open Line* in St. John's, which was also carried on CFCB in Corner Brook, and, of course, I never saw an underdog I didn't love.

Although I didn't know Gerry Byrne, and although I had no idea at the time why Tobin was showing such animosity against his former friend and assistant, it struck me that the powerful Tobin forces were trying to bully him. So I encouraged Gerry daily over the air to take on the party brass, and I decried the heavy-handed attempt by Tobin's gang to eject him. Tobin was especially offended by my labelling his style of management as "Stalinist." I even made fun of how similar to Tobin himself the guy he had put up to defeat Byrne sounded on the air. He sounded like the Tobin version of Mini-Me. Byrne got himself renominated and re-elected.

I asked Gerry why Tobin had directed such hostility at him. He told me it stemmed from a false rumour that had been floating around about Tobin. Tobin, and the other person whose name had been dragged through the mud, thought that Gerry Byrne had started the vile rumour. Byrne told me he'd had absolutely no part in it. He swore that if the rumour ever came up in his presence, he would strenuously assert that he believed it was completely unfounded.

I told Gerry that, in my experience, rumours about political leaders could flow from the most ridiculous beginnings. I cited a case from years before, of another premier who had gone from his province to Ottawa with a group of aides and advisers to negotiate with the federal government. During their stay there, a television crew filmed a strategy meeting in the premier's hotel suite one night, a portion of which was then televised. The TV film showed the meeting breaking up, and the premier saying good night to the members of his group by name as they left his suite. But he was not heard to say good night to his female communications director.

The next day, someone asked me if I'd seen the footage, and if I'd noticed that the communications director hadn't left the premier's suite when everyone else was leaving. Well, that could only mean one thing, the person said—she was spending the night with the premier. They were having a big fling. I laughed, and said that was the stupidest thing I'd ever heard. But sure enough, the story started to make the rounds: the premier and his communications director were having an affair. A person who hadn't even seen the TV footage told me a few days later that, yes it was absolutely true—he'd been informed that the incriminating evidence had been caught right on camera.

Fortunately, that yarn didn't last long in the rumour mills, but only because neither that particular premier nor that particular communications director looked like the types to have a lawless roll in the hay. Political cities like Ottawa are funny, a long-time observer of the capital scene told me. It was a wonder, he said, there hadn't been a sex-scandal rumour about Pierre Trudeau and the Queen of England after he made that pirouette behind her.

Gerry's wife was in Newfoundland with their recovering infant son, and he found himself with an invitation to the Martin government's Throne Speech to be delivered by Governor General Adrienne Clarkson on October 5. He offered it to me and, having never been at that event in the Senate before, I went.

Next day I told him it had been a nostalgia trip, but a masochistic one, complete with nightmarish flashbacks of all the endlessly dreary ceremonial occasions I'd endured throughout my own political days. Gerry concurred that attending a Throne Speech was one of those things you did once in one lifetime because of the historical nature of the occasion.

But I was glad I'd attended this event. As I sat there, tuned out and waiting, I had an insight that I thought might prove useful to our cause. It was sparked by the appearance in the Senate Chamber of the Usher of the Black Rod. This was the person the public normally sees on television once a year, bearing his or her ebony stick, that impressive symbol of authority, just before the governor general delivers the Speech from the Throne. The present Black Rod had just performed a six-hundred-year-old parliamentary tradition as the messenger of the Sovereign in Parliament by making his way down the hall to the House of Commons, where he had summoned the yahoos sitting there, the MPs, to the noble Senate Chamber. They were piled up in front of the chamber door like capelin on a beach.

Black Rod is the most senior protocol office in Parliament, responsible for security in the Senate Chamber, for acting as administrator for the opening of Parliament, and for coordinating state funerals and the investiture of a governor general. Other tasks include carrying out ceremonial duties related to the Royal Assent of bills and acting as a member of the welcoming party for all visiting heads of state and heads of government. These are very impressive things, but nowhere near as impressive as another fact I knew about the current Back Rod.

I've long conjectured that every second person you meet is ultimately, by descent or marriage, a Newfoundlander. They must be, because you encounter them everywhere, and they are so proud of their connection, however remote, to our unique tribe, that they make it known as soon as they learn that you're a Newfoundlander.

The Black Rod was a case in point. One evening, before I attended the Throne Speech, I was at a parliamentary reception when my friend and fellow Newfoundlander, Ottawa resident Herb Davis, brought me over and introduced me to retired Lieutenant Commander of the Royal Canadian Navy Terrance Christopher, the Usher of the Black Rod. Right off the bat, Christopher told me that, although he'd been born in Cape Breton, his father was from Newfoundland. We immediately bonded.

The sight of Terry Christopher as the Black Rod reminded me of the thousands upon thousands of people up here on the mainland, in high positions and low, who were somehow connected to the province, and so possessed great sympathy for Newfoundland and Labrador's cause. That, plus my realization as I listened to the Throne Speech, that, despite its bravado, the minority Martin government could fall any time—and therefore we'd better get an Atlantic Accord deal quickly—spurred me to make sure that sympathy by Newfoundlanders would be enlisted tangibly behind Danny Williams's efforts whenever possible. Later in this book, we'll see if that turned out to be a productive move.

Gerry Byrne offered to lend a hand in all this, and to give me information and advice, without breaching the secrecy of caucus or his Cabinet oath, that might steer negotiations in the right direction. That would be a great help, I said, because recent discussions with John Efford seemed to indicate that he was out of sync with the commitment made by his boss, Paul Martin. I frankly wondered if Efford wasn't sometimes off on a frolic of his own.

For instance, I'd heard him disagreeing publicly with a couple of his Cabinet colleagues in their own backyards—contradicting MP David Anderson of British Columbia on the question of drilling for undersea oil off that province, and opposing Environment Minister Stéphane Dion in Dion's own ministerial bailiwick regarding atmospheric emissions. My distinct impression from Liberal government sources was that Cabinet and caucus were often flabbergasted by Efford's quirky notions of Cabinet solidarity.

Gerry suppressed a smile, and said that he thought John Efford was growing in his extremely demanding job of Natural Resources minister. Gerry's failure to take even a little swipe at Efford surprised me, because Efford had earlier taken Gerry's seat in the federal Cabinet. Gerry had been appointed minister of State for the Atlantic Canada Opportunities Agency in January 2002, at the age of thirty-five, the youngest Member of Parliament from our province ever appointed to the federal Cabinet. He'd been removed from the position a couple of years later following a caucus revolt by his fellow local MPs. As Gerry's parliamentary biography described it, "the biggest political firestorm ever raised against him was that he was a politician who was doing just too darn much for his own riding."

Gerry told me that he was glad to be out of Cabinet these days; he and his wife, Denise, had their hands full helping their son recover from serious kidney surgery. He'd be more than content, he said, if he could just help the province benefit from a new, improved Atlantic Accord by playing the role of an honest broker between the two sides.

About a week later, I walked to Gerry's office in the Justice Building next to the Supreme Court of Canada. We were going to have a chat about Accord developments and lunch before Question Period started in the House. I found Gerry in an office all by himself, with absolutely no staff around. He was answering the phone and replying to emails. He told me that when he'd left his job as ACOA minister he'd been forced to reduce staff considerably. He had let staff go in his Ottawa office so that the people in his Newfoundland constituency office could keep their jobs, and attend to constituents' needs on the spot.

I told Gerry what I'd heard from my sources inside the Liberal caucus. At a recent meeting of Liberal MPs, John Efford had gone into a rage because he felt he was being ignored by his Cabinet colleagues regarding the Atlantic Accord. Efford hadn't even been aware of the upcoming meeting between Goodale, Williams, and Sullivan let alone been invited to it; he'd first heard about it by way of the CBC news. Efford was infuriated that Goodale had left him out of the loop. The word was that Danny and Loyola had insisted Efford not be at the meeting because his presence was so counterproductive. While neither confirming nor denying Efford's outburst and the possibility of civil strife in caucus—and I never asked him to—Gerry suggested that perhaps Danny needed to be a little conciliatory with Efford at this point.

I also told Gerry that members of the Liberal caucus and senior bureaucrats seemed to believe that everything was proceeding as it should regarding an improved Accord with Newfoundland and Labrador. They thought that a federal-provincial deal with us was imminent, but that a deal with Nova Scotia would be more problematical. I warned Gerry that these notions were untrue. I told him it would be a good idea to let Goodale and Martin know that we believed they were misleading MPs and public servants, and promoting a false sense of security.

A deal with Danny Williams was not even close at this point. The feds were simply too far away from our position. And as for Nova Scotia, both provinces were on the same wavelength, and communicating constantly. Nothing was being served by the PMO hinting one week that a deal with Nova Scotia was in the works, and that Newfoundland and Labrador was going to be left out in the cold, and then insinuating the next week to Nova Scotia that a deal was about to go ahead with Newfoundland and Labrador. It was a childish, transparent attempt to divide the two provinces.

Gerry said it was certainly not unknown for the PMO to throw a bone in among the dogs, to set them against each other. It was, in fact, a time-honoured tactic. I wondered if that was what had caused a recent outburst by the premiers of Manitoba, New Brunswick, and Quebec, who had expressed fears that an Accord deal with Nova Scotia and Newfoundland and Labrador would undermine equalization to their provinces. But Gerry said the PM and Goodale had gone out of their way to reassure the caucus that any changes in the Atlantic Accord would have absolutely no impact on any other province's equalization. He told me he would try to clear up any confusing signals coming from the federal side.

Since it was now about 1:00 p.m., with Question Period an hour away, I wondered where we could go to grab a quick bite of lunch. I was starved. Gerry said he never ate anything at midday. As we left for the House on empty stomachs, I said this lunch was on me today—it was about all the budget of our bankrupt province could handle.

A week or two later, Danny boycotted the equalization meeting of first ministers. A bunch of us, including Loyola Sullivan, got a taxi back to our hotels and offices. En route, Sullivan received a call on his cell from Gerry, offering his help to sort out the impasse. Back in my office, I had calls waiting from Gerry and George Baker, both eager to help both parties get past the roadblocks. We talked nearly every day for weeks afterwards. I was determined to make sure, knowing that the PMO would keep putting a spin on the breakdown, that the provincial position got through loud and clear, and without let-up.

After a caucus of MPs and senators from Newfoundland and Labrador met with Martin following the boycott, Brian Crawley called me to say that the PM had asked Newfoundland and Labrador senator George Furey to deal directly with Danny Williams for a while. What did I think? I told him I thought that might be very useful. I had nothing but admiration for Furey, whom I knew as a fellow lawyer; I'd sat with him for years on arbitration boards. But I and others, including Gerry Byrne and George Baker, strongly felt that Danny Williams and Paul Martin were the only ones who could overcome the stalemate. The two leaders had to put aside their personal feelings and get together. With luck, Senator Furey might make some progress toward a meeting of the minds before that happened.

By the second of November, the day of the presidential election in the United States, there was little improvement. Gerry called me that evening to talk about the terrible fix that he and everyone else on the federal Liberal side were in regarding the Accord. For the first time, he had unkind words for John Efford's lack of leadership on the issue. Gerry seemed very lonely and downhearted. His wife was still in Newfoundland with their infant son. Gerry asked if he and I could get together to watch the US election returns. I was sorry to have to tell him I had a prior commitment.

The next day Gerry called to talk about the resolution proposed by the Tories, attacking Paul Martin for his breach of commitment. He wanted to move an amendment to improve it—make it less negative, so he could vote for it.

During this stressful period, Gerry called VOCM *Open Line* in St. John's about the Accord breakdown. That was when he made the remark about giving the prime minister a smack. The PMO and many in the Liberal caucus were going nuts over it, Gerry told me. They wanted him booted out. Martin, however, as Lawrence O'Brien had said he would, managed to keep his wits and his wisdom about him.

On the night of November 15, the Tory motion condemning the prime minister for his breach of commitment on the Atlantic Accord was voted on. Norm Doyle and Loyola Hearn voted in favour of it and, in a violation of caucus solidarity which shocked federal Liberals, Newfoundland and Labrador Liberal MPs Bill Matthews and Scott Simms also voted for the motion. Lawrence O'Brien was not in the House, and Gerry Byrne and John Efford voted against the motion.

I watched the debate in the House of Commons on the resolution. Afterwards, I could not recall much of the content of any of the speeches. The note in my diary for that night reads as follows: "Extremely partisan and silly."

Gerry dropped down to see me the next day. He had proposed an amendment to remove some of the more offensive language about Martin. He told me Loyola Hearn had agreed to support the amendment. When the time came, Hearn had shouted "traitor, traitor!" across the House at him instead. He felt duped by Hearn, he said.

Gerry wondered why the federal Tories had not backed up Williams: the premier had asked for the amendment that Gerry had pushed. Gerry felt hoodwinked by it all. People were accusing him of not being on board with his own province, he said, but that wasn't true. He was squarely on side, but it took two to tango. Meanwhile, he said, the word was going around that Nova Scotia was getting ready to jump in bed with the feds. And why hadn't Lawrence O'Brien, Paul Martin's great friend, been in the House for the vote instead of letting Gerry twist alone in the wind with John Efford? Gerry wondered if he was getting paranoid.

Feeling paranoid in politics was healthy, I told him. It only meant you had a firm grip on reality. It was remotely possible, however, that sometimes there was, in fact, nobody out to get you. When Gerry had started playing the role of broker between the two sides on the Accord, he'd thought the phone in his office was being bugged because he could hear sounds along the line. But when he'd had the phone checked by security, it was clean: the sounds were being caused by an Internet connection. Maybe, I told him, his paranoia was groundless this time too; maybe no one was out to get him. Gerry looked at me very dubiously. And then we had a good laugh over how divorced from reality I had become since joining the public service.

Shortly after that, I ran into a gaggle of Conservative MPs on the Hill, a couple of whom I knew, and we fell to chatting about the Accord and the vote on the resolution condemning Paul Martin. Gerry Byrne had let them down completely, one of them said. Loyola Hearn had told him so. Another said that Byrne's vote against the motion had resulted from his paying gig as parliamentary secretary. Having already incurred the wrath of the PMO with his public statement of desire to give the PM a smack in the chops, the MP continued, Byrne knew he was on thin ice.

Gerry telephoned me to say he had called VOCM *Open Line* in St. John's and, to say the least, it had not gone swimmingly for him. Host Randy Simms had pronounced him politically dead, he said, predicting that he would be defeated by his constituents in the next election because he had sided with the federal government against his own province. Gerry was dismayed at Randy's reaction. He thought it was a serious political blow.

I told Gerry not to be so foolish. Based on the many proclamations of political death that I'd heard during my years in politics and as a host on call-in radio, such death decrees were trivial matters. There would be little, if any, impact on his political career. The people in his riding had no doubt where his loyalties lay—squarely with them. Hadn't he been ousted from Cabinet for piling too much money into his own riding? Hadn't he sent the great and powerful Brian Tobin scurrying off with his tail between his legs at the nomination battle a couple of elections ago? Hadn't he received the highest percentage of the vote in the entire province in the last election, beating even John Efford's percentage? I told him to relax: after the next election, and an even bigger majority, he could have some fun with Randy on *Open Line*. Ask him on air if he wished to revise the "political death" comment.

The next morning, the premier's office telephoned me to say that Gerry had hung Danny Williams out to dry on VOCM *Night Line* the night before. Apparently, Gerry had said that he'd voted against the Tory resolution condemning Martin because Danny Williams had wanted him to vote that way. The premier's office was planning to have a serious talk with our Mr. Byrne. In the "to do" list in my work diary that day, I wrote the following: "Tell Gerry Byrne, for Christ's sake, to stay off the talk shows for five minutes."

A few years ago, prominent provincial Liberal and former MHA Chuck Furey publicly compared fellow Liberal Gerry Byrne to a child in traffic. Gerry did give the impression sometimes of dangerous, directionless meandering off the safety of the sidewalk. But I found him very helpful in trying to resolve the Accord issues. He did his best to play the difficult role of middleman between two warring factions, and got squeezed for it now and then. But he also got the points and positions of both sides across the great divide. He was very useful to his province and to his government. And he managed to survive the Atlantic Accord war—whereas John Efford, as we shall see, tripped up on the rocky negotiations and took a plunge over the political cliff.

MEANWHILE, NEWFOUNDLAND LIBERAL MPS Bill Matthews and Scott Simms were playing controversial and important roles in the federal-provincial drama. Whether their actions were to their benefit or detriment was a good question.

The Conservative motion put the Liberal MPs from Newfoundland and Labrador in a tough spot. If they voted against it, they would be painted as traitors to their province. If they voted for it, they'd be painted as traitors to the prime minister and the Liberal Party. As one wag commented, they were between the Rock (Newfoundland) and a hard place (Ottawa). In trying to do what they believed was right, they would have to act, one way or the other, against their own self-interest.

Bill Matthews and Scott Simms both agonized over the thing for days. When I ran into Scott outside the House one day shortly before the vote, he told me that a poll of his riding indicated that the vast majority of his constituents supported the resolution condemning Martin. Therefore, he had to answer this question: Who was his boss, the prime minister of Canada, or the constituents who elected him?

He decided in favour of his constituents, and voted with the Tories. Many considered Scott's decision wrong-headed. One Liberal MP lamented to me, only half in jest, "Whatever happened to that most cherished tradition in the House of Commons—sucking up to the prime min-

ister?" Some of Scott's colleagues said his decision had had nothing to do
with his constituents. He'd allowed himself to be influenced by Bill
Matthews, they said, and Matthews had his own agenda.

Some argued that Scott was obligated to use his own judgment, and
not be a slave to the perceived whims of his constituents on every issue. If
MPs always voted to curry favour with their own ridings, politics would
become parochial and corrupt, and democracy at the national level would
collapse. MPs must vote in the House according to the consensus of
caucus. If they couldn't do that, they should get out of caucus.

It would be hard to conclude that Simms acted out of self-interest. He
was savvy enough to know he didn't need to do it to secure re-election.
Gerry Byrne would prove as much in the next election. Indeed, Simms
could have evaded the whole issue by not being in the House when the
vote was taken. But he didn't evade it. He voted for the enemy motion,
knowing that he might well be kicked out of caucus and prevented from
running as a Liberal in the next election in his strong Liberal seat. He knew
he would be *persona non grata* with his Liberal colleagues for a long time,
and that his action effectively negated the possibility of higher office—parliamentary secretary or minister—for the foreseeable future, perhaps for
his entire parliamentary career.

When I ran into Simms at a Federation of Canadian Municipalities
function after the vote on the Tory resolution, he told me that John Efford
had spotted him at a crowded reception, and had loudly declared to all
and sundry, "I never thought my own colleagues would stab me in the
back." Liberal MPs from other provinces showed strong sympathy for
Efford's feeling of betrayal.

I don't believe Simms's action was self-serving. Right or wrong, stupid
or smart, it was done honestly and sincerely and courageously, and for the
right motives.

BILL MATTHEWS'S INDEPENDENT, SELF-GOVERNING mind made him a
genuine political maverick. He had been elected in the federal riding of
Burin–St. George's as a Progressive Conservative. But in August 1999,

after a ninety-minute meeting with Prime Minister Jean Chrétien, he surprised his fellow Tory MPs and vacationing Tory leader Joe Clark by announcing that he was crossing the floor of the House of Commons and joining the Liberal Party of Canada. He could do more for his district on the government side of the House, he said; his move had more to do with his concerns about the fishery than about the Progressive Conservative Party or its leadership. Joe Clark's office said that Clark was disappointed, but accepted the decision. It wouldn't affect the rebuilding of the PC Party, Clark said. But Matthews's action in leaving the PC Party showed more foresight about its future than its leader's words did.

Bill had a strong individualistic streak that no leader or caucus was going to rein in. He told me a few stories that illustrated for him how "weird" things were in Ottawa. At one meeting of MPs, he said, the PMO's director of communications, Scott Reid, went around like a teacher giving out assignments, distributing papers containing the party "line" on different topics. This unelected functionary instructed the MPS to memorize these lines for future public statements. All you MPs, this appointed backroom boy had warned ominously, practically wagging his finger in their faces, have to be on the same page, or else.

And the childish partisanship was beyond belief, he told me, especially with John Efford as their regional political minister. It was true, Matthews confirmed, that after my appointment by Danny the Liberal MPs from our province were convened for a big discussion on whether or not they should have anything to do with me. Matthews had told the others from the get-go, and in no uncertain terms, that he'd be meeting with Bill Rowe whenever he felt like it.

Meanwhile, the prime minister was so worried about shoring up support for the federal position on the Atlantic Accord in Newfoundland and Labrador that he had actually attended two early morning Atlantic caucus meetings, which was apparently unprecedented. He even had Bill Matthews drop in on him at home for a one-on-one on the Accord over a bottle of wine. But none of it worked.

Bill's decision to vote against the Liberal government was based purely

on the fact, he told me, that his leader was reneging on an election commitment of great value to his home province. Matthews had been elected,
at least in part, on that undertaking. Partisan considerations did not apply,
he said. He didn't care about the effect on the party or the caucus or the
Liberal government as long as he knew he was doing the right thing. It all
boiled down to the integrity of a prime minister during an election campaign. He knew he had little to gain from his vote except the contempt of
his Liberal colleagues.

Some of that contempt was expressed to me by a Liberal MP, who
alleged that Matthews's act was not a result of his principles, but of frustration with the party leadership. He'd been promised a Cabinet position
in due course when he'd crossed the House, the MP said, and here it was
"five years later and still bugger all."

I doubted that. Bill Matthews would take another dramatic action in
the House of Commons a couple of years later against another prime minister, the newly elected Stephen Harper. Again, it would be on principle.
He had already decided not to run again; there was nothing at stake but
the truth.

Bill Matthews would rise in the House of Commons during Question
Period and say: "Mr. Speaker, on January 4, 2006, the Prime Minister
[Harper] wrote Premier Danny Williams promising to remove non-renewable natural resources revenue from the equalization formula. The Prime
Minister also sent Newfoundlanders and Labradorians a brochure promising 100% of oil and gas revenues. He promised no small print, no
excuses, but most importantly, he promised no cap. Regrettably, Budget
2007 tells a very different story. Why did the Prime Minister lie? Why this
betrayal?"

The Speaker ruled Matthews out of order for his unparliamentary language, and called upon him to withdraw his remark.

Matthews replied: "Mr. Speaker, it is regrettable that events have tran-
spired the way they have. I have literature here from the Prime Minister. I
have letters and brochures that clearly illustrate what he said to
Newfoundland and Labrador, and I have read the budget. If I were to

stand here in my place today and tell the people of Newfoundland and Labrador that the Prime Minister honoured his commitment, I would be lying to them. I am not prepared to do that."

The Speaker said that, henceforth, Matthews was going to have trouble speaking in the House. In effect, he was stating that he would never recognize Bill Matthews again unless he withdrew his allegation that the PM had lied. In his quest for truth from yet another prime minister, Bill would be designated a non-person in the House of Commons, to which tens of thousands of citizens had elected him. To paraphrase Voltaire, it is dangerous to be right when the prime minister is wrong.

Whatever one may think of Bill Matthews's behaviour, he certainly made it clear that he was no sycophant. Matthews will go down in history as one of the last of the gutsy independents. Some might argue that "loose cannon" would be more accurate, a type of politician considered destructive to parliamentary democracy.

Some of us are naive enough to believe, however, that if all MPs held their prime minister to the standards of honest conduct set by Bill Matthews, there might be better government in Canada, not worse.

— CHAPTER EIGHT —

Our "Magnificent" Seven
Part 2: The Minister

AFTER RUBEN JOHN EFFORD was appointed minister of Natural Resources for Canada in December 2003, I mentioned, on the air, a report from Alberta praising him for his frank position on oil development. I said I was proud as a fellow Newfoundlander that a minister from this province was creating such a positive impression in the oil patch, unlike so many previous federal Liberal ministers. But my public praise did no good. John Efford still didn't love me.

Mind you, I didn't mind. I never worked very hard over the years to make Mr. Efford develop a warm, cuddly feeling for me. Someone once told me she remembered me describing John in the media as the perfect example of "the smaller the mind, the bigger the ego." Another person said he'd heard me referring to John's position on some issue as "the absolute self-confidence of the absolutely ignorant." I didn't recall saying any of that, but I wasn't denying it either. Because something had caused a lack of affection so palpable you could cut it with a knife.

I was checking in at a hotel in central Newfoundland one evening, when Efford and his wife, Madonna, happened to enter the lobby. From five feet away, when I turned toward them, they both pointedly ignored me. When I said good evening, they turned their faces away in unison. Apparently, they had studiously conspired to snub this bastard, and their perfectly executed husband-and-wife snubbing act was worthy of a Monty Python skit.

In my experience, it was unusual for public figures to carry a grudge forever. For example, I was at the same reception years ago as Brian Peckford. Despite the fact that we had taken some pretty painful verbal smacks at each other in the House, and that, later, as a media commentator, I had been brutal in attacking some of his policies, he and I gravitated toward each other and had a long enjoyable gab.

Many observers at that function seemed surprised to see us laughing and joking together. In fact, the president of Memorial University, Mose Morgan, who had taught us both, actually came up to us and said, "You mean you two are still talking to each other?" We laughed, and Peckford replied that all the old political and media stuff was purely professional; there was nothing personal in any of it. We were just two guys trying to do our jobs, and you couldn't let that affect friendship.

Now Peckford might appear to have been an extraordinarily broad-minded politician, but, in my experience, he was a typical one. Sometimes, after expressing a critical remark in the media about, say, Frank Moores, Clyde Wells, John Crosbie, Tom Rideout, Ed Roberts, or Bill Rompkey, I might sense a certain chilliness at a later encounter, or receive an acid greeting, but the ill will, or at least the displays of it, soon passed. I'm not alleging we all adored each other—far from it—but we managed to have cordial conversations. John Efford's rancour seemed permanent, however, and it would surface in extremely comical ways when I went to Ottawa.

Before my appointment, Danny Williams had tried to make sure that there was no perceived conflict between the functions of the province's representative in Ottawa and the MPs, including Efford. He said publicly, on July 27, 2004, "While the province is well represented by our Members of Parliament, Mr. Rowe will be the provincial government's own voice in Ottawa." He mentioned to me that he had run the appointment by John

Efford, who apparently thought it would be a great boost to our MPs struggling to help the province in Ottawa. This was confirmed the next day
when Craig Westcott wrote in the *St. John's Express*: "Just before making
the announcement about Rowe, [Premier] Williams gave a courtesy call to
federal Cabinet minister John Efford, who expressed strong support for
the move." If, in fact, Efford's support was genuine at the time, it would
undergo a radical reversal later.

On August 7, 2004, a dozen days after the appointment, a prominent
Liberal co-partisan of Efford's in central Newfoundland, George Saunders,
wrote a piece for the *St. John's Telegram*'s "Forum":

> Just over a month ago, we elected seven members of
> Parliament to represent our interests at the federal level of
> government . . . Are they all so incompetent that we have
> to send a representative to Ottawa, separate and distinct
> from our elected representatives to try to achieve some-
> thing for this province? . . . Obviously, there is a tremen-
> dous lack of confidence in all seven of these representatives
> by Danny Williams and his administration. All seven of
> them are unable to accomplish what Bill Rowe will be able
> to do . . . Mr. Rowe has taken on a formidable challenge.
> He is also a symbol to our federal MPs that they are, at best,
> considered to be inept and unable to accomplish anything
> significant . . . If Bill Rowe is able to accomplish significant
> gains for this province, the seven federal MPs should hang
> their collective heads in shame and embarrassment.

Oh-oh. I guess that was a red flag to John Efford's bull.

Upon arriving in Ottawa, I sent an email to Efford at his ministerial
office in Ottawa requesting a short get-together. I received no reply. I telephoned his office and left a message that I would like to meet with him
briefly to chat about my mandate. Still no reply. On September 10, I called
his office again and told the person who answered that if Minister Efford

had no intention of replying to my communications or of meeting with me, would they simply tell me now, please, so that both his office and mine could stop wasting our time.

The same day I received a very courteous telephone call from an assistant of Efford's, who explained that the minister travelled a lot and was extremely busy. That contact led to much to-ing and fro-ing by telephone between our offices, culminating in a message from his secretary in early October. It said that Minister Efford would "slot" me in the next day, at 1:00 p.m. The Speech from the Throne was scheduled for that afternoon.

The next day I went to meet Efford at the Department of Natural Resources in the Sir William Logan Building at Booth and Carling. In the front lobby was a plaque commemorating Logan, the pioneering Canadian geologist from the nineteenth century, considered by many to have been one of Canada's top scientists. I was disappointed there wasn't more information on the wall; for instance, that Mount Logan in the Yukon, the highest mountain in Canada and the second highest in North America, was named for the great man. Perhaps the lack of info resulted from Prime Minister Jean Chrétien's misguided attempt to rename the mountain "Mount Trudeau," which exploded in an uproar of opposition.

John Efford's office was on the twenty-first floor. However, the elevator I entered only went to the twelfth floor. I had to get out at that floor and change elevators to reach his office. I was going to jokingly ask Efford if there was any significance to the fact that in this federal department the elevator didn't go all the way to the top. But the atmosphere of our meeting did not favour a joking mode.

I arrived at his floor a minute or two before the one o'clock appointment, and was ushered into his office. Tom Ormsby followed right behind. I'd known Tom for many years, ever since he'd arrived in Newfoundland from Ontario as a radio personality in the '80s, when he'd retained me as his lawyer. Over the years we'd had many an enjoyable chat; he was always full of good humour, and relished telling amusing personal anecdotes. But our last conversation, earlier that year in St. John's, had been far from enjoyable.

He had been laid off months before from his radio station, and he came into my studio before the show one day to say goodbye. He hadn't been able to find new employment in St. John's, and he was about to go back to Ontario to look for a job. I bid him a sad adieu. A few days later, I was delighted to learn that John Efford had appointed him to a position in his St. John's office. And now, half a year later, here he was, communications sidekick to the minister in his Ottawa headquarters. And no one could accuse Tom Ormsby of lack of dedication to the job: an item had just appeared in the "Cheers and Jeers" section of the *St. John's Telegram* that Efford's office had made a cold call to the *Telegram* newsroom with the electrifying news that Efford would be available to take questions on today's Throne Speech. The item essentially ridiculed Efford's office for being a mite too pushy with the blindingly obvious.

John Efford's welcome that day, however, was anything but pushy. He was standoffish and unfriendly (when he shook hands with me, I suddenly realized what Bill Clinton must feel like during a hug from Hillary). When I said I'd come to make a courtesy visit, to explain to him in person the purpose of my new job, he sat there stern-faced and frosty. He never once looked at me, and his body language verged on the hostile.

As I explained my position in Ottawa—purely that of a provincial public servant, a deputy minister to the premier, with no mandate to encroach in any way on the jurisdiction of federal MPs—Efford stared at Tom Ormsby with a sneer of skepticism and contempt on his face. Meanwhile, Tom, as he'd been ordered to do, had ostentatiously opened a big notebook on his lap, and alternated between holding his pen poised in the air like a weapon and suddenly scribbling with the alacrity of one who'd just heard something good enough to hang me from the rafters with.

Then, without commenting on what I'd just said, Efford started talking about two vacant positions on the Canada-Newfoundland and Labrador Offshore Petroleum Board (CNLOPB), the chair and a provincial representative. For some reason that I couldn't fathom at the time, he was mostly concerned with the provincial vacancy on the board. The lack of an appointment to that position, he warned, was going to blow up in everyone's face in the media. Imagine, he said, if Andy Wells got hold of that.

Why was Efford so concerned, I wondered to myself, about a matter under provincial jurisdiction possibly blowing up in the media? If, in fact, it blew up, it would be in Tory premier Danny Williams's face, not Efford's. Why was John Efford suddenly worried about Danny Williams's political well-being? I looked for a bump on his head, which might account for this aberration. Efford continued talking, and a shaft of light penetrated the murk.

He had proposed a candidate to the premier for the provincial position, he said. Someone who was "not a party person," he emphasized, but a well-qualified Newfoundlander from Brigus, which, by pure coincidence, was in Efford's own riding. Efford had called and written the provincial minister of Natural Resources, Ed Byrne, and the premier's office but, even though Ed Byrne was on side, Efford had received no reaction from the premier. Danny's lack of response perturbed him.

I managed not to burst out laughing. This was our federal minister's top priority for the province—concern that our premier had not acceded to his proposal that one of his political cronies be appointed to the federal-provincial board? I could not believe what I was hearing. Straight-faced, I stressed that such a matter was not under my personal control, but I would, nevertheless, pass on his message to the premier, even though, as he himself had said, the responsible minister and the premier's office were already fully apprised of his wishes.

Efford smirked at Ormsby. They would soon see what kind of a deal-maker this guy Rowe was. Would I produce and deliver on this test he had set for me, or would I prove that I was as redundant and useless as he thought? Evidently, Efford figured that if I had a function at all, which he doubted, it was to get the premier to do what Efford wanted. Or maybe he was setting himself up to try to undermine, for possible later use, this new Ottawa office of Danny's, and, thereby, Danny himself.

Efford then turned the discussion to the horrific demands on him as minister, which included not only his huge portfolio but also having to look after the province federally. I could not resist replying that I could well imagine how challenging the demands of office must be for him, since they were even challenging for a minister of the intellectual stature of John Crosbie. There seemed to be something in my reply Efford didn't like. His quizzical look indicated he sensed I'd made a distinction between his capabilities and John Crosbie's.

"John Crosbie," he fumed. "In two or three weeks, when the Accord clawback commitment gets signed by Prime Minister Martin and Premier Williams, I'll make John Crosbie's blunder on the original Accord in 1985 look worse than the Upper Churchill deal." John Efford threatening to expose John Crosbie as a blundering minister was entertaining, but more interesting was his prediction of an Accord signing in two or three weeks. That indicated how hopelessly deluded by their own optimistic rhetoric the feds were. At the end of Efford's "two or three weeks," the battle between the prime minister and the premier would be more heated than ever.

Before ending our meeting, Efford brought up "Danny's outburst" at the health summit, i.e. "I don't know what's wrong with this fellow's [the prime minister's] attitude. We're not even getting crumbs, let alone the scraps." Shaking his head, Efford said he hadn't heard the outburst personally, but everyone in Ottawa was talking about it. Well, I said to myself, that certainly turned out to be a good move, Danny.

Tom Ormsby led me out of Efford's office. Downstairs in the lobby, we met Lou McGuire, Efford's chief of staff, and Tom introduced us. I hustled by taxi to Parliament Hill to hear the Throne Speech. In the Senate Chamber, I was seated next to the spouse of ACOA Minister Joe McGuire. When I told her I'd just met a Lou McGuire, she said Lou was Joe's brother. Cozy little world, this federal government in Ottawa.

During a telephone conversation with Brian Crawley soon after my meeting with Efford, I mentioned the lack of a provincial appointment to the Canada-Newfoundland and Labrador Offshore Petroleum Board, and how much that was exasperating John Efford. Crawley replied that there had been absolutely no correspondence to the premier from Efford on it. But the premier's office had heard about it from Ed Byrne. Their reaction?

All Efford was concerned about was getting his political pal appointed to one of the vacant positions on the board.

As new federal stances on the Atlantic Accord emerged and the battle intensified between Danny Williams and Paul Martin, I started to pity John Efford. It looked as if the prime minister and the PMO were using Efford to float trial balloons for Danny's reaction, and were prepared to make him their fall guy whenever a balloon burst on them. No doubt they knew how easily Efford's sense of his own political popularity at home allowed him to be led down that path. Some Liberals thought that it was, in fact, Efford who had sucked in the PMO, convincing them that the high political esteem he believed himself to be held in at home—"I could get elected for the Green Party"—would allow him to beat Danny Williams at this game.

Whatever the truth, Efford's public pronouncements on the Accord moved away from the PM's original commitment, and continued to flummox Danny and his chief of staff and myself. In early September, Brian Crawley had called me to talk about it. Nobody knew what to make of the situation. There hadn't been one word from the PMO to the premier's office, or from federal Finance to Loyola Sullivan, much less anything in writing.

It was possible that Efford was speaking entirely for himself on a matter about which he knew little and understood less. His bombast had all the appearance of a solo flight, but nobody was sure. Danny was very troubled by what he thought might be a sleazy end run by the feds, and was going to speak to Martin, to find out exactly what was going on. I told Crawley I would listen, observe, and network unobtrusively to see what I might learn.

And learn a lot I did during the next month. I got Sullivan on his cellphone when he was in Montreal en route back to St. John's after the meeting with Goodale, and he told me their discussion had not been conclusive; he was coming back to Ottawa soon, perhaps the following week. I mentioned that I'd learned of Efford's rage at being left out of the loop, and wondered if there was some way we could enlist his energy and desire to be involved in helping us produce an Accord agreeable to both parties. Sullivan paused, and then said, "Bill, boy, it's sad. But I don't think so."

A week later I went to lunch with a Newfoundlander, highly successful in business in Ottawa and a big strategist and commentator for the federal Tories. He was most interested in an Accord deal for his province regardless of partisan credit. I'd just had an email from Tom Ormsby, stating that he had been promoted to full communications director for Efford, and I mentioned it to my companion, wondering aloud at the same time if there was some way to harness Efford's desire to help in producing a solid Accord for Newfoundland. Unfortunately, he said, he couldn't see any way of doing that.

I persisted in clinging to the notion that there must be some way to make Efford as relevant and useful to his province and his government as he obviously yearned to be. I made up my mind to suggest a few things to him at the next opportunity.

I felt he should make no further public statements on the Accord, its progress or lack thereof. If he was doing so at the behest of his own government, they were making him their goat. If he was doing so on his own, he was making a fool of himself and losing the respect of his federal colleagues. Either way, he was plummeting in popularity at home. He had put himself in a conflict of interest situation—toeing the federal government line while claiming to work on behalf of the province. He was sucking and blowing at the same time. In my opinion, he needed to get a grip on the issues, consult with his provincial colleagues in the House of Commons and the Senate, and then work behind the scenes to bring the two sides together. That way, he could make himself a hero federally and provincially.

That was the speech I was going to make to Efford, and I looked for an opportunity for an amicable get-together. That opportunity soon arose.

On Wednesday, October 27, Penny and I went to the Memorial University Affinity Alumni Dinner at the Château Laurier. The dinner had already started when John Efford walked into the room with Tom Ormsby in tow. Before sitting down, John stood there for twenty seconds, looking around the room to make sure he was seen by everyone. Nobody noticed, or if they did, they avoided looking at him. I waved to him; it was the only acknowledgement, as far as I could tell, he had received. He was so delighted he waved back enthusiastically for a couple of seconds. Then he recognized me and abruptly stopped his hand in mid-wave. It was certainly droll, but not a clear sign that he was warming to me.

During a pause in the proceedings, I walked over to his table to see if it was possible to break through the wall of ice he had erected. Seeing me coming, he turned away, deliberately and dramatically. I had to keep a straight face, despite how foolish it looked. Propelled now by curiosity more than anything else, I bent over the table and said, "Good evening, Minister." He turned his face to me and snarled, in that whining voice, "You never got back to me." Then he turned away again.

"Never got back to you, Minister, about what?" I asked.

"That appointment to the CNLOPB."

"I did pass your concerns on to the premier's office as I said I would. But it's hardly my place to get back to you. It's the premier or the minister at your level who will deal with you on that."

Efford didn't reply. He actually twisted in his chair with a jerk, so that his back was to me, like an eleven-year-old boy in a sook. I looked at Tom Ormsby. Tom's face was bright red, and he grinned sheepishly.

During this period, John Efford had roared down from Ottawa to St. John's and issued his famous ultimatum to Danny Williams on Paul Martin's latest offer on the Accord: "Take it or leave it." Several hours before I ran into him at the MUN alumni dinner, Danny had supplied him with a response.

Danny had held a news conference in St. John's and made mincemeat of that federal offer. He reminded everyone that on June 5, the prime minister had made a commitment to him personally, and to the people of Newfoundland and Labrador: the province would receive 100 percent of all offshore revenues, with no clawback. The premier had pulled out a letter from Goodale, which he had received a couple of days before the equalization summit. The federal proposal laid out in the letter was in clear contradiction to that commitment.

Danny said his agreement with Martin didn't include a cap, or linkage to the fiscal capacity of other provinces. And it didn't include a time frame. The federal government's latest proposal called for a cap, which prevented the province from benefiting from higher oil prices and increased production. Danny pointed out that only the feds would benefit from such a clause; like the Upper Churchill agreement with Quebec, any such deal would cost the province hundreds of millions of dollars. Then came the Danny clincher: "Minister John Efford said earlier this week that we could take it or leave it; well, let me answer Mr. Efford loud and clear. We will leave it, thank you very much."

The next day, I mentioned to Brian Crawley how John Efford had reacted to my overture to him the night before. Whining about his guy not going to the CNLOPB. Bizarre, bizarre—how could he give that a thought, when the sky was falling? We could only conclude that Minister Efford's behaviour resulted from the fact that the Accord had made a broken man out of him.

Less than a week later, on November 2, CBC Television aired Doug Letto's piece about my position as provincial representative in Ottawa. In it, John Efford wondered, "What's his purpose here in Ottawa, I don't know." He then listed the names of the Newfoundland and Labrador MPs, and said, "That's our responsibility here, to work with the federal government and work with our provincial colleagues . . . and others back home who have an interest or stake-holding here in Ottawa. The taxpayers of Newfoundland are spending in excess of a half a million dollars to keep an office open here when I can't even get a letter back recommending a name for the CNLOPB."

My God, the offshore board again! I didn't know what the hell this guy he wanted to appoint so badly had done for Efford, but it must have been huge. Because there John was, fiddling with the CNLOPB while his political future was going up in flames.

"Take it or leave it." Those five little words were the most important John Efford uttered in his long political career. They would be the nails in his political coffin.

On October 29, the *Toronto Star* stated, "It is now obvious that Natural

Resources Minister John Efford has not one sweet clue what 100 percent of provincial revenues actually means."

On November 8, the Monday after a weekend convention of the Newfoundland and Labrador Liberal Party, Campbell Clark of the *Globe and Mail* wrote the following:

> [The delegates] passed a [unanimous] resolution demanding that Newfoundland receive 100 percent of revenues from offshore oil, while Natural Resources Minister John Efford, Newfoundland's federal cabinet minister, found himself alone in defending Ottawa's offer.
>
> [Former Liberal Premier Roger] Grimes said that Mr. Efford did not make converts at a meeting Friday with the Liberal members of the provincial legislature. "He didn't convince a soul in our room that what's offered officially in Newfoundland and Labrador . . . is 100 percent. Not even in the ballpark."
>
> Churence Rogers, outgoing president of the Newfoundland Liberals, said it is a "huge issue" that could damage Mr. Martin and certainly Mr. Efford.

A Liberal observer from the mainland who had attended the convention told me that going into each room or hall there was like entering a series of tombs. All the delegates, including Efford, were walking around like zombies, he said.

The same Monday, the "Cheers and Jeers" section of the *St. John's Telegram* included this:

> Jeers: to John Efford. Still bravely pitching the party line, Efford is stumping his way around the province claiming the deal offered by Prime Minister Paul Martin is the same as this province getting 100 percent of offshore oil revenues. If his report card was going out today, Efford

would get an A plus in party loyalty and an F in mathematics.

Cheers: to former Liberal candidate Walter Noel. The former MHA offered up a few more details . . . when a campaigning Paul Martin decided to give Newfoundland and Labrador oil royalties from offshore. The details seem to support Premier Danny Williams' version of events.

The premier of Nova Scotia confirmed his solidarity with the position of Newfoundland and Labrador. Hamm stated in a news release on November 7 that "both provinces must speak with one voice that will not accept less than what we are guaranteed by federal-provincial law and by the word of Prime Minister Martin."

A day after that, Danny Williams criticized the prime minister for his plans to take off on one of his escapist international missions: "This morning Premier Hamm and I placed a call to Prime Minister Martin and requested a meeting so that we can resolve the differences that are blocking the implementation of the agreements that he made with each of us in June. It is absolutely imperative that Prime Minister Martin resolve this serious domestic issue before he turns his attention to this international mission [to South America and Africa] in mid-November . . . He has a responsibility to fix what is broken at home."

To say the least, not every politician in Canada was on the side of Williams and Hamm. In addition to the misgivings already expressed by some provincial premiers over Williams's demands, the *Globe and Mail* reported on November 10 that "some Ontario MPs are concerned that allowing Newfoundland to keep all its oil revenues and equalization payments would be tantamount to allowing the province to get richer at the expense of Ontario taxpayers." It also stated that Hamm was being criticized by Nova Scotian Liberals, "one of whom recently asked why the Premier continues to hold fast to Mr. Williams."

Many national reporters were amazed at how far the two Atlantic premiers had gotten in backing the federal government into a corner. One reporter told me that she remembered Paul Martin as Finance minister, with his government in a majority position, showing no interest whatsoever in the campaign initiated by Hamm for a new revenue agreement. And she recalled the new PM dismissing outright Newfoundland's efforts to get a better offshore revenue deal the year before. "Now Martin is starting to look like a deer caught in the headlights," she said.

Another journalist shook his head in admiration at Danny Williams's reported statement on November 9 that Paul Martin didn't have to worry about looking soft if he backed down. "There's no shame in honouring your own word," Danny had said.

"Jesus," the journalist said to me, "that was one beautiful jab straight to Martin's glass jaw."

Some reporters were calling the battle between Martin and Williams "the perfect political storm." It had so permeated the public psyche of Canada, that Rex Murphy's topic for discussion on the November 14 edition of CBC Radio's *Cross Country Checkup* was the Atlantic Accord.

John Crosbie called the show from St. John's, and described how the original Accord, which was supposed to give the province the majority benefit from its offshore oil, had turned out to be so unfair in practice. Mark Watton called from Ottawa to make some sensible points on equalization. Then John Efford came on, assuring the people of Newfoundland and Labrador that they could depend on him not to let them down.

There had been a steady stream of scorn in the provincial media for Efford after his take-it-or-leave-it ultimatum to Williams. There might have been support elsewhere in Canada for the prime minister's position, which Efford had so confidently supported, but where it counted most for him politically—at home—you could tell he knew he had lost everything. If he wasn't a shattered man a couple of weeks ago, as Brian Crawley and I had surmised, he certainly gave that impression now. The poor fellow sounded absolutely lost and pathetic.

A few days later, I had a meeting with a Liberal MP known for his frankness and independent thinking. He had recently received a call from the prime minister himself, who had asked for his candid assessment of the Atlantic Accord debacle. The Liberal MP had described to the PM flat out how stupidly the whole thing had been handled, especially by John Efford. His own federal colleagues, he said, were entirely responsible for this shitstorm between Martin and Williams.

The current assessment of many in the caucus regarding Efford, according to this Liberal MP, was that far from being a fall guy for the PMO, Efford had misled Paul Martin into believing he could persuade the people of Newfoundland and Labrador to accept the federal offer whether Danny agreed or not. And Danny had cut his balls off.

I remarked that the PM hadn't appeared to be able to rein Efford in. The MP replied that the PMO had, in fact, attempted to chain down Godzilla. A shocked Efford had told some MPs that Tim Murphy, the prime minister's chief of staff, had asked him not to attend a certain meeting between ministers Goodale and Sullivan, designed to clean up the fallout from the blow-up and near fisticuffs at the meeting between Danny and the PM. Efford went to the meeting anyway. From all accounts, his presence didn't advance the discussion. The meeting ran well into the night, and went nowhere except around in a circle of recriminations.

A federal adviser who had been present at the meeting said to me, "I now know what Flaubert meant when he described leaving a whorehouse at sunrise and feeling like throwing himself into the river out of pure disgust."

Efford's extreme partisanship was a standing joke among MPs, Liberals and Conservatives alike. A Liberal MP told me he once saw Efford go lobster red in the face, fly into a rage and stomp aboard a plane at the sight of a Liberal talking to a Tory.

The same MP said Efford had told his caucus colleagues more than once that he was under terrible stress and couldn't sleep. He thought Efford's recent discussion of his diabetes on television, complete with finger-pricking, was possibly a lead-up to an announcement of a decision not to run in the next election because of poor health.

ONE MORNING IN MID-NOVEMBER, I had a meeting with a Newfoundlander who was an adviser to a federal minister. He told me he thought that the provincial government was being very unfair to John Efford. It had been at the request of the premier's office, he said, that Efford was being kept out of high-level discussions on the Accord. Yet, Loyola Sullivan had publicly criticized Efford because the province hadn't heard from him on the Accord for two weeks. I told him it was a good point. It was unfair. Extremely so. But the Accord battle had reached the stage where no matter what poor John did or said or didn't do or say, he always seemed to shoot himself in the foot.

On Monday, November 29, I met with an outspoken Liberal senator for another view of Accord proceedings, and to solicit suggestions on John Efford's possible future contribution to a deal. We talked for an hour and a half, and it became clear to me why this parliamentarian had a reputation that disturbed certain colleagues. "While you're here in Ottawa, don't go near that Langevin Building," was just one negative reference to the home of the Privy Council office and the PMO. The senator severely criticized Efford's attitude and actions. "If John was a fish, I'd throw him back."

In mid-December, the premier's office told me there was a rumour in John Efford's riding that he might resign on the same-sex marriage issue, then before Parliament. Efford had already made a big public fuss about it, disagreeing openly with the federal recognition of such marriages. He spoke about consulting with the clergy in his district on how he should vote on the issue in the House of Commons. Liberals I talked to in Ottawa couldn't believe how seriously befuddled his loyalties were.

On the one hand, he never hesitated to come out against public opinion in his own province on the Atlantic Accord. On the other hand, when it came to same-sex marriage he was prepared to oppose his own federal government and let the clergy dictate his vote—in a secular democracy like Canada!

I too found Efford difficult to fathom. Perhaps the cynical view was correct: Efford was looking for a way, any way, out of politics on account of his disastrous role in the Atlantic Accord fiasco, and the same-sex marriage legislation presented him with a convenient red herring.

John Ibbitson of the *Globe and Mail* had another suggestion. In his column of December 16, he wrote: "Not only must Mr. Efford defend the government's position [on the Atlantic Accord]; he has lost control over the negotiations which are now being handled by Finance Minister Ralph Goodale and Alex Himelfarb, Clerk of the Privy Council, leaving Mr. Efford in a politically impossible situation. His chances of surviving the next election are said to be slim at best. Under the circumstances, voting against the government on same-sex marriage might be his key to political survival as an MP, even if it costs him his portfolio."

As it turned out, however, Efford did not vote against his government on same-sex marriage. Nor did he resign over the issue. To add to his public relations disaster—his alienation of progressives and conservatives alike—when the moment of truth arrived on the same-sex marriage vote, he toed his government's party line.

The only John Efford supporters from start to finish, ostensibly at least, were Martin and the PMO, even though, behind the scenes, they had emasculated him on the Accord negotiations. I saw this support clearly in early December, when I was finally able to arrange a lunch meeting with Melissa McInnis, the relatively new Atlantic representative in the PMO.

A Liberal MP had described her to me this way: "She's young enough to know everything." She was young all right, but she sounded savvy and extremely bright on the phone. My idea was to have a frank and confidential discussion off the record with her on the Accord, not so much on the content, but on the process and the roles played by key figures on both sides—the prime minister and his staff, Ralph Goodale, John Efford, the two premiers and their staff, Loyola Sullivan and anyone else who might be contributing to or hindering a settlement.

I had high hopes, intending to suggest to McInnis that we try to find some way of improving our use of Efford's obvious interest and enthusiasm, and minimizing his tendency to put all sides in an impossible position. But as soon as I uttered the words, "John Efford," she interrupted with, "Minister Efford is a good man." That set the pattern for the luncheon discussion: every time I mentioned his name, she would cut off discussion with another, conclusive "Minister Efford is a good man."

Obviously, all talk of John Efford had been tabooed by the PMO, and there was no way McInnis was going off-message. Our discussion went precisely nowhere.

In his memoirs, *Hell or High Water: My Life In and Out of Politics*, written four years later, Paul Martin was still loyal to John Efford. He seemed to have no idea that his office had placed Efford in an absolutely untenable and disastrous position. On page 303, Martin wrote the following: "The other thing I regret in all of this is that Energy Minister John Efford, who fought vigorously for the accords, and his native province, was attacked at home when the federal government insisted that the deal reflect a fair balance and that it have a termination date. Just as I believe that Williams and Hamm fought for their provinces, *so did Efford as the federal minister for Newfoundland and Labrador fight for his province. He also fought for the national interest, as was his responsibility, and this should be recognized.*" (My italics.)

No, that's not what should be recognized. What should be recognized is that Paul Martin, as prime minister of Canada, hadn't realized that in a no-holds-barred war between his government and the government of a province on a crucial and emotional issue, the federal minister for the province would be torn to shreds politically unless the PM and the minister were extremely careful about just how the minister was employed in that war. Ignorant of that simple fact, or simply not giving a damn about it, Martin and his gang allowed John Efford to be swallowed whole by the press and the public.

Paco Francoli wrote the following in the *Hill Times* (December 13):

> [John Efford] has been called everything from "Judas" to a "trained seal" in his home province of Newfoundland and Labrador, and been shouted down repeatedly in the House of Commons by opposition MPs who dubbed him the "Benedict Arnold of Newfoundland."
>
> Last week in an interview . . . Mr. Efford held firm to the position that giving in to Newfoundland and Labrador

Premier Danny Williams . . . would effectively kill
Canada's long-established revenue sharing scheme which
has been allowing provinces to provide comparable services since 1957.

In the House of Commons . . . when Mr. Efford rose to
answer Mr. [Norm] Doyle's question, Mr. Doyle's colleagues drowned him out by singing "Nah nah nah nah,
hey hey hey, goodbye."

It was a sad, wretched finish to a once flourishing political career. A
couple of weeks later, on January 3, John Efford would be interviewed at
his home in Bareneed by Doug Letto for CBC Television's *Here and Now*.
Efford was having trouble believing what had happened to him. "I could
never imagine that I could be so hurt and so many people would turn on
me so much over this, over this file. I mean it's a Finance minister's discussion between Finance ministers." A discussion between Finance ministers?
John once had proclaimed himself, loudly and proudly, the lead federal
minister on the file.

His own future? "I can't see it coming back to where I was in
Newfoundland as a politician . . . I've lost a lot of ground in Newfoundland
. . . I've got friends who won't even talk to me anymore. I guess what hurts
most is that people would think that I would put . . . my job as minister
ahead of Newfoundland. And that could not be further from the truth."

A Liberal MP, on hearing of John's "take it or leave it" ultimatum to
Danny Williams on the Atlantic Accord, mentioned John's earlier boast of
having so much support in his province he could get elected for the Green
Party. The MP then made a pretty accurate prediction of John's future:
"Well, as Charles de Gaulle said, 'the political graveyards are full of indis-
pensable men.'"

— CHAPTER NINE —

Danny and Bill's First Date

PRIME MINISTER PAUL MARTIN and his wife, Sheila, gave a gargantuan reception and dinner on November 30 in honour of the visit to Ottawa by the newly re-elected president of the United States, George W. Bush, and First Lady Laura Bush. Martin laid down his weapons and invited Danny Williams. Shortly before the event, the premier's office called to ask me if I'd like to accompany the premier as his guest. I said yes. The prime minister had notified Danny that he wanted all federal-provincial discussions on the Accord put on hold until Bush left, but Danny and I figured the gala function might be a good occasion for us to get a few points across in a casual way to some federal players.

The premier and his entourage were staying at the Château Laurier. Executive Assistant Steve Dinn telephoned me to clarify the arrangements. He couldn't seem to find my formal invitation to the dinner. Did I have an invitation card? I said I had nothing except a phone call from the premier's office and one from the protocol officer. There was a pause on the other end and some muffled palaver, the nature of which I would discover later, and then Steve told me not to worry—they'd sort it out. He told me to meet the premier at the hotel; he was scheduled to leave for the reception and dinner at 5:10.

En route to the Château Laurier, I got another call from Steve Dinn: he told me I wouldn't be able to get to the front door of the hotel because of the protesters demonstrating against President Bush. I would have to walk over Mackenzie King Bridge, through the Rideau Centre, over the pedway, through the Bay, then on to York Street and through the back door of the parking garage of the Château Laurier.

I got dropped off as near the hotel as I could. First I walked toward the front door to see what was going on. Metal barricades and the large crowd of protesters in front of the Château Laurier stopped my progress. I retraced my steps and walked across the bridge, feeling like a salmon swimming upstream as I weaved solo through a flow of protesters walking in the opposite direction toward the Château, many holding placards with messages that made some excellent points.

One said "With a Bush and a Dick in charge, you're fucked." An elderly lady waved a poster demanding "No more Bushit." Another placard contained an American flag with the stars replaced by a maple leaf. "Is this Canada's future?" it asked. "Wake up and resist!" Yet another placard wondered: "How many lives per gallon?" The next one I saw seemed to be slightly misspelled: "Fick Duck Cheney." My attention was drawn by movement on the tops of buildings. Many roofs had SWAT teams of snipers, with high-powered rifles in plain view. On the ground, riot police were everywhere. A later estimate on the news put the number of protesters at about five thousand.

The pedway over the street from the Rideau Centre to the Bay was crowded with people, most of them training binoculars or cameras on the protesters in front of the Château. At York and Sussex, I had to identify myself using my government of Newfoundland and Labrador card and driver's licence and explain to suspicious police what I was doing there and where I was going. Before I reached the hotel, I was stopped and put through that drill three more times. The trek took me nearly an hour of stops and starts and semi-jogs. This had better be good, I groused to myself, this frigging Bush dinner.

Steve Dinn met me at the entrance to the parking garage of the hotel and brought me up to Elizabeth Matthews's room. Danny came in and we talked about the protesters. He joked about how we were much worse at their age. What these protesters were doing was great, he said, looking out the window. Yeah, it was great, I said, unless you'd just been trying to make your way through them for an hour like a lonely sperm swimming upstream. I don't know why, all of a sudden, the image had changed from a salmon to a sperm. Calling Dr. Freud! Whatever the reason, it got a good laugh from the room.

Steve and Elizabeth approached me, rather gingerly, I thought, and passed me my invitation to the dinner. I couldn't help noticing that it was made out to Premier Danny Williams and Mrs. Williams. I understood now the hesitation on the phone earlier. Evidently I was to be Mrs. Williams for the evening.

I asked Danny if he was doing this to prove he was really sincere about getting his same-sex marriage legislation through the House. Elizabeth said, "At least he didn't ask you to cross-dress." I said I supposed I should be grateful that a sex-change operation wasn't required. We were all having a jolly old time.

There was a knock on the door; when we opened it, a female police officer in a bulletproof vest was on the other side. She was our bodyguard, and she looked very fit and alert. As she led Danny and me in no-nonsense fashion through the corridors and down in the elevator to the parking garage, I felt safe. We boarded a big SUV driven by another Ontario Provincial Police officer.

In the back seat, Danny and I exchanged a glance as the discussion between the driver and the bodyguard in the front seat centred on how to get to the evening's venue, the Museum of Civilization across the river in Gatineau, Quebec. They were studying a map and discussing the best route to take. It was obvious that neither of them was very familiar with the Ottawa region. The driver turned around and said that the tremendous demand for police personnel to provide security had brought officers in from everywhere in Ontario. Then we set off, the two of them following their route plan and their noses. They did a great job, driving up over sidewalks and through parking lots to avoid barricades, giving off-roading in an urban setting a whole new meaning. In mere minutes, we arrived at the museum.

We walked in with the massive crowd of other invitees. I couldn't help noticing that nearly every man there was accompanied by what appeared to be a female spouse or companion. I probably should have felt more special than I did.

As soon as we entered the building, an official approached us and whisked the premier off to meet the US president. Danny was part of a small group of forty VVIPs (Very, Very Important Persons). I, on the other hand, was left standing there in the middle of the room. Was this any way to treat someone on a first date?

But I had lots of company: several hundred Cabinet ministers, big business magnates, senators, Supreme Court judges, and top civil servants who had also been excluded from the top forty because they were merely VIPs. Government protocol had evolved to the point where, if you were attending an official function and you were classed as a VIP rather than a VVIP, you were a nobody. The term VIP had become a negative designation: it meant you belonged to the ragged-arsed artillery, the great unwashed, the dregs. Not the 0.1 percent that constituted the country's elite. My humiliation was complete the next day, when I read in the *Ottawa Citizen* that those forty VVIPs had come back to the reception by descending "the escalator *with their wives* [my italics] into the Great Hall of the Museum of Civilization for the official dinner."

The mob of people at the reception was as tightly squeezed together as the protest crowd outside the hotel, and the buzz was similar. The only difference was that here there was no sloganeering or screeching, and less overt hostility to George W. Bush.

In fact, I saw only two examples of manifest hostility toward anyone at this agreeable soiree. The first occurred after I glimpsed John Efford between people's legs in the huge standing crowd. He was sitting by himself on a bench by the wall, and I thought I'd stroll over and mention some good news on the Accord negotiations. The provincial government had

sent a letter late last week to the federal government containing some suggestions on how to solve the Accord impasse, including some serious com-
promises by the province on equalization. It would be pleasant for a
change, I thought, to share a sense of progress with Efford. I'd have his
undivided attention for a few minutes too, because no one else was near
him. I wended my way over and said, "Good evening, Minister." My
greeting put his hackles up. He said nothing, and would not look at me. I
tried again: "The Accord negotiations are starting to look a bit better now,
Minister."

Efford barked, "After that letter on Friday, I don't think so." And he jerked
around so that his back was turned to me, as usual. I walked away from yet
another of Efford's trademark snubs, and headed for souls less futile.

I ran into Liberal Senator George Furey and his wife, and couldn't help
but be struck by his contrasting reaction. In the past I'd made snarky comments in the media about how three Furey brothers had all won the lot-
tery in the same year. Chuck had won a Lotto 6/49 jackpot, Leo had been
awarded the top job in the provincial film corporation, and George had
been appointed to the Senate. Arguing that the Senate should be
reformed, I had decried the practice of pitchforking party bagmen into the
Upper House to be kept in grand style at the taxpayers' expense. Neither
George nor the others seemed to have a straw up their nose about it. They
appeared to have the same broad-minded attitude as most other public
persons: that they were fair game for snotty, as well as serious, remarks
from talking heads. George and I had a chat which was more affable, if
less comical, than the one with John Efford.

Rejoining Danny, I asked him if he'd had a reply yet to the Accord
letter. He said he hadn't. I mentioned Efford's very negative reaction
regarding that letter. Danny was surprised. "That worries me," he said,
"because it was a good letter."

We figured Efford's reaction must have been absorbed from the prime
minister's office or the Privy Council office or the Department of Finance,
since he couldn't have come up with it by himself. His blurt had done us
an immense favour. He had alerted us to the fact that, federal moratorium

on Accord discussions tonight or not, Danny and I couldn't just sit back and enjoy this dinner. We had to get to work, bend a few ears belonging to the top federal brass.

The second note of hostility was perhaps less useful, but provided me with an interesting insight into Danny Williams's personality. As he and I were discussing what we needed to do that night to push the Accord, Craig Dobbin and his wife, Elaine, came over to say hello. I'd known Craig for a great number of years—professionally (as his lawyer in the '70s) as well as personally—and I'd always found him to be an independent-minded, frank guy who was friendly and open with high and low alike. But tonight, his behaviour toward Danny went way beyond friendliness. He was positively obsequious. And Danny, usually friendly to everyone he encountered, was frosty to the point of hostility to Dobbin.

Later, I asked Danny if he was irritated with the Dobbins because Mrs. Dobbin had said, to thousands of people gathered at a benefit gala in St. John's, that the provincial government's fifty-thousand-dollar donation to autism was not enough. No, said Danny. He'd been irritated at the time, but that feeling didn't last. Danny had a lot of respect for those who strove to raise funds for such challenging causes.

Then why, I queried, had Craig Dobbin been so far up the premier's ass tonight that you could only see the soles of his shoes? That, said Danny, must have been because Craig was trying to make up for his fax.

It seemed that Dobbin had sent a fax to Danny after unsuccessfully trying for several weeks to have a private meeting with the premier. In the fax, he had expressed outrage at his requests for a get-together being ignored, ending with the comment that he was accustomed to timely meetings with premiers. Danny had taken out his pen there and then, and scribbled on the fax that Dobbin had given the provincial government no notice, timely or otherwise, when he decided to pull his company out of Newfoundland, and that Danny's meetings as premier were based on what was in the best interests of the province. And he sent Dobbin's fax back to him. When it came to hard-headed, no-bullshit bluntness, it seemed that Craig had met his match, if not his master, in Mr. Williams.

Our pleasant encounters with current and former prime ministers, provincial premiers, ministers, senators, and MPs before dinner included one with the leader of the Opposition, Stephen Harper. I was interested to see him make a beeline for Danny, and then carry on at length like a best buddy. Harper invited me to call his office as soon as possible to arrange a meeting with him. He insisted it was important that we get together.

That invitation must have been given merely to impress Danny, because I would attempt to follow it up by calling his office three or four times, without result or response. One of Harper's caucus colleagues later confirmed that Stephen didn't seem to like human beings very much, and avoided them unless his hand was forced.

As we were about to sit at our table, Condoleezza Rice came over with the US ambassador to Canada, Paul Cellucci. She wanted to thank the premier for Newfoundland and Labrador's hospitality to aircraft passengers during the 9/11 crisis. Rice had been recently nominated by President George W. Bush as secretary of state, replacing Colin Powell.

Her handshake was good. The palm was startlingly soft, smooth and small, but the grip was firm. Rice had charisma plus; it was easy to understand the positive effect she had on her opposite numbers in other countries, including Canada's Peter MacKay, who would later become minister of Foreign Affairs. He was here at this event, but I didn't see him mooning around Rice that night. Maybe "la belle dame sans merci," Belinda Stronach, had him in thrall.

Seated at our table were Premier Danny Williams and, according to our place cards, me as his wife, Clerk of the Privy Council and Secretary to the Cabinet Alex Himelfarb with his wife, and former Atlantic representative in the prime minister's office, Newfoundlander Mark Watton and his girlfriend. There were places set for Ujjal Dosanjh, federal minister of Health, and his wife. But, regrettably, they didn't appear. His absence disappointed me because I wanted to congratulate the man who, years earlier, had had the courage to stand up to terrorist thugs in British Columbia.

In 1985, an extremist attacked him with an iron bar after he spoke out against militant Sikhs in Vancouver. He had eighty-four stitches in two layers in his head, and had to have his hand operated on to rejoin his fingers. I wanted to tell him to his face how much I admired his courage. I've always believed that, whatever else you might think of them, politicians whose valour was well beyond the ordinary should be commended for it, both publicly and privately, whenever the opportunity arose. Politicians such as Dosanjh, and Ontario's Bob Rae, the first western leader to appear in public with Salman Rushdie after the Ayatollah Khomeini placed a million-dollar bounty on Rushdie's head.

There were eighty-one tables of diners. President Bush was seated at the large circular head table in the middle, between Sheila Martin and Supreme Court Chief Justice Beverley McLachlin. There were three black vases filled with yellow roses on the table—a homage to Bush's home state's famous folk song, "The Yellow Rose of Texas." Condoleezza Rice was seated at the Martin-Bush table.

Former prime minister Jean Chrétien and his wife were at a table near us. Mme. Chrétien looked amazingly young, and she sparkled with intelligence. I didn't see Chrétien or Martin talk to each other or even look at each other all night. Neither did their spouses.

Colin Powell was at a nearby table, seated next to John Efford. He had announced his resignation as secretary of state two weeks before. According to the *Washington Post,* he had actually been asked to resign by the president's chief of staff. Powell announced publicly that he would stay on until the end of Bush's first term, or until Congress announced his replacement. The very next day, George W. Bush nominated National Security Adviser Condoleezza Rice as Powell's successor to the second most powerful post in the country.

A big Liberal and a big Tory at the table next to mine bent their heads together, and then pulled me into their tête-à-tête. One of them nodded toward John Efford and Colin Powell conversing. He said that Powell's punishment for his fall from presidential grace was his exile to that table. The other said he had just heard that Powell was desperately listening to the earpiece of his electronic translator, trying to find an English translation for the term "Bay Wobbits."

The menu featured grub from the US and from right across Canada—New Brunswick to British Columbia. (At least it was a change from the usual practice of starting Canada in Halifax.) We seven hundred and forty "distinguished guests," according to the media count, were fed as follows: giant shrimp on a bed of Santa Fe guacamole, topped with New Brunswick lobster; asparagus and chive cream; maple dressing; roasted butternut squash and Okanagan apple bisque; mesquite-smoked medallion of Alberta beef; rich jus; Yukon Gold potatoes mashed with Monterey Jack and jalapeno pepper; thyme-roasted Taber corn kernels; hand-picked fall baby vegetables; Saskatoon berry crème nestled on dark chocolate fondant; Florida orange sabayon and mousseline; Quebec maple syrup sauce; coffee.

Philippe Wettel, executive chef of the Westin Hotel, was reported as saying, "We put in a touch of pepper and extra spicy mashed potato and corn, to give [Bush] a touch of Texas."

President Bush expressed his satisfaction with the menu. "I'm glad to see," he said during his speech before dinner, "that we'll be eating Alberta beef." I didn't hear afterwards if he thought it was as good as Texas beef.

This visit was obviously costing the Canadian taxpayer a pretty penny. But whatever the final tab, it would be enough to spark an unseemly public debate later. In keeping with our Canadian sense of dignity, the federal government and the City of Ottawa squabbled over unpaid bills from the Bush visit—who was responsible for what.

When Paul Martin got up on stage to welcome President Bush, between the two Canadian Mounties standing at attention in front of six American and Canadian flags, we got another indication of how he was being dogged by bad karma as prime minister. His first order of business was to announce that the master of ceremonies was unable to make the gig: he had dropped dead that morning.

I mentioned to Danny that when Martin had been Finance minister, cruising along on Chrétien's good luck, he'd seemed to have the Midas touch. But as prime minister, and relying on his own luck, he exhibited the reverse of the Midas touch—the Sadim touch—everything he touched turned to shit. This had to be having a traumatic psychological effect on the poor guy, something for us to bear in mind during our negotiations.

Martin made a reference in his speech to our province, saying that the museum we were in "celebrates a journey through our social history from the first Viking settlements on the Newfoundland coast." I wondered, though, how our Aboriginal citizens felt about his proclaiming that tardy start as the beginning of Canadian history. I didn't hear of any protests, perhaps because there were so few, if any, Aboriginals present.

The night's entertainment consisted of Leahy, the family of Celtic singers and dancers. I wasn't sure if all eight or so members of that family of geniuses were there that night, but a lot of them were and they were great. President Bush went nuts. When they'd finished fiddling, singing and dancing, he jumped up from his table like a teenaged groupie and rushed backstage to meet them. By presidential order, he got them to do an encore.

During dinner, Danny Williams and Alex Himelfarb were seated next to each other, and talked earnestly and at length. I was sitting next to Himelfarb's wife, whose conversation was peppered with interesting insights. She told me she worked with the inmates of penitentiaries, which I found intriguing as a career choice. I mentioned to her Winston Churchill's remark that a nation's level of civilization can be determined from the way it treats the most despised people among them—the worst criminals in the prison system.

She took the conversation from there, with some fascinating implications for us all regarding our penal system and its institutions. I almost hated to have to finish our chat in order to talk turkey with her husband. But after dinner, as soon as Danny got up from the table, I moved over to have a natter with Alex Himelfarb too. I had a wacky but, I hoped, productive pitch planned for him.

Sliding around the table, I kept in mind that although he was intellectually brilliant and greatly admired by his peers—in 2000 he was awarded the Outstanding Achievement Award, considered the most prestigious award in the Canadian public service—he could also be exceedingly subtle and ingenious.

Two months before, Himelfarb had testified before the Gomery Inquiry into the mismanagement of the sponsorship program through which millions of dollars were funnelled into Quebec to boost the federal government's profile there. It boosted the federal profile all right, and covered it with filth in the process. Auditor General Sheila Fraser calculated that one hundred million dollars had gone to ad agencies with Liberal connections, and there was no proof they had provided the work.

On September 28, CBC News reported that Himelfarb had testified that the former prime minister, Jean Chrétien, was not legally accountable. Even though Jean Chrétien had personally directed money to the program, the minister of Public Works was on the hook for it.

What? Chrétien had signed the first requests to Treasury Board for millions of dollars to kick-start the sponsorship program, his initials were on memos from the Privy Council that warned him he'd be accountable for how the money was spent, and Chrétien's chief of staff met regularly with the program's director to discuss which projects would get money. In spite of all that, Himelfarb testified to Gomery that while Chrétien was answerable, he was not accountable.

"Answerability is a form of accountability that's narrower than full accountability where you accept the consequences of your behaviour," he testified. When Himelfarb explained the "arcane" distinction between accountability, responsibility and answerability, the lawyer for the inquiry queried whether, in spite of Chrétien's involvement, it was Minister Alfonso Gagliano who was accountable because the money flowed through the Department of Public Works. "It has to be, legally, in your view, that the minister would have signed off on the prime minister's decision?"

"Exactly," said Himelfarb.

"And of course," said the inquiry counsel, "there are going to be very few ministers who are going to say [to the PM], 'I'm not signing off on your decision.'"

I could visualize Himelfarb shrugging in response.

At the Bush dinner, I reminded him of who I was and what I was doing here in Ottawa. "Bill Rowe, Bill Rowe," he murmured. "Is Penelope Rowe your wife?"

"Yes, she is," I said. "You know her? She spends a lot time in Ottawa with her work."

I was accustomed to officials in Ottawa raising Penny's name, and very grateful for it; her magnificent reputation had eased the way into several productive discussions.

"Yes, I know her well," Himelfarb said. "Penny Rowe is an absolute force of nature."

"Oh, I agree, I agree," I said, chuckling—the husband who needed no convincing. Knowing I might only have a short time to make my unorthodox sell, I started right in: "I just wanted to make sure you were aware of something crucial about Danny Williams. He—"

"When Penny Rowe walks into a room," Himelfarb rhapsodized, "the room changes."

"Right, right," I said. "Now, about—"

"That woman, your wife," he interjected, "is a national treasure."

"Okay, okay, Jesus Christ, I get it, honest—I get it." When Himelfarb looked at me, startled, I told him how I had come to the dinner as Danny Williams's spousal appendage to start with, and if that was not traumatic enough, I was now the spousal appendage of my own wife, who wasn't even here. "Can't I just be *me* for a minute?" I whined. We had a quiet laugh and settled back to talk.

He mentioned his long-term interest in Newfoundland and Labrador. He'd been there many times, often with a Newfoundland woman he'd been in a relationship with. For a time, he had even wanted to retire there.

I told him that if I ever retired to a part of Canada outside my own province, it would be Quebec. So full of ironies and paradoxes, not to mention good food—it was the most interesting part of Canada. Many Canadians thought that as Quebec's population and political power became an ever decreasing percentage of Canada's, the separation option would die. But a growing sense of powerlessness would actually make Quebec's will to separate in a future referendum stronger, not weaker. A Québécois Danny Williams, I said, could pull it off.

That scenario brought us back to the brutal reality of the present.

Himelfarb said that Paul Martin dreaded doing anything that might have the effect of weakening the Canadian federation. For example, giving one province a deal on equalization that other provinces didn't get.

Hearing that, I'm not sure I was able to hold back my snigger. Hadn't the federal government already given Quebec, at the September health summit, a deal with the right to go its own way, I asked, gently, ladling out federal billions to Quebec to spend freely and without accountability except to the people of Quebec? And wasn't Martin's new equalization deal at the October summit tailored to suit Quebec's needs, since that province would become the beneficiary of, by far, the lion's share down the road? If the federal government would only give Newfoundland and Labrador a small taste of the asymmetrical federalism Quebec was getting, I was sure that Danny Williams would stop boycotting federal-provincial summits and give up the slanging matches with Paul Martin.

This led to talk about the relationship between Danny and Paul. Himelfarb was saddened, he said, by the collapse of their great friendship. They'd been close friends, but he wasn't too sure right now whether they could ever be good friends again. I told Himelfarb he'd better disabuse himself of the relevance of that consideration. Friendship might appear to be a big deal with Danny in ordinary circumstances—he seemed to wear his heart on his sleeve—but when it came to deal-making, forget it. Himelfarb was familiar with the man's business and legal history. When had friendship ever played any role there? Friendship between Danny and Paul, I told him, had no bearing whatsoever on the Accord issue. It was not even the lowest priority for Danny.

It was then, as Himelfarb shook his head in disbelief, that I decided to give the Atlantic Accord battle my best unconventional and, I hoped, most psychologically scary shot.

The mistake Himelfarb and the prime minister and Minister Goodale were making, I told Canada's top public servant, was in thinking that Danny was a normal person. He was not. Danny Williams was crazy.

"Is that your boss you're talking about there?" queried Himelfarb. "This person you're calling crazy?"

Yes, I said, but crazy in the best sense when it came to his allies and partners—crazy in the worst sense when it came to his opponents and enemies. Crazy in the same way that Winston Churchill was crazy. Other people might try to compromise, or take evasive action, but these absolutely determined "crazy" men would never give in or back away. They would not be defeated by you. They would only defeat you.

One glance at Danny's history told you that. Beating out powerful interests as a youngster to obtain a cable TV licence; then, two or three decades later, horse-trading the cable side of his company to Ontario cable mogul Ted Rogers, and getting more than three times Rogers's $90 million offer for it. Himelfarb could ask Francis Fox, a former Rogers executive, all about that. And Danny had obtained acquittals in murder cases many observers thought were hopeless, including getting a woman completely off a murder charge for killing her husband in cold blood. Danny had argued self-defence, based on chronic spousal abuse, breaking new legal ground. Most other "sane" lawyers would have tried to plea-bargain the charge down to manslaughter. He had fought hard to get Greg Parsons acquitted on a wrongful murder conviction, and he'd taken on the Roman Catholic Church and won in the case of thirty-nine former residents of Mount Cashel Orphanage who had been physically and sexually abused, and he had negotiated their $11.5 million settlement. In case after case, Danny had emerged victorious by never giving up, never ever accepting less than he believed was due.

This guy was different from other premiers, I told Himelfarb, as Martin was perhaps already starting to realize. The PM might as well realize what he was up against, and come to the inevitable conclusion: he could not win against this crazy man. If the prime minister was truly worried about the future of Confederation, he should seriously contemplate that.

Himelfarb was too canny to indicate if he was accepting, or even absorbing, my argument as to why Danny Williams was invincible on the Atlantic Accord. I did get soothing smiles from him, which seemed to say that if there was a crazy person in the piece, it was me, and not necessarily in the best possible sense.

I have no idea if any of it, including my linking of Danny Williams with successful separation if he were a leader in Quebec, and the PM's worries about Confederation, had a direct effect on the final outcome of the Atlantic Accord. During the following weeks, however, I was gratified to see Danny carrying on true to my characterization of him. His public statements against Martin and the federal government and his description of Newfoundland and Labrador's appalling place in Confederation were extremely disquieting for Ottawa. When they culminated in his dramatic action with the Canadian flag just before Christmas, it unsettled the national media and rattled the prime minister and his advisers to the core. Media people reported on the madness of Danny's refusals to accept successive federal offers. And God alone knew, the feds whispered to each other, what this crazy person was going to do next.

Crazy? Yes. Crazy like a fox.

— CHAPTER TEN —

The Flag Flap

BY THE LATTER PART of November, media interest in the Accord negotiations had begun to die in Ottawa because nothing new was happening. Till then I had received frequent calls from reporters who wanted to interview me about the battle between Paul Martin and Danny Williams. I did some interviews but, because mixed messages from our side were always a risk, I turned down more, restricting myself mostly to providing background information off the record on our position. I told the premier's office that I thought only Danny and Loyola Sullivan should be making statements to the national media on the Accord. Everyone agreed.

Then, in the middle of the media doldrums, I received a surprise call from a prominent journalist in the national capital who proposed an extensive interview with me on the federal-provincial offshore oil imbroglio. It sounded like a way to revive some interest, so I said yes. I told them I would do the interview in the open air, with the numerous big government office buildings of Ottawa behind me as backdrop. I would be referring to them as a symbol of the billions upon billions of federal dollars pouring into the Ontario treasury from taxes on federal government incomes and expenditures in the national capital. The journalist balked at that, saying that at this time of year, with the weather so uncertain, they wanted to do the interview inside. To add colour to the piece, they would be setting up their cameras in D'Arcy Magee's, a pub.

I should have known. In a journalistic culture where most stories on any subject pertaining to Newfoundland had the mandatory tag "Canada's poorest province" attached plus the obligatory reference, however irrelevant, to the George Street booze scene in St. John's, I didn't think my sitting down in a tavern to make the case that federal unfairness had driven our per capita debt up to more than double the national average was such a brilliant idea. Oh, I realized I was a quaint and colourful Newf and all that, I told them, but could we possibly do the interview somewhere less picturesque? Of course, they said. Did I have a favourite pub—the Earl of Sussex, maybe? Oh, for goodness' sake! I replied. (I may have used a shorter and pithier word than goodness.) I forced out a chuckle and said that my job description did not include playing the role of Goofy Newfie, and I declined the interview altogether.

I didn't blame the media, though, for their dwindling attention to the Accord. The feds had proclaimed that the end was nigh too often. For example, how were reporters supposed to keep their interest up after Ralph Goodale made another big fuss in the news about flying down to St. John's with Alex Himelfarb in order to conclude the Accord with Newfoundland, only to have the negotiations come to nothing yet again?

Shortly after all that hoopla followed by that bust, I received a call from a Liberal MP who couldn't stop laughing as he described the recent caucus of Atlantic MPs attended by Goodale. Ralph had contended that the difficulty in making a final deal was because Danny Williams raised expectations way too high. My caller hooted: Goodale was blaming Danny for raising expectations when Goodale was all over the media for piling aboard the Challenger jet with Himelfarb and barrelling down to St. John's. You had to love his colleagues in the federal Cabinet, the MP concluded—they all had the face of a robber's horse.

Late on the night of November 19, I received a detailed email from Brian Crawley on the Accord talks that had gone on all that day. He concluded that they were far from a deal yet. Another meeting was scheduled for Tuesday of the following week. The next morning, Lawrence O'Brien telephoned me to say that John Efford had just called him to declare that there would be a definite deal reached on the Accord next Tuesday. Goodale, Efford had said, was sure of it. A few hours later, Crawley telephoned me from Halifax. When I mentioned the federal optimism, he was surprised. A deal at the meeting on Tuesday? That was at most a bare possibility. Talk about someone raising expectations way too high.

The next Wednesday, a day after the "deal-making" meetings, Crawley called me with an update. The most that could be said was that progress had in fact been made, but there was certainly nothing final yet. Hamm was particularly concerned about the eight-year deadline the federal government wanted to impose on any deal, as was Newfoundland and Labrador, and, of course, the two provinces were sticking together on their objection to it.

Among the current Accord proposals from Newfoundland and Labrador were two sensible ones regarding the length of operation of a new Atlantic Accord: Any review of the new deal would take place only after the province had been off equalization for five years, and only when our per capita debt became the same as the average per capita debt in other Canadian provinces. What could be more reasonable, I wondered, especially since our appallingly high debt had resulted largely from our disadvantaged position in Canada, above all from our inability to benefit from the Upper Churchill development? Those were the proposals I was referring to when I mentioned to John Efford at the Bush dinner that the Accord was starting to look good. And those were what Efford was referring to when he had responded, "After that letter on Friday, I don't think so."

But even the *Globe and Mail*, which had not exactly been a cheerleader for the province's demands over the years, was prepared to press the federal government. An editorial on November 25 stated, "But he [Paul Martin] made a promise, and even at $55 a barrel, a pledge is a pledge. Newfoundland should receive its full share of offshore oil proceeds, without time limit or cap . . . [Newfoundland and Labrador] has an enormous debt ($9.8 billion in 2002, the highest per capita in Canada at $18,867) and unfunded pension liabilities."

Behind the scenes, as evidenced by that *Globe and Mail* editorial and later editorial comments, Danny Williams was doing a tremendous job of getting our provincial position across to the editorial boards of national journals and thoughtful media commentators. In his attempts to directly appeal to the Canadian public through the mainland media, however, he occasionally missed.

One morning, I was shaking my head over the inadequacy of an article that had just appeared under Danny Williams's name in the *National Post*. My cellphone rang. It was Rollie Martin, an expert on equalization and the current Atlantic Accords, calling from Halifax. Rollie was a concerned Newfoundlander, a former top executive in many capacities in our provincial government, and he and I had been communicating regularly on the Accord problems. (I'll be mentioning more about his contribution to our cause later.)

Rollie was always frank about how the province was communicating its position. He never hesitated to assess candidly Danny and Loyola's appearances in the media and their public statements, for which I was grateful. Today he wanted to talk about Danny's article in the *National Post* (November 30), entitled "The Scales Are tipped in Ottawa's favour." We both lambasted it.

To Rollie, as well as to me, it clouded rather than clarified the issues. The thing was a boring, whiny litany of how our province had been hard done by; it meandered on for two-thirds of its length before Danny got to the crunch: "Over the life of the [offshore oil] fields presently under development, the federal government will receive 86% of the offshore benefits while Newfoundland and Labrador receive just 14%."

That was the essential point of it all, but how many readers would stick with the article long enough to reach it? Rollie and I thought that Danny should get better writers, or, if he had written it himself, better editors. I told him I'd be conveying our impressions to the premier the next time I talked to him.

When I telephoned the premier's office, Danny was in a meeting. I found Brian Crawley and gave him our reaction to the newspaper article. I asked Brian to pass it on to the premier, and to tell him I'd be keeping an ear and eye open for the reaction of others. A few days later, I called Crawley to say I had picked up virtually no reaction to Danny's *National Post* article in Ottawa. There was a bare mention of it and the Atlantic Accord in the December 6 edition of the *Hill Times*. National media interest in the Accord at every level had spiralled downward drastically.

Late the same day, I got an email from Crawley. The premier was about to dispatch him and Loyola Sullivan to Ottawa. They were going to demand a meeting out of the blue with Goodale.

The next morning, Crawley called from the Ottawa Sheraton to ask me if I could join him at a meeting with Sullivan and Nova Scotia's minister of Energy, Cecil Clarke, at noon to discuss the day's strategy. I said yes, although unfortunately that meant I had to cancel my meeting with Tom Graham, a director of Intergovernmental Affairs, on the intractable 5 Wing Goose Bay problems.

We all gathered, provincial ministers and staff, in the hotel lobby and trooped off to a boardroom for our discussion and a sandwich. There we talked over what had to be done to dramatically display our displeasure to the feds and to the media over the fact that, apart from John Efford's comment to me at the Bush dinner, our provincial governments had had no reaction whatsoever to our latest letter to the federal government on the Accord. It had been eleven days since it was sent. The ministers agreed that we would all go to Question Period to make our presence felt. Meanwhile, Loyola sent a message to Goodale, insisting on meeting with him before he and Clarke left Ottawa.

Then we walked through a horizontal sleet storm to the House of Commons, and used the passes Loyola had obtained from the Speaker's office to go to the gallery facing the ministers on the government front benches. Sullivan and Clarke sat conspicuously in the front row of the gallery, with Brian Crawley and me behind them. John Efford walked into the House and glanced up at the gallery.

He was visibly startled, or, as one of us later described his reaction, he looked like a man who had just shit shrapnel. He stomped up to Goodale, several seats away. You could see from his body language and gestures that he was asking his fellow minister what Sullivan and Clarke were doing here in Ottawa, and why he hadn't been notified beforehand of their presence. Their exchange looked rather heated. From Efford's and Goodale's point of view, it was probably a good thing their words were not being picked up for *Hansard*.

Then Question Period started. In the past, the prime minister had been questioned, often for days on end, about the Accord negotiations, but today the Opposition was preoccupied mostly with demanding why he hadn't yet fired Minister Judy Sgro for allegedly promising to help a pizza shop owner avoid deportation to India in return for his help with her re-election campaign. She had also been accused of helping an "exotic dancer" from Romania stay in Canada because the stripper had worked on her re-election campaign as well.

Someone asked Ken Dryden a question; he slowly and reluctantly unwound his considerable length to rise and answer, prompting a delighted chuckle and a comment to Crawley and me from hockey buff Loyola Sullivan about how Dryden's painfully slow movements in the House were such a contrast to his quick and engaged actions in the net.

No one was asking any questions or making any comments about the Atlantic Accord. The thing was dead here too.

After Question Period, the Speaker announced the presence of Sullivan and Clarke in the gallery. The two men rose to their feet and received a standing ovation from MPs on both sides of the House.

As we left the gallery, Sullivan mentioned that word had come through—Goodale would meet Sullivan and Clarke between four-thirty and six o'clock. When we picked up our cellphones at security, Brian Crawley had a message from the premier's office on his. Williams had just received a call from Alex Himelfarb suggesting that they needed to get together privately. Something was certainly clicking again.

We walked from the House of Commons in the sleet storm to the hotel, where Sullivan and Clarke prepared for their meeting with Ralph Goodale. It was after close of business in Newfoundland and Labrador by the time I got back to my office. My assistant, Christie Meadus, told me she'd received a call that afternoon from someone in the office of John Hickey, Progressive Conservative MHA for Lake Melville district, asking me to meet with union leaders Randy Ford and Peter Chaytor, who had come from Happy Valley–Goose Bay to discuss 5 Wing. I told Christie to say I'd be delighted to meet with them, and asked her to arrange it at everyone's earliest convenience.

Early the next morning, I received an email from John Hickey complaining that his office had not had a reply from me. In his email, Hickey said that he knew I was busy up here "despite what Anna Thessel [sic] might say in the House of Assembly." It looked suspiciously like sarcasm, appropriately described in this case as the lowest form of wit. "Thessel" seemed to be Hickey's attempt at spelling "Thistle," the name of a Liberal Opposition member who had been requesting information from the premier in the House of Assembly about my position, its duties, its costs and what I was in fact doing up here.

I sent an email back to Hickey, wording it as patiently as if I were dealing with a child. The premier's office had already forewarned me that, like them, I would be receiving blizzards of emails from his office with attachments containing interminable minutes of local meetings, and documents referring to 5 Wing Goose Bay, with no attempt to focus the recipient's attention on what was considered important.

In fairness to Hickey, though, he did give me some useful leads and information regarding 5 Wing Goose Bay, which led to productive meetings and exchanges of information in Ottawa. For example, the meeting that he initiated for me in Ottawa with the union leaders and their associates from Happy Valley–Goose Bay was excellent, and added an important perspective to my understanding of the issues.

On the evening of the abruptly arranged meeting between Sullivan, Clarke and Goodale, I attended a showing of a documentary film on the Labrador Innu in the West Block. It was produced by Ed Martin, and

Senator Bill Rompkey had issued the invitations. Penny, who was in Ottawa on business, went with me, through the sleet storm that refused to die. I wondered as I slogged from the parked car to the door, my face parallel to the ground to avoid lacerations, where the hell Ontarians got the idea that Newfoundland had all the lousy weather.

The audience was fairly small, probably as a result of the weather, but perhaps also because of indifference. There were several Innu from Labrador, including Simeon Tshakapesh, and a number from Quebec, plus Lloyd Wicks, our province's child and youth advocate. Senator Bill Rompkey acted as the host and was able to introduce, in short order, everyone in the audience.

The film was moving, if somewhat heavy-handed in its emotional manipulation. But it depicted important injustices: the Innu had never had any say or control over their own lives since Confederation because the provincial government and the Church had ruled them, and conditions in Davis Inlet had been as bad as or worse than any in the Third World.

There was a lot of ignorance in Ottawa concerning the Innu. Even the *Hill Times*, normally a reliable source of political goings-on and punditry in Ottawa, surprised me one day with a reference to "the Inuit of Davis Inlet" in an interview. I banged off an email to the *Hill Times* pointing out that anyone presuming to talk knowledgeably about Labrador should know the difference between the two proud peoples, the Innu and the Inuit: Davis Inlet had been an Innu community, not an Inuit one. I received an email back from the editor of the *Hill Times* requesting permission to publish my email as a letter to the editor, and then I received another email apologizing for the mistake, saying that it was the interviewer's error, not the person's being interviewed, and that the editor should have picked it up. A fine newspaper, the *Hill Times*, but I had found that many fine newspapers contained misconceptions and outright mistakes about Newfoundland and Labrador.

After the film was over, a number of people spoke about the horrendous conditions portrayed. One was an Innu lawyer from Quebec, who was highly placed at the United Nations. She hit hard on the past and present victimization of her people. At first I was disappointed that she didn't move away from that subject and concentrate on her own progress in life, since she was a magnificent role model for the young Innu of Labrador and Quebec. But then I came to my senses and realized that she was absolutely right.

Her personal success spoke for itself. What needed reiteration was how the artificial white man's border between Quebec and Labrador had divided her people, subjecting them to differing laws, none of their own making, in overlord languages. The damming of their river and falls and the flooding of their ancestral lands for the big Quebec-Labrador hydro project without so much as a by-your-leave. Loud low military aircraft flying over them and the game in the wilderness which they had occupied for thousands of years. The destruction of their self-esteem and sense of independence, and the erosion of culture that would lead inexorably to alcohol abuse. How could any self-respecting Innu leader pass lightly over the subject of what had been done and what was still being done to her people?

The combination of neglect and wrong-headed actions that she described, on the one hand, and the squabbling that was taking place, even as she spoke, between federal and provincial representatives of the white elite over the billions of dollars of spoils from offshore oil, on the other hand, presented a powerful and gut-wrenching contrast.

I talked to Brian Crawley the morning after Sullivan and Clarke's descent on Ottawa to discuss the divvying up of those spoils with Goodale. The meeting had been pretty much a bust. Goodale had been very angry at the unannounced arrival—the ambush—of the Newfoundland and Labrador and Nova Scotia ministers and the springing of the meeting on him. The provincial ministers threw back in his face that their premiers hadn't even had the courtesy of a letter or phone call since their last approach, nearly two weeks ago, to the prime minister. What were they supposed to do, sit on their hands and wait forever on the pleasure of the PMO?

Sullivan and Clarke did wring one thing out of Goodale: that he had no mandate as minister of Finance to conclude a deal on the Atlantic Accord with either province. In other words, the situation was as Crawley and I had been insisting all along—only Danny Williams and Paul Martin—with the able assistance, I hoped, of Alex Himelfarb—could actually close a deal. Nevertheless, Danny, no doubt remembering that his last formal meeting with Paul three weeks before had nearly resulted in bloodshed, wanted Loyola Sullivan to stay on in Ottawa till some form of progress was made. I told Brian not to mortgage the house on that hope, but then, just hours later, I learned that Hamm and Williams were to meet with Alex Himelfarb in Halifax the next day.

Meanwhile, my own networking went on. I had received a phone call from a lady with a delightful English accent, who was with the British High Commission in Ottawa and who wanted to invite me to their festive season breakfast. An English breakfast? I guess so! I accepted with alacrity, asking her how come the High Commission had invited me, a provincial representative, to a national embassy function. She replied that the High Commission kept itself informed of who the various representatives in Ottawa at all levels were, and it liked to establish contact with them. And it didn't hurt one bit, she joked, that she was married to a Newfoundlander. (I told you we were everywhere.)

Off I traipsed at eight o'clock on the morning of December 9, to the British High Commission on Elgin Street. A fair crowd of invitees was gathering there, mainly what looked like mid-level external affairs officials and diplomats. As I wandered about, a few glanced with a quick and practised eye at my lapel tag—"William Rowe, Government of Newfoundland and Labrador." Their eyes glazed over and slewed away, hunting for bigger game. I had good gabs, though, with Liberal minister David Anderson and leading Opposition light Peter MacKay, and was able to punch home some points on the Accord. Then I happened on RCMP Commissioner Giuliano Zaccardelli.

When he saw where I was from, he mentioned his years in Atlantic Canada. He had been in charge of criminal operations in New Brunswick, and then in charge of the force's overall operations in that province. There had been accusations that, under his watch, the RCMP had not properly investigated alleged criminal conduct by a former RCMP officer involved with the Kingsclear Youth Training Centre, and that they had covered up alleged sexual abuse by the same officer, saying there was not enough evidence to lay criminal charges against him. Zaccardelli had stated publicly and vehemently that the case had been fully investigated.

At the British breakfast, he talked about the need for integration of various policing services in Canada. I told him I disagreed. The last thing we needed, I said, was one big monolithic police force answerable to no one but itself, subject only to its own authority and rules. He considered this, I think, a criticism of the RCMP's methods of investigating itself.

Evidently concluding that I was a dupe of irresponsible journalism, he launched into a bitter tirade about the media in Canada being completely out of control. As we parted, agreeing to disagree, I noted the quality of the riding boots he had on. Those must have been the fifteen-hundred-dollar boots, paid for by taxpayers, that the out-of-control media had had a field day criticizing. They didn't seem to fit him very well; he simply didn't have the legs to fill them out properly. My overall impression of him was that he was a small man—nothing wrong with that—but a small man striving officiously, and vainly, to fill a big man's boots. I wasn't surprised to see Zaccardelli's Canadian career come to a sorry end, or to see him snag a senior Interpol job after that in Africa.

I brought my plate of scrambled eggs, bacon, sausage, lamb cutlet, fried tomatoes, and home fries over to a table that happened to have a number of people from the French embassy at it. Straight-faced, I introduced myself as Newfoundland's ambassador to Canada. They all picked up on it immediately, and one of them said that Canada seemed to have matured a good deal as a country since de Gaulle's cry in the late '60s of "Vive le Quebec libre." We had a good laugh.

Well, it was about time we came of age, I said, since the country was getting ready to celebrate the four hundredth anniversary of the founding of Quebec City. Yes, but even there, one of them replied, Canada was a Johnny-come-lately: Newfoundland was a hundred years ahead of them.

They were extremely knowledgeable about what was being planned in our province to celebrate five hundred years of French presence. I had to tear myself away from the pleasure of conversing with those savvy, entertaining guys to get back to my office and the task at hand.

There, I learned from an email from Brian Crawley that the premiers' travelling circus was in Halifax, where a new meeting had been held with the feds. Some progress had been made. He said he'd call me the next day to discuss it after he'd talked with Premier Williams.

That evening, December 9, there was a Canadian Press story out of Halifax headlined "N.S. and Newfoundland Resume Offshore Talks with Feds." It said that Hamm and Williams had failed to strike a deal with the country's top civil servant during talks at a Halifax hotel.

> They emerged from the meeting with Alex Himelfarb, clerk of the Privy Council, to say that negotiations will continue by telephone on Friday and through next week, if necessary.
>
> "The federal government has been very conscious of how it will look in the rest of Canada if two of the country's poorest equalization-receiving provinces are given a multibillion-dollar break on offshore revenues," Williams suggested.
>
> "The sensitivity is being overblown," said Hamm. "We haven't had opportunities here in Atlantic Canada. When huge investments are made in the automobile industry in Ontario, I don't object. I don't object when huge amounts of money are made available to build airplanes at Bombardier."
>
> When [the] meeting was over, Himelfarb refused to comment to reporters, insisting that he had to catch a plane.
>
> Williams said all sides have agreed that the talks cannot drag on indefinitely. "There may not be a deal," he

said. "[But] there is certainly consensus that before Christmas this will be finalized one way or another."

Both premiers refused to discuss details of the talks, but they remained upbeat they can reach an agreement, which could be worth a minimum of $1.2 billion to Newfoundland and $640 million to Nova Scotia over eight years.

"The fact that we have been discussing and we intend to talk again means we are making progress," said Williams.

Hamm said the talks with Himelfarb were more detailed and precise than any exchange with the federal government to date. "We are exchanging creative ideas that could lead to a deal," he said.

The next day, Friday, December 10, I got another email from Crawley. They had tried to fly back to Newfoundland, but had to return to Halifax because of bad weather. This, he said, had turned into the week from hell.

Early the following week, I had a long telephone conversation with Crawley. The Accord negotiations were not going as well as he had hoped after the meeting in Halifax. A couple of days later he called to say the Atlantic Accord seemed to have gone bottom up, and that Goodale and the officials in his department were the problem. As hard as it was to believe, they did not seem to understand the position of the two provinces. Goodale was still annoyed by Sullivan and Clarke's ambush in Ottawa; he couldn't see past that. Williams, Hamm, and Himelfarb would meet on Sunday, December 19, but only if the feds indicated beforehand that they were going to be flexible and give.

I told Brian that interest in the Accord continued to be on the wane here in Ottawa, both politically and in the media. Perhaps the apathy was caused by the nearness to Christmas, but I didn't think so. Although chatting behind the scenes with Himelfarb was well and good, it wasn't enough. We had to do something publicly to attract the prime minister's attention and the media's, something that would raise alarm—something crazy, in fact. Danny was giving the impression of being far too level-headed, too rational.

But nothing crazy happened. In the week before Christmas, media attention to the Accord dispute had evaporated entirely. Before calling Brian Crawley on December 20, to find out what had happened at the meeting between the premiers and Himelfarb the day before, I talked to Rollie Martin in Halifax. I wanted to confirm my own sickening impression that there hadn't been, in any of the year-end interviews that Paul Martin had done with the media that week, any mention whatsoever of the Atlantic Accord.

Rollie had the same impression I did: as a public issue, the Accord was dead as a doornail. The way things were going, there would definitely not be, as the provinces and the feds piously hoped in tiny items relegated to page twenty of the newspapers, any agreement before Christmas—if ever. Something was definitely needed to stir things up—something that would make Paul Martin want to put this crap behind him once and for all. We juggled ideas. Perhaps one or two MPs from Nova Scotia would have to vote against the prime minister on the Accord, as the Newfoundland MPs had done. I called Brian Crawley and told him that as far as the prime minister and the Ottawa press gallery and the national media were concerned, the Accord had dropped off the radar completely. Clearly, Danny had to make some dramatic moves to resurrect it. Why the hell should Paul Martin be permitted to enjoy a quiet and pleasant Christmas holiday over in Morocco while we were forced to cool our heels back here? Brian replied that there was some breaking news that would probably make that unnecessary. He'd get back to me as soon as the ducks were in a row.

On this freezing December day in Ottawa, I downloaded the online news from home—VOCM and CBC and the *St. John's Telegram*—as I did every day. The *Telegram*, dated August 3, 2003, was full of stories on the Quidi Vidi regatta and the balmy summer weather. It was a glitch, temporary but nonetheless delightful. The temperature outside my window, with the wind chill factored in, was minus 38 degrees Celsius.

Brian Crawley called back. A deal on the Accord was highly likely after Himelfarb's meeting with Danny and Hamm the day before. All hands were now flying to Winnipeg—Williams, Hamm, Himelfarb, Regan (Nova Scotia's federal minister), Efford, and Goodale—to conclude the deal and to sign it.

"Winnipeg?" I gasped. Talk about sending the fools further. But Crawley replied that the possibilities looked good, so much so that some provincial supporters found it galling that Efford and Regan were going to be there for the signing when neither of them had done a goddamned thing to further the new Accord. The prime minister was so certain of a deal that he'd asked Himelfarb to find out from Danny if Efford, once the new Accord was signed, could be saved politically in Newfoundland. Danny said no.

I told Crawley that, based on the dead-issue feel in Ottawa and the fact that the PM was not even going to be there, I was very surprised at, not to say skeptical about, this "positive" turn of events. John Efford himself was all over the media, but it was about same-sex marriage, not the Accord.

The CBC story on the Winnipeg meeting, which took place on Wednesday, December 22, indicated how far apart the federal and provincial governments were.

"Newfoundland's Premier says he expects the fate of offshore-oil reserves to be decided at a meeting on Wednesday, even as federal officials downplay the significance of the talks. Premier Danny Williams—who is in Winnipeg with Nova Scotia Premier John Hamm to meet federal Finance Minister Ralph Goodale—has characterized this meeting as 'do or die.' Williams said the meeting will either nail down a new offshore oil deal, or will mark the end of formal negotiations. However, a spokesperson for Goodale said the federal government sees the meeting as important, but not the end of the road. The spokesperson said talks could well move into 2005, and Hamm has said he believes talks could spill over into the New Year."

Meanwhile, John Efford, far from going to the Winnipeg meeting to reap undeserved credit, played down the importance of the meeting for CBC—a meeting he said he would not be attending. But he still claimed to be the kingpin, even though Goodale had been made the lead minister many weeks earlier. "Nothing can be signed in Winnipeg, nothing can be signed without my signature," said Efford, who described his department as taking the lead on finding a deal to replace the Atlantic Accord, even though he said he hadn't been told of the meeting. "Give me a break . . . It doesn't make any sense flying to Winnipeg."

The PMO had said, however, that Himelfarb and Goodale had the authority to sign a deal, and both men were going to Winnipeg to negotiate with Williams and Hamm. Listening to the story, I could only shake my head. It could be a Groucho Marx comedy—too bad the matter was so important.

Meanwhile, I left for St. John's, my first trip home since August. In the taxi to the airport, the driver had the radio on. I heard John Efford complain on the national news that he'd only found out about the meeting in Winnipeg between Danny Williams and Ralph Goodale from the media; he confirmed that he wasn't attending it himself.

When I got off the plane in St. John's, there was a message from Brian Crawley on my cellphone. He said he'd tell me all about the Winnipeg meeting the next day. He did not sound upbeat.

The following morning, December 23, I taped a half-hour interview on Rogers Television's *Out of the Fog* about my job in Ottawa and my take on the battle over the Atlantic Accord, to be aired that night.

When I finished, there was a call waiting from Brian Crawley. He told me that Danny regarded the meeting with Goodale in Winnipeg as absolutely disgusting. He had gone all the way out there just before Christmas on the assurance of progress from the federal government, and nothing whatsoever had happened. I stifled the urge to say to Brian that things were pretty bad indeed—John Efford and I had both turned out to be right.

Brian told me that the feds had attached seven conditions to their offer, all of which eroded their commitment to make annual offset payments equal to 100 percent of any reductions in equalization payments resulting from offshore revenues. Ultimately, the equalization clawback would be completely reinstated. The federal position was a despicable charade, he said, and Danny was going to show his feelings about it in the strongest possible terms: he was going to remove all Canadian flags from all provincial government buildings, and he was going to encourage everyone in Newfoundland and Labrador to do the same. How did I feel about that?

"Finally!" I bawled into my cell. "Hallelujah!" Of course, there would be a godawful backlash across the country, I said, including the risk that some Newfoundland and Labrador supporters upalong might be offended, but I agreed with the move wholeheartedly. Something dramatic was necessary, not only to show our outrage at the way the feds were treating us, but to attract the attention of the rest of Canada back to the Atlantic Accord. This, I said to myself, might be just crazy enough in the eyes of Himelfarb and the PM to work.

Brian said he hoped I wouldn't mind if Danny pre-empted the showing of my interview that night—he wanted and needed as much media as he could get. Go for it, I said. After I talked to Brian, the guy who had interviewed me for Rogers informed me they wouldn't be using my interview that night, but would show it over Christmas. They were going to interview Danny later that day. They'd been told, he whispered, that something big was up.

Danny called his news conference, and solemnly announced his protest action. Every Canadian flag flying over provincial government property would be taken down, folded up respectfully, and put away.

Danny's announcement sent the PM, the mainland media, and much of the Canadian public right off their heads. "Traitor," "separatist," and "total asshole" were some of the milder epithets flung at the premier. The "flag flap" had pulled Danny and the Atlantic Accord out of the media black pit. I pictured Alex Himelfarb on the phone to Paul Martin, who was trying to enjoy a family holiday in Morocco: "Prime Minister, we must end this war with Williams—there is no way to win it, because we are dealing with a crazy person." Anyway, I hoped that was what he was saying.

FOR ONE BRIGHT DAYLIGHT hour on Christmas Eve, Penny and I enjoyed a meandering walk over the light snow covering Signal Hill, taking in the view of the ocean and the cliffs. We often said to each other that these walks may be good for the body, but they were even better for the soul. I made no bones to anyone about how much I missed my hikes there.

That evening we had our traditional party at the house for four generations of family members on both sides. The night was as delightful as always, but my mother's deteriorating health was strikingly noticeable. I could see that her life might very likely end during the next year, and I didn't want that to happen while I was away from St. John's.

I decided that night that I would stay in Ottawa until the province either had a definite Accord deal or we knew for sure that we were not going to get a deal. My hope was that the situation would resolve itself one way or the other within the next couple of months so that I could be back in St. John's for at least several months before my ninety-three-year-old mother's death.

Between Christmas and New Year's, I received hundreds of emails, direct or forwarded, about the flag debacle. Many of them, even from Newfoundlanders on the mainland, expressed shock. Danny called me to get an update on my thoughts about the fuss.

I told him my views hadn't changed; the more I thought about it, the more right I thought the flag-lowering was. How many Canadian flags were flying above provincial government buildings or non-federal institutions in Quebec? Not that we could or should mimic that province, but the government of Canada had to realize that there would be serious consequences if they treated *any* province in the union with contempt. Yes,

Danny said, the contemptuous failure of the Winnipeg meeting had made a dramatic gesture absolutely necessary.

I said that, in the minds of the gang in the Langevin Building, the Privy Council office, and the PMO, the Accord dispute had, much to their cynical delight, withered on the vine. The Winnipeg meeting had been pure cosmetics from the start—even John Efford agreed with that. The feds had wanted to be seen as being really interested in trying to conclude a deal, but in reality they had absolutely no intention of doing so. Therefore, Paul Martin had to be made to feel all this in the gut—that his failure on the Accord had led to this action that everyone in Canada felt so keenly— because only Paul Martin and Danny could solve this. For Danny to meet with anyone else would simply be an exercise in futility; he should refuse to meet with anyone but Paul Martin ever again. The benign influence of the festive season did not prevent us from concluding that further drastic action might be necessary, even if it entailed out-and-out political war.

I spent much of New Year's Day reading emails on the Accord and the flag kafuffle. The local support for Danny's action was vast, but, for variety, there were some contrary emails from the mainland: "To paraphrase Mark Twain—In the first place God made idiots. That was for practice. Then he made Danny Williams."

One correspondent from Ontario wanted to replace Canadian democracy with tyranny to deal with the premier of Newfoundland and Labrador. "I wish the federal government would apply Joseph Stalin's simple but effective solution to the Danny Williams problem—'No man, no problem.'"

I went to a party that afternoon at which a fair number of St. John's movers and shakers were present. Several substantial businessmen, big supporters of Danny ordinarily, were not at all pleased with his action on the flag. I couldn't help recalling that many of them were the same people who had disliked Clyde Wells's position during the Meech Lake crisis. They never liked anything that threatened to ruffle the smooth surface of the local or national economy. The rightness or wrongness of the position in principle seemed to be irrelevant. Danny had told me months before that he rarely went to "high society" cocktail parties. I could see why. It was hard to enjoy a drink when you were being subjected to don't-rock-the-boat whining.

Many other people at the party, however, were delighted with Danny's actions. Some even expressed the need for Newfoundland and Labrador to consider its options in Confederation. One respectable lady said she hoped we never got a deal on that "frigging old Accord," so that Danny could use the federal affront to pull Newfoundland out of Canada altogether.

On January 4, I went to the Confederation Building for a meeting with Brian Crawley. As I parked, I listened to John Efford talking to Randy Simms on VOCM *Open Line*. I heard Efford say, "The main interest I have is to make sure that the commitment of the prime minister—that Newfoundland and Labrador can retain 100 percent of its revenues with no clawback on the equalization—is fulfilled."

"Based on what the premier is telling us," Simms remarked, "and based upon, certainly, the outline of the agreement I saw that was tabled in Winnipeg, it doesn't seem to be that we're anywhere near that."

Efford replied, "I haven't seen that agreement you're referring to, but I can assure you . . ." I sat there in the car in total disbelief. The federal minister for the province was on the public airways discussing the Accord dispute between his own government and his province. Yet he had not even seen the latest federal proposals tabled two weeks ago, which had caused the premier to lower the Canadian flag, and had led to a nation-wide storm of controversy.

And this was the person that the prime minister, in the face of objections from his own Department of Finance, some of his own MPs, and the provincial government, wanted to keep on the file as a lead minister? I couldn't help recalling a Liberal MP's remark to me, when we were discussing how his leader had continued to mishandle the Atlantic Accord battle: "It boggles my mind that out of a hundred million sperms, the one that produced Paul was the quickest."

I went up to the premier's office to meet with Brian Crawley. This was the meeting where, during our frank discussion about my year-end report on the sluggish indifference and/or incompetence in the setting up of the Ottawa office, and the waste and potential hazard such traits might represent in essential government services, Crawley replied that both he and the premier were already making phone calls, and heads were going to roll, if necessary, at high levels.

Then we got down to the latest briefing notes on the Atlantic Accord. I told Crawley that it was hard to disagree with the assessment I'd recently had from an expert on the Accord in Nova Scotia: that the negotiations were completely off the rails. I told him what I'd heard on VOCM *Open Line* that morning from our federal minister Efford, a man who was no more in this loop than Robert Mugabe of Zimbabwe was.

Crawley said he'd be getting a transcript of Efford's remarks. He agreed that the possibility of a federal-provincial meeting of minds did not look good. Moreover, the prime minister was making it clear, privately and publicly, that he would not meet with Williams as long as the Canadian flags remained down. We both thought that was okay. Our point had been made loud and clear, and in another few days Danny could find a good reason to put the flag back up.

The only real hope was a marathon meeting between the prime minister and the premier, with an agreement beforehand that it would not end until a deal was struck. This time, I added, no one should be allowed to step in if a bare-fisted brawl threatened to break out between the two; the survivor's position on the Accord should be the prize. We shook our heads at the idea that, unfortunately, my ridiculous suggestion came a bit too close to the truth of what might be needed to break the impasse.

On my way to Ottawa the next day, I got a call from Christie Meadus, who was back in the office after a Christmas holiday at home. She was very surprised at what was going on. There seemed to be, she reported, a general enthusiasm among people in the government in St. John's about the Ottawa office; people whom she had found apathetic in previous dealings were suddenly obliging and eager to help. I thought of Voltaire's observation that the British navy would shoot an admiral now and then to encourage the others. The threat from the premier's office to make heads roll seemed to have jump-started the zombies, like a bolt of lightning to Frankenstein's monster. At least for the moment.

Back in Ottawa, there was still no furniture or equipment in our new office. I worked out of my apartment and Christie worked out of hers as we waited for it to arrive. I couldn't stand the idea of leasing temporary office space again, and paying two amounts of rent.

The reaction in Ottawa to Danny's flag-lowering from advisers and supporters of Martin, especially from some Ontario members of the Liberal caucus, continued to be colourful. I was receiving comments from plugged-in political friends who reported getting an earful.

One of Martin's supporters said to a mutual Newfoundland acquaintance, "No one can have a higher opinion of your Premier Williams than I have, and I think he's a vicious little prick." An adviser to the PM apparently wanted him to send this reply to the next letter from Danny: "Dear Premier Williams. I am sitting in the bathroom adjoining my office. I have your latest demand in front of me. Soon it will be behind me." Another said that having to listen to Danny Williams's rhetoric was like "lying awake during a long stormy night listening to the shithouse door banging." A Liberal senator from central Canada stated, "What Einstein was to physics, and Gretzky was to hockey, that's what Danny Williams is to horse manure."

Although some antagonists seemed unable to rise above the level of excrement, I reminded myself of Bertrand Russell's insight that the first man who hurled a vicious, filthy insult instead of a rock was the founder of civilization.

Media reaction was divided. One national reporter asked me the following: "When Danny Williams lowered our Canadian flag, will you please tell me what was going through the poor fellow's mind, if you will pardon the overstatement?"

On the other hand, Paul Jackson of the *Calgary Sun*, in his January 2 column entitled "Flag Flap No Flop," wrote that the "Newfoundland premier deserves praise after striking a blow for Confederation." Two days later he wrote the following: "This was not an anti-patriotic act, rather the reverse, an act of sheer pluck and true patriotism. Williams has put Martin and crew on notice Newfoundland is neither going to be ignored nor pushed around anymore. More provinces should do the same . . . [Martin had] better wake up or we will have a real constitutional crisis. Newfoundland may leave, and with that, the break-up of our country will have begun."

Margaret Wente, however, issued this exhortation in the January 6 edition of the *Globe and Mail*: "Oh Danny Boy, pipe down." Then she wrote, "Angry [Newfoundland and Labrador] citizens are flooding open-line shows and threatening that . . . Newfoundland should go it alone. My grandpa had a saying for moments like this. He would have said, 'Here's your hat, what's your hurry?'"

According to Wente, Newfoundlanders' "sense of victimhood is unmatched." Danny Williams, she said, "reminds me of a deadbeat brother-in-law who's hit you up for money a few times too often. He's been sleeping on your couch for years, and now he's got the nerve to complain that it's too lumpy . . . Those of us not blessed to be born on the Rock have sent countless cakes its way in the form of equalization payments, pogey, and various hare-brained make-work schemes . . . In return, the surly islanders have blamed us for everything."

She went on to state that rural Newfoundland was "probably the most vast and scenic welfare ghetto in the world." She wished Danny Williams "would explain why it's a good idea to keep picking the pockets of Chinese dry cleaners and Korean variety-store owners [in Scarborough, Ontario] who work 90 hours a week in order to keep subsidizing the people who live in Carbonear, no matter how quaint and picturesque they are."

She ended her column with an offer to strike a deal with the people of the Rock: "You can keep all the oil and gas revenues. And you can pay us back all the money we've sent you since you joined Confederation. Fair enough? I thought not."

Even Paul Martin had to take issue with Wente's simple-minded abuse. He put out a statement registering his "total disagreement," condemning her remarks and stating his desire to reach a final deal on the offshore oil and see "the people of [Newfoundland and Labrador] succeed and prosper . . . It's not welfare. It's the right thing to do."

The actual reaching of a final deal seemed more problematical than ever, though. Danny warned that the Canadian flag would not fly over provincial buildings until Paul Martin agreed to a meeting on the Accord. At the same time, the prime minister's office was saying that the Maple Leaf had to be hoisted over government offices again before any substantive talks could resume.

A couple days after Wente's column, Edward Greenspon, editor-in-chief of the *Globe and Mail*, published a letter from the editor: "This has been the week of the angry email," he said. "In her take-no-prisoners style, Peggy [Margaret Wente] apparently gave offence to a record number of readers for a single column. By yesterday afternoon, we had been inundated with 900 emails."

> Mr. Williams . . . has been a regular visitor to the *Globe and Mail* in recent months, presenting his case to the editorial board twice—most recently this past Tuesday.
>
> We have supported Mr. Williams in his argument that Paul Martin is honour-bound to abide by his election equalization commitment, an intervention that some say persuaded Ottawa to remain at the bargaining table and sweeten its offer. We have condemned Mr. Williams for some of his more histrionic tactics, including his flag caper.

Not all Ontario commentators disagreed with Danny's "flag caper." The January 7 edition of the *Ottawa Citizen* contained two diametrically opposed opinions. The editorial was against: "Newfoundland and Labrador Premier Danny Williams may be right that his province's equalization payments shouldn't be linked to its oil revenues, but his fiddling with the Canadian flag has been abhorrent . . . His abuse of the Canadian flag, a symbol of our country and our nation, not of Mr. Martin's government, is odious. The prime minister is right to have nothing to do with Mr. Williams until the Maple Leaf is flying again over St. John's."

Susan Riley, however, wrote the following in her column: "Maybe I have a recessive Newfoundland gene or something, but I am instinctively behind Premier Danny Williams in his ongoing fight with the federal government over resources—the stormy denunciations, the dramatic departures, the flag-lowerings, everything."

Early in January, as part of our after-hours reconnoitring among influential opinion-mongers, Newfoundlander Herb Davis and I decided to go to a reputed watering hole of the famous and powerful in Ottawa, D'Arcy Magee's. Penny had just arrived in Ottawa on business, and she and Herb's companion, Chantal, agreed to go with us.

The place was exceedingly crowded and loud. The average age of the patrons appeared to be about twenty-three. All the men seemed to be wearing identical dark blue suits, giving the place the appearance of the South Korean parliament. Sparking conversations with anyone turned out to be a lost cause. We couldn't hear ourselves speak to one another.

Everyone there, male or female, was glancing repeatedly over the shoulder of whoever was facing them, and all had expressions of either expectancy or disappointment on their faces. The expectancy resulted from the hope of seeing someone important. The disappointment resulted from seeing no one more important than themselves. The four of us had a great laugh over what a failure this brilliant reconnoitring adventure of Herb's and mine turned out to be.

On January 10, I emailed Brian Crawley a copy of the *Hill Times* that contained a lucid article by Newfoundlander Tim Powers on the province's position on the Accord. It was another reminder of the value of intelligent and knowledgeable Newfoundlanders everywhere.

Brian called to confirm that the Canadian flag was going back up that day. This would clear the way for a meeting between the premier and the prime minister. Danny had written to Paul Martin a week earlier about the discussions leading up to the abortive Winnipeg get-together. The feeling in the premier's office was that the feds were now likely to come back with a proposal that would meet our demands partway, but still leave Danny in a position where he had to refuse on principle. The mood was strong that no deal was likely on the Accord dispute.

That night, Danny was appearing on Don Newman's show, *Politics*, on CBC television. The media had been using this sound bite from the premier: "We're not a have-not province. We're a keep-not province. We have it; we're just not allowed to keep it." The message was powerful and novel, yet simple. I anticipated more of the same from the Newman interview.

On camera that night, the premier looked very stiff. His face seemed, not earnest, serious, and determined, as he no doubt intended, but angry, if not downright surly. His explanation of the province's position on the Accord, I thought, would have sounded convoluted to the everyday viewer, and it was all over the lot—the opposite of simple and understandable. Don Newman was unusually testy, as if he was fed up with Williams's foolishness.

Several Newfoundlanders called to offer their analysis of Danny's performance, which were similar to mine. Herb Davis suggested that Danny needed to boil down to a couple of clear sentences exactly what Newfoundland and Labrador wanted. He'd been talking to the publisher of an Ottawa journal, who told him that although he'd tried valiantly, he simply could not understand precisely what Danny and his province wanted.

I thought about those reactions long and hard before calling Brian Crawley with my final assessment. My conclusion was that those reactions were largely irrelevant to our ultimate end. Our supporters were with us on Newfoundland and Labrador's getting a fair deal from our offshore resources, whether or not they fully comprehended the complexities. The real question was what the impact of Danny's performance had been on the prime minister and his crew.

If Danny won his war with them, the public relations with our supporters and even the general population would take care of themselves. And I believed that the impact on the PMO was a good one. Danny's explanation of our position did not have to be spelled out for them.

By now, the prime minister and his top advisers knew all the complicated issues inside out. The important thing was that the image presented by Danny reinforced the message that they were dealing with an angry and aggressive premier who would be a continuing nightmare to Martin as long as the dispute continued. Sure, Williams had put the flag back up, but what in God's name might the madman do next?

I conveyed these sentiments to the premier's office along with a suggestion that now might be the time for Danny to throw the feds a lifeline, get that final meeting going with the prime minister. On the basis of recent conversations in the capital, I felt that Paul Martin did indeed want to solve this thing desperately, and that the flag brouhaha had intensified his desire to put the lunacy behind him.

But lots of commentators thought that the flag caper would not redound to our benefit. Premier Canadian columnist Jeffrey Simpson, who always displayed a complete understanding of all sides of the Accord issues, headlined his column in the *Globe and Mail* of January 11 "Why the Flag Stunt Hurt Newfoundland." In it, he wrote the following:

> Yesterday, the typically unrepentant Premier insisted that the flag-lowering had got the attention of Canadians, who, in turn, made sure Newfoundland's grievances got Ottawa's attention. Complete baloney.
>
> If anything, the stunt hardened attitudes against Newfoundland, and those attitudes will do the province no good in the future.

Then, after an insightful analysis of the federal and provincial sides, Simpson concluded, "Those who defend Newfoundland's essential position argue that the province has one chance, and only one, to improve significantly its economic standing. The offshore is that chance . . . The flag stunt, an insufferable insult, made the making of that case harder."

On January 13, Martin finally responded to Williams's letter—ten days later. The PM was calm and deliberate and hard-nosed; he stuck to the federal proposals already made. The tone of the letter was remarkably free of rancour under the circumstances—not a word about flags. There was a touch of "you've-hurt-my-feelings" in his missive: "Since the Atlantic Accord was originally signed over 20 years ago, I am the first Prime Minister that has been willing to make such a commitment to your province and I have honoured it in the proposal that we have provided." Martin assured Williams that he was, of course, prepared to meet with him, and despite his apparently unbending attitude earlier in the letter, the conclusion sounded as though he was ready to be flexible: "I look forward to further discussions . . . to arrive at an agreement on new offshore arrangements." That conciliatory note reminded me of a warning from an astute Ottawa observer, given when the feds had appeared to be agreeable once before. "Tell Danny," he said, "to remember that federal-provincial relations often consist of the PMO saying 'nice doggie, nice doggie' until they can find a rock."

Soon after Martin's letter reached the premier, I received an email from Brian Crawley saying that Danny was asking for a definitive meeting with the prime minister. Then, because life was still going on, I went to a meeting with Tom Graham, the director of provincial Intergovernmental Affairs who was responsible for 5 Wing Goose Bay.

We had a good long talk, which included a discussion of whether a federal-provincial Crown corporation or development corporation to umbrella the issues was necessary, or whether a provincial-only corporation would be better. We were both of the firm opinion that the time for action had arrived. We wished each other luck on that: despite the involvement of powerful people at the highest levels, a solid interest in actually doing something regarding 5 Wing seemed to be sorely lacking in the Department of National Defence.

Shortly afterwards, Brian Crawley phoned to say that Paul Martin and Danny Williams had agreed to meet in Ottawa on January 28. That was great news, but the fact that the PM had agreed to meet with alacrity was even better news. It showed just how eager the federal side was to solve the impasse. Despite that, though, the premier's office found it hard to be optimistic that a deal would be struck at the meeting. Danny was going to insist that Martin keep his word 100 percent; the PMO, the Department of Finance and the Privy Council office were simply not prepared to do that.

The PMO was moaning that Martin was having nightmares over potential damage to the federation if he acquiesced fully to Danny's demands; there continued to be a lot of inside grumbling from some provinces, notably Ontario. This was the same cock and bull I'd been hearing all along. Why was no one worried about the damage done to the federation by the separate, asymmetrical, one-sided, bilateral deals forever being made by the feds with Quebec? It was all rubbish. The PM's "worried about damage to the federation" red herring reminded me of Samuel Johnson's pronouncement that resorting to an argument from patriotism was the last refuge of the scoundrel.

Meanwhile, the media were reporting that Nova Scotia was zeroing in on an Accord agreement with the feds. A Canadian Press story on January 12 contained the following: "Ottawa and Nova Scotia are close to a deal on sharing off-shore energy revenues—an agreement that would leave Newfoundland still on the sidelines. Premier John Hamm emerged Wednesday from a full-day meeting with the federal Finance Minister Ralph Goodale sounding confident that a long-awaited deal will be reached within the next few weeks . . . Goodale sounded equally upbeat." I recalled the warning about the nice doggie and the rock.

I had believed that Premier Hamm was determined to stick stalwartly with us to the bitter end. He had started the Accord ball rolling with Ottawa in the first place, and I thought that he was too honourable to make a unilateral deal at this stage, although my faith was weakened somewhat by a strong hint from him after his meeting with Goodale that we were now on our own: "What I have been able to achieve will be useful to Premier Williams."

The apparent success of the feds' divide-and-rule tactic since the flag fuss worried Danny Williams and Loyola Sullivan. Despite being on vacation outside Canada, Danny telephoned Hamm and spoke to him at length. The day after the Goodale-Hamm announcement, Sullivan had a long meeting with Nova Scotia's Cecil Clarke.

Later, despite the gloomy private prognosis in St. John's, Sullivan stated publicly that he was confident a deal between Newfoundland and Labrador and Ottawa could be achieved, provided John Efford stayed out of it. "He has been a detriment to getting a deal," Sullivan told CP. "I think we would be well served if Mr. Efford went away and hid until we got a deal because every time he opens his mouth, he complicates it. He doesn't understand it."

That was frightening to read. Brian Crawley had just mentioned on the phone to me that he'd heard John Efford was going on the *Open Line* show in St. John's the next morning. But the next day a miracle occurred: Efford did no damage on the show. In fact, I got an email that night from Brian saying there was a positive new development on the Accord. He would call me in the morning.

Early the next morning, I went to our new offices to observe what was going ahead there. Christie Meadus was already in the empty rooms, giving instructions to a technician. Brian Crawley called. Alex Himelfarb and Danny Williams had talked. Now Crawley and Loyola Sullivan were going to Toronto, confidentially, to meet with Himelfarb and narrow down the tangly issues the prime minister and Premier Williams were going to tackle on January 28.

Rollie Martin contacted me to give his views on what was going on with the Accord. In passing, he mentioned that he'd heard Loyola Hearn make an on-air call for a meeting of Newfoundland and Labrador MPs and senators to discuss the Atlantic Accord dispute. Hearn believed that together they could make an impact, and that the provincial government's representative in Ottawa, Bill Rowe, should spearhead the effort. I laughed. I had heard the same story on VOCM days before, I told Rollie, and I was touched by Hearn's new, unshakable faith in me as a miracle worker. But no, this Accord mess was a job for the super-pols.

The main reason for Rollie's call was to tell me that he was writing an article for a national newspaper on the Accord. He wanted to discuss a few issues with me first. I told Rollie I was delighted, and would do whatever I could to help. What a boon it was to have Newfoundlanders like him, not only willing to use their expertise to help the province, but eager to put their respected opinion out in the national public domain.

Sheila Copps, former MP, Cabinet minister, and deputy prime minister, might not have been a Newfoundlander, but she was the next best thing, as she disclosed in her column in the *National Post* on January 14: she'd married a Newfoundlander more than a decade ago. She wrote a glowing tribute to Newfoundland and Newfoundlanders, jumped on Margaret Wente for comments that "were akin to racial stereotyping," and concluded with this: "Newfoundland has long gotten the short end of the Canadian stick. It's time for the carrot. If Danny Williams had to resort to flag-lowering, maybe we should get beyond histrionics and find out why the only province that surrendered its nationhood to become part of Canada is having second thoughts."

Newfoundlander Rex Murphy, in his column in the *Globe and Mail* on January 15, made Margaret Wente look like an intellectual pygmy tricked out in giant's garments. On the question of the province's contributions to and from Canada, he wrote the following for his national readership: "As for the money being poured into Newfoundland while we guzzle cod tongues and stare out at the scenic bay, keep in mind the billion dollars a year going 'outward' from Churchill Falls. Churchill Falls alone nullifies the equalization 'debt.'"

By January 18, Margaret Wente was writing in the *Globe*—half-heartedly *mea culpa*—that in the two weeks since she had written her notorious column, she had heard from more than two thousand Newfoundlanders. Responses ranged from basic—"You, my dear, are stun as me arse"; "You should be slapped with a cod and drenched in Screech"—to thoughtful: "Racist remarks like yours about Newfoundland can only be emitted from a very sad, unhappy, uninformed and bitter person. At least that is what I tell my kids when they ask why you wrote such hurtful things about the place that they love."

One morning, just after six o'clock, I was listening to the Ottawa CBC morning show, when Newfoundland writer Kevin Major came on. They interviewed him from St. John's about the flag flap and the current status of the Atlantic Accord. He made a very articulate case for the inequities our province had suffered since joining Confederation.

A Newfoundlander in Washington, DC, Kevin McCann, set up a website a few days after the flag-lowering. It contained a letter that people could send to the PM, urging him to make the deal allowing the province to keep 100 percent of its offshore revenues. He told the media that by mid-January more than twenty thousand people had forwarded the letter to Martin, and nearly half of them were sent from outside Newfoundland and Labrador.

This kind of visible and audible support inside and outside the province, from natives and those with a fellow-feeling for the cause, could be felt in Ottawa as it made an impact on the Canadian public, boosting our position and morale tremendously.

Newfoundlanders and Labradorians living outside the province who supported the effort out of the public eye had a terrific effect as well. All of us on the provincial side were extraordinarily aware of that throughout the negotiations, and Danny Williams acknowledged it at a news conference late in January 2005, when he thanked the "expatriate Newfoundlanders and Labradorians who stood strong behind their home province." Their support, said Williams, was "unflappable and more important than you all will ever know."

— CHAPTER ELEVEN —

With A Little Help From Our Friends

MANY NEWFOUNDLANDERS AND LABRADORIANS I met in Ottawa would mention right from the start their great interest in helping their home province in the Atlantic Accord battle. This was so much the case that one mainlander, listening to a bunch of us gabbing after we'd just met, said this: "God I wish I was a Newfoundlander. Every Newfoundlander belongs. They all want to increase the well-being of the homeland. Everybody is automatically a member of the tribe. I'd love to be part of that."

I heard about Newfoundlanders' activities and advocacy and solidarity regarding our province all the time, and how much they advanced its various causes. I regret I don't have the space to mention them all, but in this chapter I'm going to talk about a few of the compatriots who made a special contribution to the well-being of our province in the nation's capital.

WHEN I ARRIVED IN Ottawa, I rediscovered that Newfoundlander Max Keeping was one of the most celebrated names in the region. Max was anchor of the *News at Six* and vice-president of news at CTV Ottawa—one of the longest-serving suppertime news anchors, who enjoyed some of the highest viewer ratings anywhere. I was glad when he called. He wanted to arrange an interview about the public scrap that was emerging between Premier Danny Williams and Prime Minister Paul Martin. I was delighted to learn from him that, after announcing on-air the year before that he'd been diagnosed with prostate cancer, he was making a full recovery.

I'd first known Max more than forty years ago, when he'd worked with various St. John's media before moving to Halifax and then to Ottawa to continue his work in radio and television. By 1972, he had become news anchor for television station CJOH in Ottawa. I renewed our acquaintance during the 1980s, when he suggested I become a regular commentator on Mike Duffy's national public affairs program.

Max had a fling away from journalism. He'd gone back to Newfoundland for the federal election in the fall of 1972 to run in the riding of Burin–Burgeo, which contained his birthplace of Grand Bank, as a Progressive Conservative. Max garnered an amazing twenty-five percent of the votes in his run against the Liberal incumbent (and Cabinet minister), the invincible Don Jamieson.

Max's television and charity work made him a celebrity. One estimate credited him with being behind more than a hundred million dollars in charitable donations in the Ottawa area, resulting from a mind-boggling two hundred personal appearances a year on behalf of charities, service groups, neighbourhood associations, and schools.

Little wonder that he was made a member of both the Order of Ontario and the Order of Canada, had the new wing of a children's hospital named after him, received a Gemini Award, was inducted into the Canadian Association of Broadcasters' Hall of Fame, was presented with the keys to the City of Ottawa, and received an honorary doctorate from the University of Ottawa.

I drove out to television station CJOH on Merivale Road to do the interview with Max for broadcast on Thanksgiving Day. When I approached the receptionist in the lobby, I was questioned and closely scrutinized. Then I was sent over to the security desk for similar treatment.

It seemed a bit excessive, until I remembered later, talking with Max, that they had a good reason for such vigilance.

Max came out wearing his trademark grin, his hand outstretched and, as one Newfoundlander will do to another, greeted me like a long-lost buddy. My bona fides established, the receptionist and security guard smiled and waved us inside.

I told Max that the drive out to CJOH on Merivale had made me home-sick because it reminded me so much of driving out Freshwater and Kenmount to VOCM—mile after mile of back-to-back strip malls. We chuckled at the comparison, but agreed that Merivale was impressively larger and longer.

Max brought me into the makeup room, and he soon had the female makeup artist there in stitches, describing the Newfoundland restaurant in Ottawa, "owned and operated by a man from China." Max's take on a restaurant run by a Chinese man who'd never been to Newfoundland, but who was serving up first-rate salt fish, brewis, scrunchions, seal flippers, Jiggs' dinners, cods tongues, moose, bakeapples, turrs, and other subtle Newfoundland delicacies nearly brought the makeup woman to her knees.

When she finished doing us up, I marvelled at how she had managed to turn two sow's ears into a couple of silk purses. That was true, Max said—ever since he'd got cancer, they'd been piling the makeup on him to cover up the ravages of chemotherapy, and viewers kept saying to him, "Max, you never looked better."

We did our interview, in which I answered Max's questions—ones that clearly defined the issues between the province and the federal govern-ment on the Atlantic Accord. The interview became rather spirited. Max has the great skill of being able to focus on important points, and bring out fully alive responses from his guests. For days after the interview appeared on TV, acquaintances would say "Saw you on with Max," and express their sympathy with Newfoundland and Labrador's position on the Accord.

As we walked out to the lobby after the interview, Max passed me my security tag so that I could get out of the building. I mentioned the extraordinarily tight security at the entrance, and he nodded. Less than ten years ago a colleague had been shot in front of the building.

On August 1, 1995, a man—later diagnosed as a paranoid schizophrenic—lurked in the CJOH parking lot waiting for a face he recognized from the media. Brian Smith, a former NHLer turned celebrated CJOH sportscaster, rushed out the door after his evening sportscast to go to a charity banquet for the Children's Wish Foundation. With a precision that astonished investigators, Jeffrey Arenburg followed the orders from the voices inside his skull and shot Smith in the head with a twenty-two-calibre rifle. Smith died in hospital the next day.

The shooter had not singled Smith out for death. It might easily have been any of the other media personalities in the building: Arenburg had been thrown out of the Ottawa press club three times before the shooting for demanding to see people on his "list." Max, who had hired "Smitty" back in the early '70s, told me it was pure chance that his sportscaster was the first out the door that day. Usually, Max's female news partner stepped out into the parking lot before everyone else. On that sad evening, one person's tragic death was another person's chance survival.

The killer was sent to a mental hospital. Max told me that he had come to forgive the murderer because, owing to the man's psychosis, he wasn't responsible for the terrible tragedy.

A year or so after that conversation with Max in 2004, I would read that the killer had been released from the mental hospital with no restrictions on his freedom. In 2007, he was arrested for assaulting a US border guard, and sentenced to two years in an American prison.

Where Smith's killer might be, exactly, when I last enquired, or what he might be contemplating doing next, no one seemed to know. Some Ottawa media people worry about the safety of Max and his colleagues.

Meanwhile, Max Keeping kept directing and delivering the news and raising money for charity. He was a speaker at the Affinity Newfoundland and Labrador Memorial University alumni dinner I attended in Ottawa, and inadvertently referred to me as Bill "Roberts" before correcting himself. He'd been thinking back to the last days of Joey Smallwood's government, when Ed Roberts and I had teamed up to resist Joey's attempts to put money into a couple more hare-brained schemes. Roberts and I became so indistinguishable in Joey's eyes—Ed Rowe? Bill Roberts?—that, in order not to mix up our names as Max had done, he began to refer to us jointly as one entity, the Bobbsey Twins.

It was hard not to have a great laugh in Max's company. And it was harder again to overestimate the contribution of that proud Newfoundlander to the causes of his compatriots in the nation's capital, and to the province of Newfoundland and Labrador.

MY OPTIMISM WAS BUOYED by how many Newfoundlanders and Labradorians in Ottawa contacted me right off the bat with offers to help with the Atlantic Accord. It was like having a huge family up there, eager to pitch in.

A case in point was Herb Davis. He got in touch with me as soon as I arrived, with a spontaneous offer to lend a hand. I'd known Herb when he'd lived in St. John's, and I had a warm spot in my heart for his father, the late Newfoundland activist Walter Davis.

Walter and I had talked many times, often on the radio, about his life-long struggle against appalling injustices, murderous conflicts, and disease and deprivation at home and around the world. What endeared me to Walter most was that he had mortgaged his home to run as a Tory against Joey Smallwood's hand-picked candidate in a federal election. I knew that the only thing protecting Tories from Joey's Liberals in the riding Walter ran in was the Small Game Act. Not surprisingly, Walter lost his election. But his selfless, courageous and, some might argue, foolhardy, act was something I would come to admire greatly for its contribution to democracy in our province in the teeth of lopsided odds.

In Ottawa, Herb talked about his father, and the things they'd done together in his youth. Those ranged from the inspiring to the humorous. He had travelled the coast of Newfoundland and Labrador with Walter on board the MV *Christmas Seal* during the battle against tuberculosis. And on hot summer days, while other kids swam or played ball, he'd stood with

Walter on the side of the Trans-Canada Highway holding up a placard which advocated, "Children, drink your milk. It's good for you."

Herb had an excellent knowledge of our province, augmented by his earlier career with CBC's *Fisheries Broadcast* and *Land and Sea*. He recalled an attempt back then by the CBC brass in Toronto to cancel the *Fisheries Broadcast* because, they argued, it was "ghetto broadcasting."

We talked nearly every day, in person or by phone. Herb was very familiar with Ottawa, and had many contacts. He was always on the move all over the capital city region, finding out what people, high and low, were thinking. As a result, he was an unfailing source of information, opinion, and advice, especially on the Atlantic Accord. And it was all leavened with good humour.

Once I was at a meeting in Ottawa with Danny Williams and John Hamm, and there was some gloominess in the room over the difficulty in getting our position on the Accord across to the Canadian public. I'd been among those urging greater creativity in keeping our story in the media. But it wasn't all bad, I told the premiers: Fellow Newfoundlander Herb Davis had been talking to the man who rang the bell at the top of the Peace Tower on Parliament Hill. The man in the tower was right behind Williams and Hamm on the Accord, Herb had said, "and you can't get any higher up than that." We all had a little laugh. It was foolishness, yes, but the gloom lifted, and we went on with our serious business with a lighter perspective.

Our concern about communicating the province's position clearly and convincingly was a legitimate one. I told Danny that the main problem Newfoundlanders like Herb and others who moved about trying to put our case across to fellow Canadians had was that it was hard to get a grip on precisely what that position was. A lot of people in Ottawa from the province, and many mainlanders who sympathized with Danny Williams in his battle with the Martin government, were perturbed by the constant federal counter-argument that Danny wanted to have his cake and to eat it too; that he wanted to go on receiving equalization even after our province became one of the richest in Canada from offshore oil revenues.

Newfoundlanders like Herb wanted to have a good, short, clear statement of the province's position on the Accord, that they could use in their conversations with other Canadians. That was the only demand that Herb ever made of me but, as I told him, it was a huge one.

The equalization formula was complicated enough in and of itself, but equalization plus the clawback plus the offset of the clawback for royalties received from the non-renewable offshore resources plus various time frames for it all, including scenarios for fluctuating crude oil prices, was far too hellishly complex for anyone who had a life outside of federal-provincial financial relations to even contemplate, let alone master. The damn thing was convoluted enough to warm the heart of the most sadistic federal economist. And assuming you did come to understand some of it by diligent study, any attempt to explain the basic concepts to normal human beings—as I once tried to do—caused their eyes to glaze over and roll back in their heads.

We seized upon the reasonable notion that no matter how rich our province became from the offshore oil, we were so saddled with an enormous debt from having been prevented from realizing our economic potential in Confederation—some ten billion dollars and more, twice as high as the national average for provinces per capita—that we had to be allowed to use our short-lived non-renewable resources to reduce it. That meant stopping the clawback of equalization until we had lowered our public debt to the average provincial level. Herb and I both found that a lot of people comprehended that idea clearly, and found it fair and reasonable.

Meanwhile, Herb arranged a meeting between me and a man who, in years past, had held some mysterious job in Ottawa with the Newfoundland government that may have been similar to my own. Herb thought his painful experience might be instructive for me.

The man was blunt and candid. He told me he'd spent some three and a half years as the Newfoundland and Labrador government's person in Ottawa with a mandate to stimulate economic and business activity for the province. Apparently, he'd been appointed by the provincial Liberal minister for Industry and Trade, Chuck Furey. He described to me his hectic activity on behalf of the government, trying to drum up business for the province. And he'd been quite pleased with the impact he was making. All his hard work had been reported to the minister's office in St. John's, and fully documented. Then his minister changed.

Furey was appointed to another portfolio; his new minister was Judy Foote. She summoned him to St. John's for a meeting. The man told me she looked at him skeptically for a long time from behind her big desk and finally asked, her words dripping with suspicion and doubt, "What is it that you do up there in Ottawa, exactly?"

Her attitude knocked the wind out of the guy. Obviously, he said, she hadn't bothered to confer with her predecessor, or look at the extensive files documenting his work. Or, if she had done either, she was not impressed. After that, he said, his telephone would be cut off from time to time by the phone company for non-payment, and some months he'd receive complaints from the landlord that the rent for his Ottawa office had not been paid. Finally, after three and a half years of solid work on behalf of the province, he said, he'd had enough. He quit his thankless, unappreciated job.

His opinion of my new position in Ottawa, based on his own experience, was that it would not work. To begin with, just dealing effectively with the public service in St. John's from Ottawa was impossible. And the normal situation in Newfoundland and Labrador was one big crisis after another, which preoccupied politicians and bureaucrats and made it difficult for someone up here to even get a look in.

When he had finished, I explained that there were essential differences between his former position and mine. The premier himself, not just one of his ministers, had created my position, and since I was answerable only to Danny as a deputy minister in the premier's office, it had the full clout of the premier's office behind it, and blahdy blahdy blah.

When I finished my spiel, and asked him what he thought, he opined that the role I had described, in contrast to his, sounded like it might work. Privately, I found that funny because his problems with the provincial bureaucracy were the same as mine. In fact, the man was eerily prescient.

His description of bureaucrats back in St. John's failing to pay the bills would actually apply to me as well. I thanked Herb for arranging the get-together. It was more sobering to me than he could realize. My exchange with a former provincial representative in Ottawa showed that you had to be constantly alert to one brutal reality in this racket: governments might change, but the bureaucracy remained the same.

Because Herb Davis was such a help in Ottawa in enlisting support for Danny Williams's Accord battle, I would find it ironic to watch what happened to Herb later at the hands of the premier. In the October 2008 federal election, Herb would decide to run for Stephen Harper's Conservatives. As Opposition leader, Harper had been a big ally of Williams in the Accord battle. Herb would run in Random–Burin–St. George's, against Liberal candidate Judy Foote.

He was a good candidate with broad support. Even a former federal Cabinet minister in Jean Chrétien's Liberal government, retired MP David Kilgour, supported him with a letter to the *Coaster*, a weekly newspaper in southern Newfoundland, urging people in the riding to vote for Herb. Kilgour said Davis was knowledgeable and compassionate, and stood a good chance of making it into Harper's Cabinet.

Herb's battle against a superb, experienced Liberal candidate like Judy Foote in that riding would have been uphill at the best of times. But this time, of course, Danny Williams's "Anything But Conservative" campaign against Stephen Harper and the federal Conservatives was in full swing, and at least partly as a result of that ABC campaign, Herb would lose the election. Not that Herb was looking for gratitude, but he certainly found out that there was no gratitude in politics. All is fair in love and war, and candidates for public office quickly discover that politics is both love and war by other means.

TIM POWERS WAS ANOTHER Newfoundlander who contacted me when I first arrived in Ottawa, and he also wanted to meet to discuss what he could do to help the province with the Accord. Tim was only in his mid-thirties, but he was already a vice-president of Summa Communications, after a packed career in Canadian politics acting as an adviser to federal Cabinet ministers (including cousin John Crosbie) and to national party leaders, and as an Aboriginal affairs negotiator.

Tim's opinions were influential in Ottawa. He was all over the media as a Conservative commentator, frequently on CBC with Don Newman or on CTV with Mike Duffy. I used to especially enjoy seeing him tearing strips off Martin's director of communications, Scott Reid, with his wry humour. His regular columns in the *Hill Times* were a fount of information and chuckles. And Tim's point of view could strike any time of the day.

I turned the radio on about six-thirty one morning and recognized the voice. A debate was going on between Tim and a couple of other guys over the same-sex marriage legislation then coming before the House of Commons. One of the speakers said, in near panic, that legalizing gay marriages was going to lead to polygamy—what would keep the law from allowing men to have two or three wives? He shuddered to contemplate what his dear mother would think. Whereupon bachelor Tim replied, "The thought of me having two wives is not a big problem with my mother. She'd be delighted if I had one wife." It was hard to take the other guy's arguments seriously after that.

Tim told me he got back to Newfoundland and Labrador eight or ten times a year, to keep in touch with family and friends and for business reasons. Still homesick after all these years, he read the *St. John's Telegram* and VOCM's website daily.

Tim Powers's interest and knowledge and his desire to contribute, backed up by his experience and influence in Ottawa, made him a great help in our efforts to enlist public opinion while we tried to wring a reasonable deal out of the feds on the Atlantic Accord.

THE VERY DAY I was appointed as provincial representative, I received a call from Mark Watton, a young Newfoundlander in the prime minister's office, in charge of the Atlantic desk. He wanted me to get together with him when I arrived in Ottawa. When I asked around the premier's office about him, I quickly discovered that he was highly thought of. He may have been a Liberal partisan, but Danny and his staff considered Mark a reliable straight-shooter whose judgment was good, and who was able to come up with solutions to impasses between the two leaders' offices.

There was real disappointment in the premier's office when, very shortly after his call to me, Mark was tapped to become chief of staff of a minister of State (Families and Caregivers). This was no doubt a promotion for Mark, but Brian Crawley feared we had lost a liaison with clout and influence in the PMO. I would discover that his fear was well founded.

Still, I wanted to meet with Mark, so a few weeks later I trundled off to his office at ten o'clock one morning for a gab. Easier said than done. Of all the offices—including those of MPs, senators, deputy ministers, military brass, and ministers—I visited in Ottawa, this one was the hardest to get into. The security rigmarole was incredible. Henry Kissinger once quipped that the reason university politics are so vicious is that the stakes are so low. He might have added that the reason security was so tight at this ministry was that its importance to terrorists was so low.

Then it occurred to me that the reason for such precautions must have something to do with the department's function—dealing with families and caregivers. After phone calls and electronic searches, a security officer was finally sent down to accompany my ascent to the office upstairs.

Mark Watton was in a small cubicle with six-foot-high walls in a room containing other personnel and piled-up stacks of documents. Temporary quarters, he explained, shaking hands. He was gazing at a computer screen containing his name and the amount of ten dollars. This was his expense claim, a taxi fare, and it was open to full public scrutiny on the Internet—a federal attempt at transparency in the wake of the sponsorship scandal.

As I sat down, Mark said that in the interests of full disclosure he should tell me that he couldn't stand open-line or call-in shows where callers could say anything they liked about anything and anyone without having to identify themselves. I replied that I'd heard that complaint before, especially from aides for the powerful political elite, who hated the idea of some lowly anonymous citizen publicly bringing up blunders and skulduggeries that the bigwigs had hoped were safely buried. We laughed and agreed to disagree. Then we chatted away usefully for an hour and a half.

Mark mentioned that he was still called upon from time to time to give advice to the prime minister, but I couldn't help thinking that if he had actually been in the PMO as an adviser during these crucial months, a fair amount of the grief between Danny and Paul might have been avoided.

After his years in Ottawa in senior posts in the offices of ministers and the prime minister, Mark went off to Dalhousie's law school, graduating in 2008 with a specialty in maritime law. Based on my experience during the Accord battle, he will continue to make a large contribution in high-level politics to the province and the nation.

JOHN FRECKER WAS ANOTHER example of interested and helpful Newfoundlanders in Ottawa. He was the son of a colleague of mine, Dr. Alain Frecker, a minister in Joey Smallwood's Cabinet in the 1960s. John had kicked over the old man's traces early. One of my first memories of him was from around 1969–70, when, as a student at Memorial University, he led a big group of students to the Confederation Building, to demonstrate against the Smallwood government. They claimed it was fascist, and needed to be toppled. This "fascist" government had built the new university, and tuition was heavily subsidized by the government.

Ed Roberts and I were government ministers at the time, and John singled the two of us out by name as the ones they were going to concentrate on defeating no matter how long it took. That was because, if I remember correctly, we two young men had betrayed the youth of the province by joining that untrustworthy over-thirty gang.

Alas for John, though, when Joey's government was, in fact, defeated a couple of years later: Ed Roberts and I were among the handful of Liberals who managed to get re-elected. John and I shared some amusing reminiscences about those days when we'd meet in Ottawa.

John's tendency, apparently unmellowed by age, to compare relatively small, local acts of authoritarianism to the atrocities of true fascists abroad, landed him in difficulty on the mainland. A lawyer, John became deputy chair of the Immigration and Refugee Board during the '90s. In September 1997, mocking an argument over restructuring policies at the Toronto office, he uttered "Sieg Heil!" and gave a Nazi salute.

Ten months later, board member Jeanette Goldman, a Holocaust survivor, launched an official complaint, and John apologized to her. Goldman, however, was dissatisfied with an individual apology, and Jewish organizations expressed concern about the lack of appropriate process. A third-party investigation was deemed necessary. B'nai B'rith Canada, Jewish Canada's leading advocacy and human rights organization, called upon the Immigration and Refugee Board and the investigator to broaden the scope of the report and make all findings and recommendations public.

The investigation released a report on October 1, 1998. It concluded that John Frecker's actions were "neither racially motivated nor were they symptomatic of a racist environment." It added, however, that Frecker's actions, even if done in jest, were offensive to more than one individual and recommended that Frecker apologize to the entire Toronto regional personnel of the board.

Frecker apologized. "For a person in my position to parody a Nazi situation, even if it is an ironic reply to the suggestion that Board management was acting in a Stalinist fashion, was clearly wrong. I am sorry for any pain my words have caused to anyone who may have taken my comments as trivializing Nazi atrocities in the Holocaust."

Gay and lesbian organizations now entered the fray, criticizing the report because its mandate didn't include allegations of homophobia. The chair of B'nai B'rith's board made the following statement: "We would concur with the conclusion of the investigation that this one incident was not symptomatic of anything untoward in the organization. However, the way it was handled and the further complaints of anti-Semitism and homophobia are symptoms of what may be bias in the organization. Such allegations deserve an independent, public and thorough investigation of the board and its management."

Talk about it hitting the fan. A year-long nightmare for John Frecker. And there was no one of my acquaintance less prejudiced and more disposed toward equality and human rights than John. No doubt he learned the hard way that the kind of lampooning that had gone over so well when he compared Joey to Hitler and Stalin as a student in the '60s in St. John's could put your nuts squarely in the wringer in '90s Toronto.

When I got together with John in Ottawa, he was working as a legal policy and management consultant, having served as executive director of the Ottawa Chamber Music Society and as a commissioner with the Law Reform Commission of Canada. To have a Newfoundlander of his intelligence and experience, some of it learned in the merciless school of hard knocks, available for advice and dedicated to the advancement of his home province was a great boon to Newfoundland and Labrador's efforts in Ottawa.

WHEN I ARRIVED IN Ottawa, Heidi Bonnell was an executive with Hill & Knowlton, one of the nation's leading communications and public relations consultancy firms. She had been communications director for Brian Tobin when he was premier and a federal minister under Jean Chrétien. During the federal election campaign of 2004, she was a strategist and spokesperson for the federal Liberal Party. Her frequent appearances on national television debating with representatives of the Conservatives and New Democrats did herself, her party, and her province proud.

Our exchanges of opinion were often pointed—she being a Liberal and supporter of Martin's government—but her vast knowledge of government and politics at the federal level and her penetrating insights were a tremendous help in fine-tuning my own thoughts regarding a resolution to the Atlantic Accord problem.

One of the many good things I heard about Heidi Bonnell's work in Ottawa had to do with a presentation she made as director of government relations with Rogers Communications. Head honcho Ted Rogers was reported as calling it the very best presentation he'd ever heard during his long career. I found Heidi to be a wellspring of reliable information and insightful, frank opinions.

* * *

DENIS COLBOURNE, A NEWFOUNDLANDER whom I'd known at Memorial University in the early '60s, rekindled our acquaintanceship by inviting me to lunch at the Rideau Club. I'd never been to that historic joint and I was glad to visit it. The Rideau Club is older than Confederation by nearly two years, having been founded in September 1865. Its formation was an initiative of Sir John A. Macdonald's, and other political notables at the time, and Macdonald was its first president, a post he held for two years before becoming the first prime minister of Canada. A lot of pre-Confederation discussions took place there.

Denis Colbourne had spent over forty years in the information technology industry since I'd known him at Memorial, including filling senior positions with Nortel Networks, from which he retired in 1998 when Nortel was riding high and was probably the biggest employer in Canada. In 2004, a couple of years after the tech bubble had burst, Nortel was fast becoming a shadow of its former self; I joked that he should go back and straighten the company out. But by then he'd moved on to other corporate activities.

In 2002, he received Ottawa's Business Person of the Year Award; in 2003, a Global Traders Award for leadership from the Ontario government; and in 2004, an Information Technology Association of Canada (ITAC) award for Outstanding Service to the Canadian Microelectronics Industry. He was also member of an advisory board with the National Research Council and a member of the Board of Governors of the Ottawa Hospital. And decades after graduating from Memorial, he was still an active alumnus in Ottawa. Denis was another of those able and highly esteemed Newfoundlanders in Ottawa whose successes the general public back home hardly ever heard about, but whose dedication to the province, regardless of individual political affiliations, was invaluable.

ANOTHER NEWFOUNDLANDER LIVING AND working in Ottawa whom I found most helpful was Tom Bursey. We'd never met, but within a day after my appointment, he got in touch with me in St. John's from Ottawa to offer help in settling in and meeting people there who could be of benefit to the province. And he followed up his offer with action—from the beginning to the end of my stay in Ottawa, he was full of practical advice and knowledge, including email addresses and phone numbers for, I'm sure, every Newfoundlander and Labradorian in the region, and notices and invitations regarding events and functions useful to my work.

I wasn't in Ottawa long before I discovered that Tom was a sought-after consultant and front-runner in the field of human resources, where he'd received numerous recognitions for innovation and leadership. He'd served as chair of the Ottawa Human Resources Professionals Association, and received an Ottawa Business Journal's Forty Under 40 award.

But Tom's greatest involvement there from my standpoint derived from his role as a founder and chair of the Ottawa Affinity Newfoundland and Labrador Dinner, in association with the Alumni Association of Memorial University. Since 2001, this annual social event and others connected with it had been bringing together business, government, academic and cultural communities in Ottawa with an affinity for Memorial and the province for the purposes of networking and contributing to a scholarship fund.

Hosts of the function have included Seamus O'Regan, Rick Mercer, and Jonny Harris. The event has attracted such guest speakers as General Rick Hillier, President and CEO of Canada Post Moya Greene, and Premier Danny Williams. Tickets for the dinner Penny and I attended in Ottawa in company with Tom in the fall of 2004 had sold out at once; the event was completely packed with Newfoundlanders and Labradorians from the region and outside.

MUN president Dr. Axel Meisen delivered the opening remarks; he and I would meet afterwards to discuss joint initiatives. Newfoundlander and Memorial alumnus Dr. Bob Roberts, president and CEO of the Ottawa Heart Institute, received a Lifetime Achievement Award at the event.

Dinner included Little Heart's Ease scallops, Heart's Desire beef, Heart's Content bakeapple treats, and Heart's Delight very berry partridge-berry cheesecake. It was a better scoff than the Bush dinner.

The nearly twelve thousand Memorial University alumni living in

Ontario, Alberta and Nova Scotia required that the Affinity Newfoundland and Labrador program expand to Toronto, Calgary, and Halifax. And then on it went, to London, England. Dedicated volunteer committees of alumni and expatriates organize the Affinity Newfoundland and Labrador event in each city.

To give an idea of alumni interest, these were some members of the Ottawa organizing committee and its advisers for 2005: Heidi Bonnell, Herb Bown, Tom Bursey, Lynn Cadigan, Cyril Cochrane, Denis Colbourne, Jeff Dodge, Carol Doody, Rod Elliott, Andrew Foti, Rob Frelich, Dwayne Goudie, Chris Hardy, Joe Hickey, John Kelly, Raf Khan, Iris Krajcarski, Keith Langille, Ted Parsons, Dr. Bob Roberts, Senator Bill Rompkey, Glenn Sparkes, Dr. Maureen Woodrow. Many of these people and their associates, I found, were valuable sources of candid opinions and ideas regarding our negotiations with the federal government and its public impact.

The Affinity Newfoundland and Labrador dinner brought home to me the importance of the dedication to our province of people like Tom Bursey and an army of expatriate Newfoundlanders and Labradorians on the mainland united by a sense of identity and a desire to see our homeland prosper.

Despite his tight schedule, Tom and I met regularly to discuss what was going on in Ottawa and St. John's. And he suggested, or introduced me to, or gave me contact information for, many people. I used to joke to Tom that he should join CSIS, because he could track down any Newfoundlander anywhere and he knew everything that was going on in the capital.

TOM INVITED ME TO a Canadian Club of Ottawa lunch at the Château Laurier to hear a speech by a fellow Newfoundlander, Chief of the Land Staff Lieutenant-General Rick Hillier. We sat at a table with TD Bank executive, Newfoundlander Ted Parsons, and listened to our compatriot's gripping description, illustrated with slides, of his term as commander of the NATO forces in Afghanistan. Everyone in the audience seemed to be struck by Hillier's down-to-earth narrative, delivered in a slight, but still delight-fully discernable, Notre Dame Bay accent.

After Hillier's speech, I joined the lineup of people waiting to meet him. When I introduced myself, he expressed immediate interest in the rising tensions between his home province and Ottawa over the Atlantic Accord. I told him I'd like to discuss that and 5 Wing Goose Bay with him, and he agreed to meet with me as quickly as possible on those issues, and other (military) matters pertaining to our province.

A few weeks later, I went to Hillier's headquarters in Ottawa for a meeting. The premises were unostentatious. He was not yet chief of staff for the Canadian Forces, but close to it. From the exchanges I had with staff and military personnel at the offices, I could tell they were obviously devoted to him.

During our chat about Newfoundland and Labrador, Hillier said "We're hardly even on the radar up here." The province was getting a triple whammy of disregard in Ottawa, I said. First, as he'd mentioned, most of the time we were not even on the radar to start with. Second, if we did happen to creep onto the screen, the bureaucracy considered us a pimple on the arse of Nova Scotia. Third, when we tried to get some attention, the feds thought we were a bloody nuisance—begging for more money with one hand while bashing them in the face with the other. Hillier agreed that we had our work cut out for us, and that it was hard to win.

On that hard-to-win note, I segued into the difficulties the province was having in getting the federal government to seriously gear up opera-tions in 5 Wing Goose Bay, mentioning the crushing competition from other Canadian bases for attention and scarce resources. He responded that, as chief of land staff, his bailiwick did not include 5 Wing Goose Bay, but he wanted to be aware of the issues on general principles, and he lis-tened with interest as I briefed him on the provincial government view-point—in case, I said, he got wind of an adverse decision regarding Goose Bay.

He smiled politely at that, and promptly made it clear that, while it was all very nice that he was a Newfoundlander, his overriding duty to the

men and women in the Canadian Forces was to use the scarce resources
for their best benefit and safety, and not to succumb to the blandishments
of politicians wanting to spend money in their favourite places for political reasons.

Anyone who expected our province to see increased military activity
because of Hillier's high office, especially after he became chief of the
defence staff, was in for a disappointment. One of the reasons he rose to
his lofty position, I knew from talking to MPs and ministers, was his reputation for blunt, professional, non-political integrity, which had earned
him the trust and confidence of Cabinets and prime ministers, as well as
the rank and file under him.

I mentioned the television profile that the CBC had done on him while
he was in Afghanistan as commander of the NATO forces. Yes, he'd heard
of it, he said, but he hadn't seen it yet. He had intended to watch it the
night it was telecast, but prior to the broadcast he had received intelligence that a suicide bomber, mandated to kill him, was in the process of
attempting to carry out his mission. Instead of watching a TV program on
himself, Hillier was forced to become preoccupied with a higher priority—
saving his own skin.

A few days after our meeting, Hillier's office contacted me to say the
general was going to St. John's, and while he was there he would like to
get together with Premier Williams. Could that be arranged? I contacted
the premier's office to ask them to set up a meeting, and I heard later that
Hillier had been extremely impressed with Danny's deep and wide-ranging
knowledge of matters military affecting our province, and the Goose Bay
situation in particular. Evidently, Rick and Danny became fast friends, and
Hillier even tendered him an invitation to tour Afghanistan.

A few weeks later, Paul Martin's government announced that
Lieutenant-General Rick Hillier was being appointed to the top military
post in Canada, chief of the defence staff, and I was delighted but not surprised. That night I went to a pub for a beer with a Newfoundland friend
living in Ottawa. The place was pretty crowded. As we stood around gabbing with a couple of my friend's Ontario civil servant acquaintances, one

of them made a comment on Hillier's appointment. "First we had a Chinese immigrant, Adrienne Clarkson, appointed as governor general and commander in chief of the armed forces, and now we have a Newfie as chief of staff—this ethnic thing in the Canadian military is getting completely out of hand."

They had a good laugh. I told them they'd have another laugh in a few months when they had to listen to the ridiculous whining of their boss, Premier McGuinty, because Newfoundland had gotten its multi-billion dollar Atlantic Accord deal and had started to go ahead of Ontario as a "have" province. But they didn't seem to find that prospect very funny.

ONE FELLOW NEWFOUNDLANDER, WHO didn't live in Ottawa but who was as helpful to our cause on a daily basis as if he did, was Roland Martin.

I'd known Rollie for many years, since our university days at Memorial. In fact, it was Rollie, while a professor in the Faculty of Business, who suggested that a certain graduating student might be the just the executive assistant I was looking for when I was a young and callow minister in the Newfoundland Cabinet. This was Bruce Peters, whom I hired and who was one of the best people I ever worked with in politics. He later went on to fame as the mariner, Captain Bruce Peters, one of his exploits being to join a descendent of the *Bounty*'s Captain William Bligh in retracing Bligh's legendary 6,710 kilometre Pacific voyage in a twenty-three-foot open boat. So I'd always considered Rollie Martin an astute judge of character and ability.

Rollie came to Ottawa from Halifax frequently, and he never failed to call for a get-together to talk about how we might be able to advance our Atlantic Accord cause. Every time there was a development or regression in the Accord talks, he was on the phone or firing off emails to me to discuss it. I never met anyone so knowledgeable about offshore oil benefits to the province and their impact on equalization, and so eager to give freely of their time and knowledge.

His vast experience in the government sector had involved the reorganization of the Newfoundland budget process as special adviser to the minister of Finance, serving as comptroller and deputy minister of Finance, and as a director of Newfoundland and Labrador Hydro Corporation and Churchill Falls (Labrador) Corporation.

Rollie participated in developing Newfoundland's offshore energy policies and was chairman of the Newfoundland and Labrador Industrial Development Corporation. He served as corporate director of over thirty private and crown corporations, and was president and CEO of some of them. He had also advised several provinces on offshore energy.

Equalization being a complicated subject, and the formula used to compute it a convoluted and tangled thing, I often joked that the only two people in all of Canada who could understand the equalization formula were the guy who invented it and Loyola Sullivan—and Loyola wasn't too sure about that other guy. But I learned there were three people who fully understood equalization in all its details and ramifications: the inventor, our Finance minister, and Rollie Martin.

He'd written a major report on it—*Equalization: A Milestone or Millstone for Canada's Future?*—which was published in 2001. Rollie treated me to many explanations of equalization and the Atlantic Accord's impact on it. Those chats were genuinely fascinating, and if Rollie saw my eyes glazing over at some arcane computation, he was too polite to say. I was very grateful for his advice on equalization. It was invaluable to me in Ottawa as ammo for firing at insinuations that we were a bunch of greedy-gutted grab-alls in Newfoundland and Labrador, who just wanted to have our cake and eat it too.

Rollie and I sometimes went among the politicians to watch them at work, allegedly putting polices into practice. Sitting in the House of Commons gallery during Question Period, we'd be amused and appalled in equal measure by the Tories' savage attacks on Paul Martin and the federal position on the Atlantic Accord and by the general discourtesy, ignorance, and loutishness of that great institution of parliamentary democracy. The House of Commons, it has been said, regards the truth as its most valuable possession; therefore, MPs are very economical in its use.

Rollie was open and straightforward about how the provinces were communicating their position to the public. After we discussed media points made by Newfoundland's spokespeople, I would convey our impressions to the premier's office. They appreciated this as part of the general feedback, and Danny told me they tried to use our reactions for improving the clarity of public communications.

Rollie also possessed entry to high levels of the Ottawa bureaucracy and access to political advisers around the prime minister, which he made use of to ensure that the feds clearly understood the positions of Nova Scotia and Newfoundland and Labrador. I used to kid Rollie Martin that it was time for him to go over to the PMO again and set his deluded "cousin," Paul Martin, straight on a few things.

At the MUN convocation in the spring of 2006, Rollie would be awarded an Honorary Doctorate of Laws (LLD) for his contribution to the public (government and university) and private sectors of Newfoundland and Labrador and Canada. Based on my experience, he deserved that honour just for his Atlantic Accord support.

For example, on January 27, 2005, the day before Danny, John Hamm and Paul Martin had a last big Accord summit meeting, an article by Rollie entitled "A Possible Solution to the Offshore Accords Debate" appeared in the *Globe and Mail.*

In it, he used irrefutable data and logic to make an economic and policy case for the provinces' position. Summarizing, he wrote, "Simply put, the solution is for Nova Scotia and Newfoundland to receive 100 percent of offshore revenues with no clawback until each province has achieved the five-province standard used in the equalization formula, and has sustainable economic health. At all times, of course, the federal government will continue to receive 100 percent of federal offshore revenues." Rollie defined the term "sustainable" economic health in a way that was similar, he said, to a formula "proposed by none other than Prime Minister Pierre Trudeau." Those who claimed that Newfoundland and Nova Scotia were demanding something unique, lopsided, unprecedented, and unfair, were left to ponder this: "Let's also remember that the Western Accord of 1985 (signed after the original Atlantic Accord, and still in effect) gave the economies of Alberta, British Columbia and Saskatchewan tremendous benefits by removing federal taxation and cancelling the National Energy Program, thereby leaving taxation of natural resources to these provinces."

Rollie's conclusion touched on Martin's possible place in posterity: "Paul Martin is the first prime minister since Brian Mulroney to reopen this debate, and for that he should be commended. If tomorrow's meeting is a success, the Martin government will have every right to take credit for its role . . . And Mr. Martin will be Canada's only prime minister in two decades with the nation-building vision to tackle this difficult task."

This widely read piece in the *Globe* had a huge effect on the federal side, boosting the position of the provinces during the final, do-or-die negotiations that took place the very next day.

— CHAPTER TWELVE —

The Final Do or Die Meeting

EVERYONE CONSIDERED THE MEETING between Danny Williams and Paul Martin scheduled for January 28, 2005, to be the very last kick at the very last can at the end of the road. Before this crucial get-together, I got a call from Dan Donovan, the owner and publisher of *Ottawa Life* magazine. He wanted to get together with me to discuss the province's case and its prospects. This wasn't for publication in his magazine, but simply because he was interested in our cause and wanted to help. He had great affinity for Atlantic Canada, he said. Although his parents were from Cape Breton, he had been born in St. John's. (I told you we were everywhere.)

Donovan and I met for lunch at the Parliament Pub, of which he was part owner. The various dishes on the menu were named for current politicians, and many politicos gathered there, delighted to find themselves satirized on the carte du jour. Paul Martin's entrée was an Everything for Everyone Sun-Dried Tomato Pizza, Stephen Harper's a Right-Wing Voodoo Chicken Sandwich. Peter MacKay's dish was something described as "a real heartbreaker"; Belinda Stronach's was a Belinda Shrimp Wrap. (Some observers considered Belinda's shrimp wrap to be more of a comment on Peter than on Belinda.)

When I mentioned that people with close connections to Newfoundland were everywhere and involved in everything—Donovan himself being a case in point—he concurred. Newfoundlander Peter Gill, he told me, had been behind one of the biggest stories to break internationally in recent times. The young man conducted an interview for *Ottawa Life* with the Saudi Arabian ambassador about Bill Sampson, the Canadian Englishman who was in a Saudi Arabian dungeon on trumped-up charges, suffering torture which had led to a false confession. Peter Gill got the ambassador to state that Bill Sampson would be beheaded. Donovan gave the story to the *Globe and Mail*, who broke it, and it stayed in transatlantic media headlines for months. It may have been instrumental in securing Sampson's release.

Donovan had an interesting background. After attending France's University of Strasbourg, he worked at high levels in Paris, and later as a director in a federal agency advising the prime minister and the environment minister and as a ministerial chief of staff in the federal Liberal government.

When I described to him the frustration I'd encountered in getting anything done by officials in the provincial government and asked for a comparison from his experience with the federal government, he told me to consider myself lucky. Six months to get my office set up? That would be lightning speed in the federal bureaucracy. We both agreed with a laugh that it was quite possible that neither of us was cut out for a lifetime in the civil service, federal or provincial. Committee meetings? No thanks. A committee, we agreed, was a dark alley down which ideas were lured and quietly strangled.

Donovan proffered a great deal of advice on what Danny should do to push the Accord along. Based on his considerable Ottawa experience, he believed Paul Martin would ultimately cave in on the Accord if Danny was aggressive with his public points. But they had to be kept out there until the upcoming summit, he said. There were so many demands on the PMO's attention that nothing dropped off the federal agenda quicker than something that was not an incessant irritant or embarrassment to the prime minister. Paul Martin, as a former corporate chieftain whose word was his bond, could not bear being forced to hear constantly from the media or in the House that he had gone back on his word.

Donovan thought there would be another federal election in the fall of 2005. (In fact, an election would be called in November 2005 for January 2006.) We both agreed that if that happened, neither Martin nor Harper would come back with a majority, and we argued over which of them was likely to return with a minority government.

Donovan said that Danny Williams had better get his deal with Martin now, even if it was a bit less than he wanted or thought he deserved, because he'd never get anything near a similar deal with Harper if the Tories got in. Even if Harper promised Danny the best deal in the world pre-election, he was too dogmatic to show any flexibility whatsoever on equalization, and he didn't have the sense of honour that Martin had. (Talk about calling it right.)

Needless to say, I fired Dan Donovan's wise advice into Danny's hopper.

Monday, January 24, was my mother's birthday. She was ninety-four. I telephoned her, and found her in fine fettle. She'd gone out to dinner the previous night with my brother Fred and his wife, Sandra, and several grandchildren and great-grandchildren to celebrate. Mother said there had been about seventeen family members at the restaurant, and they'd had a great time. She had the best spare ribs, she said, that she'd ever tasted in her life. I told her I was looking forward to going out with her myself on her ninety-fifth birthday. (And I fervently hoped I had inherited her taste buds.)

During the week, Rollie Martin and I called each other to talk about the Accord. I congratulated him on his article in the *Globe and Mail*. The timing, I told him, could not have been more excellent.

The day before the summit, Brian Crawley called. Danny was arriving in Ottawa that night on a charter flight, and would be staying at the Château Laurier. He and Himelfarb would meet after he got in, and he'd be seeing the PM at eleven the next morning. Danny had invited Premier Hamm along, in the hope that both provinces would reach a deal.

Dave Cochrane of CBC Radio in Newfoundland and Labrador came by my new office for an interview. The furniture had arrived just in time: if he'd come a few days earlier, we would have been forced to hold the interview on the floor, in the lotus position or downward-facing dog. In the middle of the interview, Cochrane got a call on his cell from Scott Reid, the prime minister's communication director. Cochrane had requested an interview with Reid earlier, and Reid told him he could fit him in for a few minutes before he went in to see the PM. But it had to be right away.

I had seen Scott Reid on television—CBC's *Newsworld*—recently, with three other spokesmen for political parties. Watching the exchange, I realized Reid had never been present on any of the occasions in which I'd been with Danny Williams when he was meeting with the prime minister, or any other federal official. Other members of the PMO were often around, but never Scott Reid. Obviously, Paul Martin was savvy enough to know he had to keep his own communications director, of all people, out of Danny's sight if any communication of a positive nature was going to happen.

On television, Reid seemed like someone straining to look as if he was really "with it." He had on jeans plus a jean shirt, and one of those white T-shirts underneath, sticking out at the neck. Newfoundlander Tim Powers, the Conservative Party talker on the show, used a rapier on him; Powers's wit seemed to go straight over Reid's head. The bluster Reid came back with told me that this was a fellow who was intent on looking like he'd won a debating point even if it meant losing the argument.

This was a guy who was supposed to be bolstering his master's image with the media, yet he was treating a leading Newfoundland journalist as if he were there to suit Reid's convenience. Cochrane had to ask me if he could interrupt our interview for five or ten minutes so that he could accommodate Reid.

I thought back to the day following Danny Williams's boycott of the first ministers' equalization summit, when Paul Martin, the prime minister of Canada himself, had given an interview to another Newfoundland journalist, Doug Letto of the CBC. Yet here was Reid, the PM's mouthpiece, condescending to squeeze Cochrane in for five or ten minutes on the day before his boss's critical meeting. I told Cochrane to go right ahead. Reid was sure to say something that would be of benefit to our side, anyway.

I heard from Elizabeth Matthews. Danny's communications director had forgotten to bring the digital camera. She wondered if I had one they could use. No, I said, unfortunately I didn't. She seemed surprised: I should buy one for the office, she said. I laughed out loud. A digital camera for the office? I had striven for months to obtain the office itself, plus a chair and a desk. I told her I'd call my assistant. Christie Meadus was willing to lend her camera, and I asked her to contact Elizabeth with that intelligence. I could never figure out why she didn't just nip across to the Rideau Centre and buy a camera for her boss's big day.

Doug Letto called that night to talk about Alex Himelfarb's role in the negotiations. What I admired about the Newfoundland and Labrador journalists—CBC's Letto and Cochrane and the *Telegram*'s Rob Antle had arrived in Ottawa for the summit—was that they were never content with the surface of events, but dug deep into the nature and causes of positions taken, and who might be behind them.

I was at my office early the next morning, expecting a call from Brian Crawley on the status of the meeting. While I waited I read an article in the *Globe and Mail* by Calgary's Patrick Brethour headlined "Royalty Spat Weighs on Oil Patch Nerves." It contained the following: "The scrap between Newfoundland and Ottawa over how to divvy up offshore energy royalties is making oil companies 'nervous' about committing the billions necessary for new projects, the head of Petro-Canada says."

I could only shake my head. There were no entities in the universe, I thought, more "nervous" than oil companies over political differences of opinion on anything involving the public interest, and yet so full of false bravado and self-serving bullshit when it came to their own interests.

This article stated that even though the Ottawa-Newfoundland dispute had no bearing on the amount of royalties the oil companies would have to pay for offshore production, the clash between the two levels of government was "unsettling" to them. Two or three years later, I, like most Newfoundlanders, would be gratified when Danny Williams took the oil

companies on over provincial benefits from future offshore developments—and won. How was that for "nervous" and "unsettling"?

As I waited for a report on the status of Danny's meeting, a call came
through from a national reporter, who wanted to check some background.
This street-smart journalist expressed grave doubts about today's negotiations: "These two dorks only get together like this every now and then
because they're like the guy in Billy Ray Cyrus's song, 'I'm so miserable
without you it's almost like you're here.'" I could see his point.

It was nine-thirty and I still hadn't heard from Brian. I phoned his cell;
there was no answer, so I left a message. At 10:15 he called me. They were
leaving at 10:40 for the Langevin Block to meet with the prime minister,
he said. By all means I should come if I felt like it but, after Danny's
meeting with Himelfarb last night, I would, in all likelihood, just be
wasting my time. He sounded down and exasperated. I would get an idea
why later.

I walked to the Château Laurier in the biting winter cold that always
came as an excruciating surprise to a Newfoundlander in Ottawa. Some of
our gang—Terry Paddon, Robert Thompson, Ross Reid, and Stephen
Dinn—were in the lobby, tense and fidgeting as they waited for Williams
and Hamm to come down.

We hung around, gabbing; they were worried about being late for the
assignation with the prime minister and his team. One of them hoped out
loud that someone with the premier would think of making a call to the
PMO to explain that there was a delay.

Brian Crawley came down and revealed the reason for his gloomy
exasperation: the delay had been caused by a big problem with the numbers the prime minister's negotiators had given us. Could I believe it? Our
provincial people had actually found glaring mathematical mistakes in the
federal figures, figures that the negotiations were supposed to be based
on. It was mind-boggling.

Elizabeth Matthews appeared, very much the mistress of ceremonies,
as usual. I went over to give her the digital camera Christie had brought
from home at her request. Matthews looked down at the camera she had

asked for as if I were offering her a dead rat. Give it, she decreed, to Steve Dinn. I had to smile. The Little Princess.

Terry Paddon told me he hadn't slept a wink. He'd gone over and over the numbers and projections in his head, making sure they hadn't overlooked anything. Bob Thompson looked pale and tired. On top of all the Accord hassle, Thompson had been cross-examined harshly as a government witness in a Supreme Court trial during the last few days. Christ, I thought, I'd better try to cheer everyone up.

I told them not to sweat it—sure the very worst that could happen was that, twenty years down the road, we'd be looking back on another Upper Churchill. There was a startled, pregnant pause. "Oh, thanks," said one team member. "That makes me feel a fuck of a lot better." Another was at least somewhat comforted. "Twenty years, you said? That'd be all right; I'll be long retired by then."

Premiers Williams and Hamm finally came down, and we walked en masse over to the Langevin Building. On the way, we encountered a couple of scrums—national and provincial media. Among them were Doug Letto, Dave Cochrane, and Rob Antle.

Danny projected optimism, telling them that there seemed to be a genuine will to bridge the gaps, and that he would stay at the bargaining table for as long as necessary. He also, perhaps for the very first time, signalled a willingness to compromise, to accept less than 100 percent if and when Newfoundland came off equalization. Rob Antle reported the premier's remarks in the next day's *Telegram*: "'With regard to the offset, there's a question of interpretation . . . The deal, the compromise, the solution works somewhere in between, and that's what we're working towards.'"

Approaching the Langevin Block, I recalled that a Liberal senator had warned me weeks before about her political colleagues inside it: "Watch out for that gang in the Langevin Building. Don't go near that Langevin Block." She might have been talking about the Lubyanka, the dreaded KGB building in Soviet Moscow. But I was able to tone down my apprehension as we approached the fearful edifice by bringing to mind the sweet, loveable faces of Martin, Goodale, Efford, and Himelfarb, waiting for us inside.

A federal official met us at the door and led the two provincial entourages to a doorway. As directed, we trooped into a large room containing a big table covered with breakfast food, juice and coffee. There were already people in the room. As we entered, an appalled silence descended, as if Attila the Hun's soldiers had just stormed a nunnery.

"This," proclaimed one of them in an affronted tone, "is a federal room." The official with a short future ahead of him as a federal employee had made a grave blunder in bringing us there. Without ceremony, we were immediately ushered from the federal chamber of plenty to two foodless provincial closets, across from each other down the corridor.

Right away, Danny Williams was asked to meet with Paul Martin. He wasn't gone long, and when he got back, he described the meeting as "really weird." It had been very tense but low-key. It had cleared the air a little, he told us, but feelings on the other side appeared to be extremely strained. Part of the weirdness was that Martin wanted to talk about John Efford. He said that Williams had destroyed him. But Danny was having none of that bull. He replied, quietly but emphatically, that Efford had done it to himself.

The to-ing and fro-ing went on all day. Danny was at every meeting. Some sessions were with the prime minister, some with Himelfarb, some with Goodale and Efford. Danny was accompanied by Loyola Sullivan, Robert Thompson, and Terry Paddon, either as a group or in various combinations. Ross Reid, Brian Crawley, Elizabeth Matthews and I remained in the room, providing a sounding board for Danny when he got back from each meeting.

Danny absolutely relished the day's cut and thrust. He'd come back from each session where an impasse had been reached with an air, not of anxiety, but of buoyant delight. While we looked at each other in consternation, or voiced caution, over the imminent collapse of the negotiations, Danny was animatedly trying to divine the other side's next move. Someone said to him, "You really love all this, don't you?" He replied, through a huge grin, "I must confess, I do. I really love this process."

He listened attentively to all advice asked for or tendered. Sometimes he'd become a little impatient if an answer was soft or out of focus, but mostly he was affable. He laughed readily at everybody's silly, nervous jokes. I never saw him look at his watch. I couldn't swear that he even wore one. His demeanour was that of a man laid-back and in the zone.

After each session between our guys and the feds, Brian Crawley usually grilled Thompson and Paddon as to what exactly had been agreed to, what exactly was meant by such and such language or this or that figure. Crawley was taking a no-nonsense approach—no fuzzy edges permitted—an approach doubtless stemming from his having been burned before at similar sessions on exactly what the feds had or had not agreed to. Like Sullivan, Thompson, Paddon, and Danny Williams, Crawley seemed to have a complete grip on the ramifications of every single point, cipher, graph and scenario.

Ross Reid and I, on the other hand, not having been involved in countless Accord meetings for months on end, sat there listening fairly knowledgeably, but lacking the absolute facility with figures, formulas, and future scenarios that the others shared. Every now and then, after one of their fast and spirited exchanges, Ross and I would look at each other, wide-eyed: What the hell was that all about? Once Ross ran his hand, palm-down, over his head and said, "Whoosh!"—indicating clearly where that particular point had gone.

He and I agreed that the best role we could play in this drama was to push the envelope rather than filling it with content. The actual substance of the deal was a matter for the expert numbers guys and the powerful negotiator. But if we had any doubts about the usefulness of our being present (basically just sitting around the table and only speaking when spoken to), they were alleviated by the look on Alex Himelfarb's face when he came into our room after the first, apparently fatal, deadlock between Paul Martin and Danny Williams.

He entered wearing his usual calming smile. Then he saw Ross Reid and did a double take, no doubt remembering Ross's thirty-year political career: supporter of and aide to the powerful John Crosbie, chief of staff to a federal minister of Finance, adviser to a prime minister, an articulate

MP, and a no-nonsense Cabinet minister. His gracious nod to Ross indicated he well recalled those days.

Then Himelfarb did another double take when he saw me sitting by Ross. He looked at the premier and then back at me. I trusted that my presence reminded him of our chat at the Bush dinner a few weeks before, when I had depicted Danny as a man so extraordinarily determined, so "crazy" in his Churchill-like perseverance, that he would never be defeated—he could never be defeated.

Alex Himelfarb was amazing, himself. No wonder he had survived the coup in which Martin's forces had pried Chrétien out of office with all the gentleness of a crowbar. He was much too valuable to any prime minister to be fired. A number of times when it seemed clear that an impasse would sink the session—at least twice we were actually standing with our coats on, gathering up our papers—he would appear at the door and ask politely if he could come in. Then, in a soft, even voice, he would inquire about the province's current difficulty, and convey it to the prime minister.

Danny was more than amazing. He relished guessing, after each session, what the next federal offer on the upfront money would be; e.g., "They'll come back now with $735 million." His predictions were frighteningly accurate, especially his last prophecy of the evening: "We'll saw off at two billion dollars." But at the very end, something happened that no one predicted, and it threw a monkey wrench into the works.

Just before that, though, there was some regrettable low comedy involving John Efford. He was given the privilege by his rueful boss, Paul Martin, of slotting in what was hoped would be the final three pieces in the deal—sort of the last spikes, designed to redeem the Newfoundland federal minister. But when Efford came to perform the task, he was confused about the agreed-upon points.

It reminded me of what one of Efford's caucus colleagues had said to me a few weeks before: "Whenever I look in John's eyes, I always get the feeling that someone else is driving." After sending Efford back with the correct version, Danny said to us that you couldn't help but pity poor John, even though everything that had happened to him was all of his own making.

At last, early that evening, a final deal was reached. Or so we thought. While we waited for the typed memorandum of agreement to come in for approval, Danny asked an aide to phone St. John's and make sure all available Cabinet ministers were assembled for an oral briefing; he needed their consensus. This was Friday night in St. John's, but the ministers came together in jig time to hear the premier.

After Danny had described the deal he'd reached, his telephone receiver emitted a jubilant cheer so loud that, even without the speaker phone being on, we could hear it clearly on the other side of the room. We deduced that the premier had obtained a consensus from his Cabinet colleagues. Then, a document which was supposed to be the final draft of the agreement came in from the feds.

Danny and Sullivan read it with pens practically poised to initial the thing. But instead of writing on it, they went off their heads. A point that had already been orally agreed to regarding the transition to equalization during the second eight years of the Accord's operation, they raged, had been omitted. This was a deal breaker, and they sent word to that effect down to Paul Martin.

Alex Himelfarb came up, accompanied by a fit-looking female official—witness, secretary, bodyguard, I wasn't sure which—and this time Alex was not smiling. He insisted that he had told Danny during negotiations, with the PM's clear understanding, that the point in contention was off the table. Danny and Sullivan objected strenuously. They had never agreed with that, they said. They could never agree with that. They were incensed that anyone could even think that they would ever agree with that.

Himelfarb went back to Martin. We waited—you could cut the tension with a knife. After having notified his Cabinet that we had a final deal, Danny faced the prospect of calling them again to say his beautiful new Accord had collapsed.

At last, Himelfarb came through the door. His face was grimmer than I'd ever seen it. When he had confronted the prime minister with this latest "misunderstanding," he reported quietly, the PM had hammered the table with his fist, bellowed that there was no way he was going to monkey with the principles of equalization, and stomped out of the building. He was gone, Himelfarb said; it was all over. Finished. He turned and walked out.

We stood there looking at each other. Someone said, "Jesus Christ, you can't believe this crowd when they say 'good morning' to you." Someone else spoofed Paul Martin: "'Hello,' he lied."

Then our side went into a big huddle. Danny threw question after question at Thompson, Paddon, and Sullivan about the effect of varying price scenarios for crude oil on the province's net take from offshore oil in the years to come. They answered quickly and, at least to my relatively inexpert ear, very knowledgeably. Danny told all of us to ask any questions and make any points we wanted to.

Gradually, the conclusion was reached that the worst risk would be the possible, but unlikely, loss of some four hundred million dollars in the second eight years. The ultimate question was whether the province should live with that risk, or allow it to torpedo the entire deal which, up front, would put more than two billion dollars in our provincial coffers.

Danny didn't hesitate. We would compromise, put the deal back on the rails. Himelfarb was called in again, and Danny told him we would accept the document as presented, with the addition of a few alterations to the language, which both sides had agreed on. They were written in by hand, and then, following assurances from the Nova Scotia contingent that they fully agreed, the document was initialled by both sides. Danny had one of his assistants call the ministers back home to confirm the good news. A final, signed deal.

It would strike me as interesting, nearly four years later, that the prime minister could so badly misinterpret Williams's ability to compromise. In his 2008 memoirs, *Hell or High Water*, Paul Martin wrote: "Unfortunately, our ability to reach a deal was complicated by the fact that we had a negotiating partner in Danny Williams, the Premier of Newfoundland and Labrador, whose negotiating style was not exactly built around 'getting to yes.'"

In fact, I remember clearly that Danny Williams and Loyola Sullivan had gone out and come back from the final meeting firmly believing the feds had agreed with them on the point that nearly scuppered the deal. It was simply impossible that those two men could have been mistaken about such an important thing. All our officials had believed the federal government was onside as well. The fact was that the feds went back on their word, and the province decided to accept that and compromise. It's hard to see how compromising in the face of federal reneging could be characterized by Martin as a negotiating style that was not exactly built around "getting to yes."

Around seven-thirty, we all trooped away from the Langevin Block and crossed to the Centre Block for the big news briefing by the federal and provincial leaders. We would end up hanging around outside the prime minister's office until it got under way two hours later.

Every now and then I'd catch a glimpse of Paul Martin going from one room to another in what appeared to be an agitated hurry. I had seen him walking the corridors in the Langevin Building, and he seemed without poise or presence then too. I wouldn't see him smile until he got in front of the cameras. It was as if the semi-scowl on his face all day was supposed to indicate seriousness, statesmanship, *gravitas*.

But I never did see Martin exhibit the *gravitas*—unhurried, unstressed dignity—of a leader in control of a situation. As far as never letting them see you sweat went, Martin had work to do—he always seemed to be in a sweat, or verging on one. A friend of his said to me once, laughing, "Sometimes Paul tries to force himself to loosen up, but he seems more comfortable tense."

At one point, when Martin was approaching the negotiating table with Williams and Sullivan to begin a fresh set of talks, he lurched to a stop, looked confused, and whispered to Himelfarb, "Which side of the table do I sit on?" When I mentioned to a former Liberal adviser that I could not imagine a Chrétien or a Trudeau asking his deputy for instructions on where to sit, he replied that the situation was even worse than that: When you gave Paul a map to show him how to get somewhere, you found out he didn't know how to drive the car. An unfair exaggeration, perhaps, but it does capture the essence of the leader that the *Economist* characterized as "Mr. Dithers."

Premier Hamm was upstairs in the Centre Block, looking, as usual, understated and dignified. He had been the sole initiator of the whole campaign, and had been demanding justice for Nova Scotia under the Atlantic Accord for four years. Hamm would say, "After four years and eleven days, I'm very, very glad that it's over."

When I'd first met Hamm, he gave me the impression of being soft and yielding, especially compared with Danny Williams and his sharp, hard edges. I doubted whether he could be relied on not to cave in if it came to the rough stuff. A member of our group said, "I know what you mean—he does seem kind of mushy."

But he proved to be strong and very persistent. He mostly hung in there with Danny, even though the feds did their level best to divide and conquer. Murray Brewster of the Canadian Press, in his *Globe and Mail* story on the deal on January 31, wrote the following: "One official, who spoke on the condition of anonymity, said federal bureaucrats often tried to drive wedges between the provinces, on one occasion hoping to persuade Nova Scotia to sign separately when Newfoundland Premier Danny Williams was away on vacation." That had been during Danny's flag-lowering phase, when Hamm feared our premier was out of the negotiating picture entirely. Generally, the premiers had played, with great success, good cop/bad cop, with Danny publicly admitting he was a natural in the bad cop role.

Hamm was approaching retirement, and the signing of the deal was a tremendous vindication of his perseverance: a lonely start, Danny's hijinks, federal inducements and blandishments to sign a separate deal. In his memoirs, Paul Martin said that Ottawa came close to a deal early with Hamm, but "the problem was that Hamm would not sign until Williams did." Paul Martin's "problem" became part of Danny Williams's salvation.

Loyola Sullivan looked pleased to have it all over with. Not only because a good deal had been reached at last, but also because he would no longer have to listen to Ralph Goodale pronounce his name "Lee-ola."

Loyola played a tremendous role, both leading and supporting. He knew as much about the financial figures and their consequences as the expert officials. Deputy Finance Minister Terry Paddon and I bantered with Loyola about that. When I listened to him reel off the dollars and the barrels of oil, I said that it was very clear he'd never met a number he didn't love. Paddon added, "or ever forgot."

I told Loyola that during one election, someone had phoned me on *Open Line* to say that he was voting for Charlie Power because he was the second-smartest guy on the Southern Shore. "Second smartest?" I'd replied. "Who's the smartest? You should vote for him." The caller replied that he would, if he ever got the chance. "The smartest guy on the Southern Shore," he said, "is Loyola Sullivan. Sure, everyone knows that." Loyola laughed and modestly denied the allegation, but I found his disclaimer weak.

Nothing involving the negotiations had ever been too much of an effort for Loyola. Late one night, I received a call from him: he was at the Ottawa airport, having just gotten off the plane, and about to get a taxi downtown. He sounded exhausted, and for good reason. He'd been beating around the province as minister of Finance for days, doing budget consultations. He'd had three sessions over the past day alone in Labrador, he told me, after which he had to drive down the Northern Peninsula to Deer Lake to hop a plane and make his way, through convoluted connections, to Ottawa for meetings with federal officials, in order to keep the pressure on regarding the Accord. Yet he still took the time to call and brief me. The next morning, he was up at dawn preparing for a full day of meetings.

Loyola could also be a man of few words, apparently—not all that often perhaps, but sometimes. Brian Crawley described one marathon meeting between Ralph Goodale and Loyola on the Accord, which had lasted some fourteen hours. At the end of it, a weary Goodale had summed up the federal offer, and said, "Surely that must give you what you want, Lee-ola." Without even pretending to cogitate on it, Loyola responded in his handsome Southern Shore accent, "Bayessically, noah."

He told me the night of the Accord deal that he wasn't going back to St. John's with the premier and the negotiating team the next day, to share in the accolades and celebration. He had no need for praise, he said, and besides, he had a Finance ministers' meeting in Ottawa on Monday, and he wanted to save the price of another plane ticket.

Nova Scotia's Clarke was smiling. Like his boss, he seemed laid-back and easygoing. Once, as we talked over items for a crucial meeting, he spotted my fifty-nine-dollar Timex Ironman watch and asked what marathons and triathlons I'd been in. He was always there, sharp, prepared, on the ball, and ready to dig in.

Federal minister Geoff Regan, the son of former Nova Scotian premier and federal minister Gerald Regan, was getting ready for the news conference too, although nobody seemed to know why. Regan was Efford's counterpart. Some members of the Nova Scotia team questioned why he was at meetings and briefings—and always on hand to take credit for anything positive on the Accord—since he never, ever said anything. A member of our group said that Nova Scotia should thank their lucky stars. It could have been much worse—what if Regan had, in fact, been saying something all the time, like Efford?

Ross Reid looked happier. Like me, he had not been a substance man but a process man during the Accord battle. We had pushed the envelope that others had filled. Part of Ross's pushing had consisted of sitting at the table in our room at the Langevin Block with his face turned to the heavens and his eyes closed when the deal threatened to collapse because Danny couldn't wring the last drop of blood out of the federal turnip. He didn't say anything aloud, but his face was eloquent. It said, "This offer is a reasonable compromise—take it." Danny looked his way frequently, and no doubt absorbed the message.

Brian Crawley was off by himself, texting on his BlackBerry. He was absolutely Danny's man, but he was realistic, and did not hesitate to express his sensible opinions to Danny and those around him. Brian told me before we went into the final session that there was only a twenty-five percent chance of success, which I considered pessimistic, but only for purely political reasons—I felt Paul Martin needed a deal, needed to put the fuss behind him.

But from a negotiation viewpoint—taking into account the narrow but deep gulf between the parties—Crawley was absolutely right. He knew exactly where the negotiators were at any given time. He'd dig right in with questions after each session, to make sure he understood exactly what the negotiators were saying and doing, and that they did too.

Danny relied on him a lot and turned to him often; perhaps too much. Brian did give the impression of being on top of everything, especially when it came to the Accord, but I wondered if it was possible to be on top of everything important going on in the government. For myself, I can only say that he usually kept me informed of all developments, day and night, and he was inordinately accessible despite the load he was carrying.

Elizabeth Matthews was hovering around the premier, often whispering points to him. I figured the reason Danny was usually so well briefed, and often able to emit a turn of phrase that made a good sound bite, was partly a result of her input. She definitely acted as if she occupied a privileged position in the premier's office. At one media briefing, as she walked up to Danny to pass him a paper, she dumped his winter coat and hers, and some accessories she was carrying, into the arms of a deputy minister she passed, without so much as a by-your-leave. I had to grin. The Little Princess.

I noticed, though, that a chagrined Brian Crawley was shaking his head at her and grimacing: a signal that she shouldn't be doing that. Still, as long as the demanding top boss admired how she carried off her job— the fast and effective media releases, the constant and clever briefings— what odds?

THIS NEWS BRIEFING ON the Accord deal began outside the House of Commons at nine-thirty. Standing there, smiling and looking proud, were Prime Minister Paul Martin and Premiers Hamm and Williams, flanked by the equally beaming federal and provincial ministers Regan, Efford,

Sullivan and Clarke. Ralph Goodale was there too, but he was not smiling. In fact he looked as pained as if someone had just stuck a thumb in his eye.

As the others burbled Oscar-night praises into the mikes, Goodale remained as silent as a pillaged bank vault. About the only thing he didn't do was turn his pockets inside out to show how badly he'd been robbed.

By contrast, Danny Williams, after negotiating and arguing and haggling all day, looked fresher, and certainly happier, than he had at the start, twelve hours earlier. He spoke with the vigour of success.

A scrum took place with reporters from Newfoundland and Labrador, including, as usual, Rob Antle of the *St. John's Telegram* and CBC's Doug Letto and Dave Cochrane. Looking at the media coverage from the inside, I thought that the stories developed by those three were terrific—accurate and solid. Loyola Sullivan told me he'd been saying to everyone that if they wanted to understand what the deal and the dispute were all about, they should read Rob Antle's articles in the *Telegram*.

After the briefings and scrums, we walked back in the cold January night to the Château Laurier. The others freshened up, and then we all went into the bar off the lobby, pulled a couple of tables together, and sat around for a celebratory drink. The premier and Brian Crawley and Elizabeth Matthews were at one end, and Loyola Sullivan and I were at the other end; the other officials sat in between. We spent a couple of hours, not boisterously celebrating but quietly talking about the successful end to a tumultuous, often traumatic, six months.

I was the first to take my leave. It was one-thirty in the morning. Danny got up and walked out with me to the lobby; we talked for a moment before I got into my taxi. Now that the Accord was done, he said, we'd concentrate on my position. "My God, Bill, we've got sixty years of experience between the two of us." A lot had happened since the first time he'd made that same enthusiastic comment in St. John's a year and a half before.

I agreed that the office was important. I told him that whenever I'd been asked about the office by the media, I'd always replied, sincerely, that any provincial government that didn't have a representative in Ottawa was being derelict in its duty to its people. Danny said that Hamm had come to the same conclusion from watching ours in operation. The Nova Scotia premier had told him that day that he was going to put a provincial representative in Ottawa as soon as possible.

DANNY FLEW HOME THE next day, climbed atop a table in the St. John's International Airport, and bawled out through the rapturous applause and shrieks of approval from a six-hundred-strong welcoming committee, "We got it! We got it! We got it!" Then he once again replaced the "have-not" in former premier Peckford's slogan with the term that had caught the fancy of many supporters in Ottawa. "*Keep-not*," he yelled, "will be no more."

On January 31, Danny held a news conference to detail what he had achieved in principle for the province in the new Atlantic Accord agreement. "What an awesome day to be a Newfoundlander and Labradorian!" he said.

The main elements of the deal guaranteed that Newfoundland and Labrador would receive 100 percent of its offshore revenues, free from any equalization clawbacks while we remained an equalization-receiving province, for the full life of the sixteen-year agreement. A review would take place after that period. If, during the second eight years of the term, the province no longer qualified for equalization in any year, it would receive sixty-six percent of the previous year's offset payment in year one, and thirty-three percent in year two. If the province requalified for equalization, the 100 percent offset would be restored.

Meanwhile, the province would receive an upfront payment of two billion, plus interest, which represented a floor on future offset payments above and beyond the original Accord offset payments. That would protect the province if oil prices dropped to between thirty and thirty-five dollars US per barrel, but would in no way restrict the province's ability to benefit from oil prices above that range, which the earlier federal insistence on an Ontario cap would have done. The two billion dollar payment would allow the province to reduce its outstanding debt.

I was intrigued by this sentence in Rob Antle's comprehensive story on the deal: "The only question being raised in Ottawa circles prior to Friday's talks was not whether Williams was crazy, but just how crazy he was for turning down previous offers." Gosh, I wondered to myself, how on earth did "Ottawa circles" get that idea about our Danny?

When some commentators, including John Efford, publicly doubted that the final deal was any different from the one proposed by the feds just before Christmas, Danny made the following statement to the media:

> "Some have reported that this agreement is not sub-stantially different from the offer that the federal govern-ment made in Winnipeg on December 22, but I can assure you that it certainly is a vastly improved deal. Through extensive discussions, we have improved the Winnipeg proposal by getting a $2 billion floor plus interest, securing a 16-year deal, eliminating the onerous balanced-budget requirement and achieving agreement to include a review mechanism after sixteen years.
>
> We were also successful in getting the existing Atlantic Accord benefits extended by an additional year, and we have a transition mechanism negotiated into the second eight years—a huge win for the province, which could translate into hundreds of millions of dollars. We have also negotiated a key element, which is the inclusion of all new projects into this deal. These are just some of the improve-ments between the two deals."

Could John Efford's career be salvaged? Martin had appealed to Danny again on that score at their final meeting on January 28. Indeed, he wanted to make a recognition of Efford's contribution by the premier a condition of the deal. And Danny Williams did try to reverse, somewhat, the result of his months of attacks on Efford by issuing some bland remarks of gratitude at the news conference. "He added a great deal to this file, and was instrumental in concluding this matter today."

Other federal politicians had survived conflicts between their federal duties and provincial expectations by fancy footwork. But Efford seemed to go out of his way to exacerbate the conflict at every turn, even at the very end, after Williams had buried the hatchet, and that certainly doomed him.

On February 14, 2005, in St. John's, the Honourable John Efford, minister of Natural Resources Canada, signed the new Atlantic Accord 2005 "for the Government of Canada." But this token, formal recognition was too little, too late to save him.

That wasn't because Danny Williams was a vindictive man. At the news conference detailing the new Accord, Danny said, "I would also like to thank those individuals over the past several months who have supported us vocally and morally: Federal MPs and Senators, Mayors—specifically Mayor Andy Wells—and town councils across the province."

Mayor Wells, who had earlier signed Paul Martin's nomination papers for leader of the Liberal Party of Canada, had threatened to vote against him for not fulfilling his commitment to Williams on the Accord. In thanking him, Danny had travelled a long way from his immortal statements that getting into an argument with Wells was like "getting into a pissin' contest with a skunk," and that what His Worship needed most was "a good shit knockin'."

Danny would strive mightily to have Wells appointed chair of the Canada-Newfoundland and Labrador Offshore Petroleum Board. After failing to achieve that objective, he would appoint him chair of the Public Utilities Board.

A Tory MP once told me that Danny never held a grudge—all you had to do to get back in Danny's good graces was to come back to the team. "And to Danny," he added, "a team effort is everyone doing what he says." He went on to speculate that if Danny Williams had a motto, it would be this: "It matters not whether you win or lose. What matters is whether I win or lose."

One person who, for unfathomable reasons, considered himself an Accord loser was the premier of one of the most favoured provinces in the

entire country, Dalton McGuinty. On the very day of the formal signing by
the federal and Newfoundland and Labrador representatives, the "gracious" Ontario premier was all over the media yet again, whining about
how unfairly Ontario was being treated in Confederation.

MEANWHILE, THE TIME HAD come for me to decide my own future. The
question had recently been brought to a head by my ninety-four-year-
old mother's continuing decline in health. Now that the Ottawa office
was fully set up and operational, and now that the province had concluded a satisfactory Atlantic Accord deal, I could reasonably consider
my mission in the nation's capital accomplished. I sent those thoughts
to Danny Williams, and when he came to Ottawa soon after his successful final meeting with the prime minister, we had a chance to discuss them.

Rick Hillier had invited me and the premier to his swearing-in ceremony as chief of the defence staff in early February. Danny Williams flew
to Ottawa from Toronto, where he'd made a speech the day before to the
Empire Club. The ceremony for Hillier was taking place in a hangar at the
airport, so I got a taxi out to meet Danny. On the way, the taxi driver
informed me that Rick Hillier was being installed in the top military job in
Canada at the airport today. He knew the general very well himself, he
said, because he used to drive him around Ottawa a lot; he was a great
guy with a good word for everyone, top brass and small fry alike.

Steve Dinn was at the airport with Danny, and he told me that the premier's speech in Toronto had received a standing ovation. By the sounds
of it, the Toronto establishment, in contrast to their own premier, liked the
feisty premier from another province who took the feds on frontally. Dinn
had been told by organizers that it was the first standing ovation awarded
by the hard-nosed audience at the Empire Club in twenty-five years.

I asked Dinn who the last applauded speaker had been, and he set
about to find out, on his trusty BlackBerry. The last standing ovation
before Danny's had been accorded to Sir Edmund Hillary, the first con-
queror, with Tenzing Norgay, of Mount Everest—pretty good company for

our premier. Dalton McGuinty's bellyaching over Danny Williams's success didn't seem to be cutting much ice at home.

Waiting to be taken to Rick Hillier's ceremony, Danny and I chatted about the remarkable contribution being made to Canada by people from Newfoundland and Labrador. By coincidence, Dr. Noreen Golfman of Memorial University went by to catch a flight home. Danny had an enthusiastic chat with her, not holding back on how greatly he admired her work at home and abroad. And truly, she was a superb ambassador for our province with her wide range of interests and participation. Earlier, I'd seen her at an Ottawa event for the Canadian Film and Television Producers Association where I'd joined my son Dorian of the Newfoundland contingent, and again at the awards night of the Social Sciences and Humanities Research Council of Canada of which my wife, Penny, was vice-president. Noreen and I laughed at the frequency of these chance encounters up here. We had to stop meeting like this, we kidded.

An army captain drove us to the hangar, where a reception was being held before the installation ceremony. We were so early that hardly any other guests had arrived. After some pleasant chat with attending officers in uniform, including fellow Newfoundlanders, we moved off to a corner to discuss our business.

Danny said he was sorry to hear of my plans to go back to Newfoundland, but he understood completely. When the other guests started coming in, Danny made no move to join them. I realized again how little love he had for socializing and small talk. We stayed where we were even when Paul Martin arrived with Governor General Adrienne Clarkson. Then the man himself, General Rick Hillier, spotted us in the corner and left the group he was with to walk over and say hello.

Danny said, "We're not being anti-social over here, Rick, but we had an urgent matter to discuss." Hillier replied that he knew all about that sort of thing, and he understood fully. His grin indicated that he was not much for small talk either.

The crowd started to move into the drill hall for the ceremony. On the way in, Danny spoke briefly to Paul Martin and said hello to Governor

General Clarkson. When she was introduced to me, Adrienne Clarkson said, "*Clapp's Rock*, right?" This was a reference to my first novel, published twenty years before by McClelland & Stewart, just before she had become CEO of the firm. I was astonished at her memory and her thoughtfulness.

In the drill hall, Danny and I were shown to seats in the second row, right behind Rick Hillier's mother, wife, sons, daughter-in-law, and grandchildren. It was an exceedingly proud moment for them.

An exhibition of ceremonial marching now took place, during which Danny remarked on the fairly large number of female soldiers. He loved to see that, he said. Danny was progressive on all issues—as small "l" liberal as anyone in the Liberal Party itself. Even before the Conservative Party of Canada—no longer "Progressive"—gained the government under Stephen Harper, Danny made no bones to me about his dislike of its right-wing policies and dogma. I wouldn't be surprised if he agreed with John Stuart Mill's assessment that "conservatives are not necessarily stupid, but most stupid people are conservative."

The outgoing chief of the defence staff, Raymond Henault, got up to start the ceremony. I pitied him: the acoustics in the drill hall were atrocious, and you could scarcely understand a syllable of the man's remarks. Danny and I expressed amazement that this place, as the captain had informed us while driving here, was used for these kinds of ceremonies all the time.

Governor General Clarkson sounded better, pacing her speech to allow the echo resounding through the hall after each word to die down. But she needed all the skill and experience from her media days to make her remarks quasi-comprehensible. What could the Department of National Defence have been thinking, I wondered, when it decided on this cavernous, cacophonous room, where nearly every speaker sounded like a yowling cat trapped in a garbage can? By fiercely concentrating, I picked up a few bons mots.

Paul Martin vowed that the next time he sat down to negotiate with Danny Williams, he would be bringing his own Newfoundlander with him: the head of the armed forces.

Rick Hillier confessed that when he was approached about taking his new job, right in the middle of the Atlantic Accord battle, his paramount thought was, "Oh no, my first peace-keeping mission as chief of staff is going to be in my own native province."

As we were leaving after the ceremony, Danny stopped and spoke to each member of Rick Hillier's family at length. I remarked to Danny afterwards that I couldn't help noticing he'd spent way more time with Hillier's family than with the prime minister or the governor general. He acknowledged that he didn't have much inclination for hobnobbing with the high and the mighty. His greatest satisfaction in politics, in addition to putting together deals beneficial to the province, derived from talking with ordinary people. That's why he loved a political campaign.

As I've noted, Rick Hillier always gave the impression that he couldn't wait to get away from the big shots and their ceremonial events, and go back to his enlisted men and women. Little wonder that Danny and Rick hit it off. Three years later, after Hillier retired, Danny appointed him chancellor of Memorial University.

After the ceremony, the military vehicle took us back to the departure gate at the airport. En route, we got tangled up in a traffic jam, and it looked like Danny was going to miss his flight. The driver followed alternative routes not immediately obvious to our civilian eyes, and got us there just before Danny's departure time. You definitely had the feeling that there was no way the officer was going to fail a guest of General Hillier's.

Danny's plane, as was often the case for anyone trying to get to St. John's from Ottawa, took off for Toronto first—the exact opposite direction. Good old Air Canada. Meanwhile, for the first and last time in my life, I was chauffeured to my office in a Canadian Forces vehicle, at the request of Canada's chief of the defence staff.

THE DAY AFTER THE public announcement from the premier's office that I was resigning my Ottawa position to return to St. John's for personal reasons, I got a call from my daughter Toby with great news—an excellent omen that I had made the right decision. She and her husband, Colin, were expecting their first child in September—a first grandchild for Penny and me.

I received a pleasant "Dear Bill" letter from Premier Williams, which said, "I want to thank you personally and sincerely, on behalf of the people of Newfoundland and Labrador, for the remarkable skills, counsel and patience that you brought to the negotiations in which we secured . . . the historic Canada-Newfoundland and Labrador Atlantic Accord 2005."

That was a generous statement, and I appreciated it, but Danny Williams had had a lot of extraordinary support in his endeavour from many dedicated people. Moreover, without his own dogged perseverance and guts from start to finish, and backing from Loyola Sullivan and Premier Hamm, there simply would have been no Atlantic Accord 2005.

Danny concluded his letter to me with "looking forward to many more opportunities for us to work together, in the months and years ahead to accomplish even greater things for Newfoundland and Labrador." But that sentiment was for the sake of form. I had already made it clear that I desired no future role in the public service. What I wanted to do was return to public commentary, and to devote considerably more time to writing.

Calls came through from producers, editors and managers with the media in St. John's—CBC and NTV television, the *Independent* and the *Telegram*, and the major radio network, Steele Communications—with kind offers of regular contributions to their public affairs programming. In order to leave more time for book-length writing, I accepted only a weekly column with the *Telegram/Western Star*, and a new daily afternoon call-in show, *Back Talk*, with Steele Communications.

As to my relationship with Danny Williams, it became non-existent. Our get-together for Rick Hillier's installation as chief of defence staff was our last. On what basis could one remain close friends with someone so powerful, controlling and driven, anyway? Put as delicately as possible, it would not be my cup of tea, nor, I'm sure, his.

Because of my public commentary, we didn't even remain chummy at a casual level. Mostly, that had to do with the nature of my radio show, *Back Talk*. I was determined to pull no punches on any public issue, including Premier Williams's policies and statements, and I encouraged callers and email correspondents to act the same way. Occasionally, I'd hear through the grapevine that Danny was perturbed over one of my critical rants, which he perceived as unfair, or over my tolerance (perhaps even encouragement) of callers who unjustly, he thought, tore political strips off him.

His disenchantment showed directly on a couple of occasions. I ran into him and Elizabeth Matthews by chance once at VOCM; he was there to record an announcement. I said hello, which he acknowledged without enthusiasm. Then he immediately turned away from me to talk to someone else. I walked on, chuckling. How the wheel turns, I thought. John Efford couldn't have snubbed me better.

During the federal election year 2008, the Cable Public Affairs Channel, CPAC, arranged with VOCM to televise my show across Canada, and to take calls from viewers in every province. They also wanted me to discuss issues by phone with federal and provincial politicians on different sides. Most of those we invited agreed with alacrity to call in.

When I told Danny's contact man that it would be a good opportunity for the premier to get his position across to the nation on Harper's breach of commitment to remove non-renewable resources from equalization, he seemed eager, and said he would get back to me shortly. I never heard from the premier or his office again. Not only was I no longer on the team, but evidently I was being boycotted.

Once, in late 2009, when Danny made a rare call to my show to take issue with some criticism I'd made, I greeted him by saying that it had been a long time since he'd called. "I was starting to think, Premier, that you didn't love me anymore," I said jokingly. We had a little chuckle over that, and I felt a small spark of our former easygoing relationship, which was otherwise ashes.

I have mentioned the above in order to put the following statement in context, and to try to indicate my objectivity in making it:

I was in the House of Assembly, or had political involvement outside the House, with every person who was or became premier of this province—Joey Smallwood, Frank Moores, Brian Peckford, Tom Rideout, Clyde Wells, Brian Tobin, Beaton Tulk, Roger Grimes, and Danny Williams. Some I liked, some I disliked. But they were all fine men, and those who had sufficient time in office to do so, made significant contributions to the well-being of Newfoundland and Labrador.

Based on years of close observation of those leaders, it is my opinion that Danny Williams has already proven himself equal to the best of them. And if he manages to overcome the challenges of putting the Lower Churchill on stream—with benefits to this province comparable to those he gained in the Atlantic Accord negotiations—I believe he will take his place as the greatest of our premiers.

Acknowledgements

My wholehearted thanks to superb writer Susan Rendell for graciously taking time from her own creative demands to edit the manuscript; to esteemed photographer Paul Daly for his photos of Danny Williams and the author; and to highly regarded graphic designer Adam Freake for his design of the book cover.

My boundless gratitude to Garry, Margo, and Jerry Cranford and Laura Cameron at Flanker Press for their enthusiasm and their earnest attention to the task of publishing this book. Their dedication to Newfoundland and Labrador writing over the years has made Flanker Press a provincial treasure.

Index

Born in Newfoundland, Bill Rowe graduated in English from Memorial University and attended Oxford University as a Rhodes Scholar, obtaining an Honours M.A in Law.

Elected five times to the House of Assembly, Rowe served as a Minister in the Government of Newfoundland and Labrador, and as Leader of the Official Opposition.

He practised law in St. John's for many years, and has been a long-time public affairs commentator, appearing regularly on national and local television, as well as hosting a daily radio call-in show on VOCM and writing weekly newspaper columns.

Rowe has written three books: *Clapp's Rock*, a bestselling novel published by McClelland and Stewart and serialized on CBC national radio; *The Temptation of Victor Galanti*, a second novel published by McClelland and Stewart; and a volume of essays on politics and public affairs published by Jesperson Press of St. John's. He is a member of the Writers' Union of Canada and has served on the executive of the Writers' Alliance of Newfoundland and Labrador.

He is married to Penelope Ayre Rowe CM of St. John's. They have a son, Dorian, a daughter, Toby, and three grandchildren.